LIVING IN EXISTENTIAL PARADOXES OF LIFE:

MY AUTOBIOGRAPHY

SEGUN OGUNGBEMI

UNIVERSITY OF TEXAS - DALLAS
Commencement
January 5, 1985

LIVING IN EXISTENTIAL PARADOXES OF LIFE: MY AUTOBIOGRAPHY

Copyright ©2024 **Segun Ogungbemi**

Paperback ISBN: 978-1-957809-77-9

All rights reserved. No part of this publication may be reproduced, distributed, or transmitted in any form or by any means, including photocopying, recording, or other electronic or mechanical methods without the prior written permission of the author except in the case of brief quotations embodied in reviews and certain other non-commercial uses permitted by copyright law.

Published by Cornerstone Publishing
A Division of Cornerstone Creativity Group LLC
Info@thecornerstonepublishers.com
www.thecornerstonepublishers.com

Author's Contact
To book the author to speak at your next event or to order bulk copies of this book, please, use the information below:

seguno2013@gmail.com

Printed in the United States of America.

FOREWORD

It is an honor and privilege to receive a telephone call from Professor Segun Ogungbemi inviting me to write the foreword message to this book. I am qualified to attest to the veracity and authenticity of the information contained in his autobiography. First, I would like to define our relationship. Professor Segun Ogungbemi and I are natives of Idofin. He is much older than I am; thus, our paths did not cross during my formative years of development.

I occasionally saw him in high school, reporting at the Idofin Descendant Union annual meetings. I observed him as articulate, meticulous, and knowledgeable of his facts. Hence, I grew up admiring him as a teenager. Coincidentally, we met in 1974 during my first year at the University of Ibadan. Although there were several Isanlu natives at the University of Ibadan, Professor Ogungbemi and I were the only Idofin natives. At the time, there were six Isanlu students at the University of Ibadan - myself, Ignatius Ifelayo, the late

Simon Agbore, Kunle Adegboro, Segun Ogungbemi, and the late Francis Ikudaiyenu. I was the youngest among them. We often socialized on Sunday afternoons at Professor Eyitayo Lambo's house at Bodija - Professor Lambo was a Lecturer in the Department of Economics at the University of Ibadan. We always had a great time with the Lambos. Ms. Lambo always cooked delicious meals for us, and we enjoyed each other's company by discussing our future career aspirations and reminiscing about community life in Isanlu.

Professor Ogungbemi graduated with a Diploma in Religious Studies from the University of Ibadan in 1976; he left the country a few years later for further studies in the United States. As fate would have it, I also arrived in the United States in 1980 for graduate education at the University of Pittsburgh. This development allowed us to grow closer. At the time, Professor Ogungbemi was in Dallas, and I was in Pittsburgh - about 1,223 miles apart. During that era, there were four Idofin natives enrolled as students in different universities across the United States – myself, Segun Ogungbemi, Bamidele Solomon and Samuel Omokore.

As Nigerian Federal scholars, we could not afford the price tag of air or land travel. Hence, we primarily discussed, over the phone, news from the homeland, our tribulations, and our accomplishments. Upon completing our doctoral degrees, Segun Ogungbemi, Bamidele Solomon, and I returned to

Nigeria when the country was "unstable" politically and at a personal financial loss because we were already gainfully employed in the United States. On arrival in Nigeria, Professor Ogungbemi was employed at Ogun State University, Ago-Iwoye, and Professor Bamidele Solomon and I at Obafemi Awolowo University, of Ife Ile-Ife. Second, I would like to address the book's content.

The book is divided into twelve parts: The genesis of his existence, formative years, waiting on the providence, blue-collar work experience, the pursuit of higher education, his academic career in African universities, community service, reflection on his western education experience, becoming a United States citizen, reflections on marital life, and benefactors. I am glad that Professor Ogungbemi wrote this inspirational book that comprehensively documented his genealogy, life story, and academic accomplishments. The depth of the scholarship fascinates me that Professor Ogungbemi brought to bear in writing this book. Notably commendable is the history of the East and West Yagba Local Government areas of Kogi State, Nigeria, that he eloquently described, including his detailed recollection of the stories on Idofin, which his father handed down to him.

As chronicled in the book, Professor Ogungbemi attained academic stardom through hard work, determination, and God's blessings, which he referred to on many occasions as

"Providence." He is a self-made man with nothing handed over to him on a platter of gold. Even as a student, he financially cared for himself, his parents, and everyone within and outside his nuclear family. Without any equivocation, Professor Ogungbemi is a generous person with a big heart, selfless, and sympathetic to social justice issues. Interestingly, as most African children will do, his son - Segun Junior - is caring for his dad in retirement. Professor Ogungbemi started his academic career at Bishop College in Dallas, Texas, in the United States, where he was on the faculty from 1983-1985 before returning to Nigeria. As a visionary academic, his legacy is his unique contributions to African Philosophy literature.

He has undoubtedly left desirable footprints in the sand of time. His passion for his profession is palpable in so many ways, as narrated in this book. During his academic career, he pioneered the establishment of the philosophy department in four African universities - Ogun State University, Nigeria (1985-1990); Moi University, Kenya (1990-1993); Lagos State University, Nigeria (1997-2000); and Adekunle Ajasin University, Nigeria (2004-2016). Professor Ogungbemi rose through the academic ranks from the Instructor position to Assistant Professor at Bishop College, Texas, United States, to Associate professor of philosophy at Moi University, Kenya and full professor at Adekunle Ajasin University, Nigeria.

During his meaningful academic career, which spans over four decades, he mentored several students and junior faculty members who are now full professors at different universities worldwide. He also served in various administrative roles as Head of Department, member/chairman of several Faculty and University Senate Committees in the five institutions he had worked during his academic career. In this autobiography, Professor Ogungbemi described, from the heart, his service contributions to the Sudan Interior Mission, Idofin, and Ere communities, with the verve and authority of a griot engrossed in the story he is narrating. The book also discusses the essence of education, family relationships/peaceful co-existence, moral values/knowledge acquisition, spiritual forces and holistic wellness, and respect for the natural environment.

The elephants in the room this book calls attention to are the decision to become a permanent resident of the United States later in life, candid reflections on marital life, and benefactors. Finally, I offer here my opinion about the book. The book is easy to read, and the chapters are sequenced to enhance the flow from one primary topic to another. The reader can peruse each of the parts independently without the knowledge of the previous section. The writing style is lucid and engaging and keeps the reader in suspense in several areas. The reader cannot but wonder where the author will land the plane of the story he is telling. I have learned a lot from reading the book. You will, too, if you read it as closely as I did! Professor Ogungbemi's autobiography is a "must read" for every "Okun" indigene and those desiring to learn about the challenges associated with developing the academic philosophy program at Ogun State University, Moi University, Lagos State University, and Adekunle Ajasin University particularly, during their formative developmental era before the academic programs attained their present levels of development.

I recommend the book very highly to alumni, friends, associates, and lecturers in the four institutions mentioned above, as there are many examples of ways to reposition the universities for greater effectiveness contained in the book.

Joseph Abiodun Balogun
PT, PhD, FACSM, FNSP, FAS, FIMC, FRSPH, FAcadMedS, FCADP Former dean and distinguished professor,
Chicago State University.
Tinley Park, Illinois, USA
December 2022.

DEDICATION

To my Roots, Ancestors, Descendants and Humanity.

Iyagba L.G.A Map

Source: Google Maps

CONTENTS

FOREWORD ii

DEDICATION viii

PREFACE xiii

ACKNOWLEDGMENTS xvii

PART ONE
THE ROOTS OF MY EXISTENCE

1. Genealogy 3
2. Ancestral Homes 9
3. My Parents 17

PART TWO
FORMATIVE YEARS

4. Living In A Pluralistic Religious Society 37
5. Western Education 59

PART THREE
WAITING ON THE PROVIDENCE

6. Career Path Trajectory 81

PART FOUR
FORGING AHEAD

7. Blue Collar Work Experience 105

PART FIVE
THE PURSUIT OF HIGHER EDUCATION

8. University Of Ibadan (UI) 125
9. United States Of America... 141

PART SIX
GOING BACK HOME

10. Reasons For Going Home.. 159
11. Experience On Returning To Nigeria 163

PART SEVEN
ACADEMIC CAREER IN AFRICAN UNIVERSITIES

12. Ogun State University Ago-Iwoye, Now Olabisi Onabanjo University 171
13. Moi University Eldoret, Kenya................................ 209
14. Lagos State University Ojo, Lagos 227
15. Adekunle Ajasin University..................................... 241

PART EIGHT
MY SERVICE TO COMMUNITIES

16. Idofin-Isanlu Community... 283

PART NINE
THE PATH OF EDUCATION

17. Self-Reflection 303

PART TEN
BECOMING A U.S. PERMANENT RESIDENT

18. Becoming A U.s. Permanent Resident 325

PART ELEVEN
REFLECTION ON MY MARITAL LIFE

19. Reflection On My Marital Life 351

PART TWELVE
MY BENEFACTORS

20. My Benefactors 363

APPENDIX
PERCEPTIONS OF SEGUN OGUNGBEMI

21. The Great Chains Of Family Members 371
22. Colleagues In The University System 395
23. Young African Entrepreneurs And Professionals In Houston 409
24. Special Friends 413

ABOUT THE AUTHOR 447

PREFACE

This historical trajectory of my life in the wilderness of existence spans over seven decades is a response to my father's conception of historical significance of human life. According to him, every individual is first and foremost a child of history, no matter his or her geographical location, social and economic circumstances and status in this universe. Considering my obscure location in Yagbaland with attendant economic challenges; it is worth telling my story, having succeeded in my academic pursuits and reached the apex of my professorial career, and made contributions to humanity towards human capacity building and infrastructural developments, as a child of history. My historical narratives entitled, *Living in the Existential Paradoxes of Life: My Autobiography* is an explicit documentation on interesting topics and written in a coherent language for easy reading with understanding.

I have lived in the United States for many years and got assimilated into their culture of capitalism, liberty, freedom, education and patriotism that are inherent in their democratic system of values and governance. This is also rooted in their constitution that the country is a home of immigrants. Therefore, anyone from any country in the world can come to the United States and become an American. My fear is that my children who have become citizens of America may one day be unwilling to go back to Africa and their children and great grandchildren may become chronically influenced by their country and forget that their ancestors came from Yagbaland in Africa. This book is written as a record of their history to remind them of their roots. As my father used to tell me; a man without history is lost and I don't want them to be lost. I want them to be proud of their historical inheritance of great values. I also want to leave behind those institutions and individuals behind my successes in addition to hard work on my part for emulation because without hard work and support of Providence, I believe one cannot have anything with enduring legacy of value. It is not only my successes and values that this book is about but also a record of reminder of the inherent human dispositions of enigmas, 'facticity and possibilities' in the wilderness of existence. The paradoxes formed the basis of encouragement, psychology and philosophy of courage to be in my existential life.

This book encourages self-reflections on how we live has negative and positive impacts on others. As Socrates says, 'a life without self-reflection is not worth living.' A self-reflection is a compass of life without which we will be lost in this wilderness of paradoxes of existence. It ought to be part of our cultural identity and value.

The book comprises twelve parts that are further subdivided into 20 chapters. The first part gives details of my roots and ancestral homes. Part two is about my formative years and part three deals with my dependence on Providence and the beginning of career path trajectory experience. Part four is an enabler to forge ahead in the pursuit of work experience to prepare me for a better future. Part five is about my pursuit of higher education at University of Ibadan, Nigeria and several universities in the United States of America. These institutions gave me the opportunity to excel in my academic endeavors.

Part six is about going back home after my years of studies in the United States to contribute to its development. I gave genuine reasons for going back home and my first experience on getting back home. I have had the view that wherever I go, home is the best. In other words, my country is the best no matter its deficit infrastructures. It was an irreversible determination and commitment. Part seven is a detailed academic career in African Universities that spanned over three decades. Part eight is my community service to SIM/ECWA, Idofin-Isanlu and adjacent communities, national service, Senior Special Adviser (Research) to the late Honorable Minister of Labour and Productivity, Dr. S.O Ogbemudia, and National Universities Commission. Part nine deals with my reflections on traditional system of education and western education experience. Part ten is about my second coming to the US as a permanent resident/citizen. Part eleven is a reflection on my marital life and Part twelve is a concise record of my benefactors. The appendix is about perceptions of me from family members, relations, and colleagues in the universities, friends and special friends.

ACKNOWLEDGMENTS

It would have been impossible for me to write this book without the initial encouragement from individuals very close to me: late Chief Bolaji Iyekolo and his cousin, late Elder Sunday Iyekolo. As I began to assemble the materials together in my library at Arigidi-Akoko, Ondo State, and a serene environment with gentle breeze from the hill behind my house, I had an inner feeling that the task was achievable. I was also planning to attend the 2016 Annual conference at The University of Texas at Austin, Texas, USA and I had to put finishing touches to my paper for the conference, while my wife was busy preparing to go with me for the conference. I felt her trip with me to the US in 2016 would be a unique contribution to the autobiography when I started writing it.

My parents had infused in me from childhood a moral habit of appreciation. I want to thank Segun Ogungbemi Jr. for creating the enabling environment for me to write this book. He has also been concerned about my welfare, always making sure of my good health. His friend, Jackie Herrera freed me from the nightmare of dread in 2014 when he had a close shave with death. I am very grateful to her for the spontaneous decision and action taken in my presence. She has also been instrumental to my good health by assisting Segun to provide good medical services in their hospital. Temidayo and her husband, Dr. Ademola Oridate have been very supportive of my well-being by their regular calls, visits with gifts. They have done their best to keep me happy in my retirement. Tinuke Bisola Ogungbemi is my Internet Technology mentor, and she has assisted me in this book project. Her calls from school in Nashville, Tennessee calmed my nerves when I didn't hear from her on time.

I am very grateful to my longtime friend Keith Morgan for proofreading the manuscript and Dr. Sunday Layi Oladipupo for reading several parts of the book and made useful observations on my services at Adekunle Ajasin University Akungba-Akoko. I want to thank Professor Samuel Oloruntoba for sparing his precious time and busy schedules in the cold winter in Canada to proofread the manuscript with eagle eyes and making sure no human error was spared from being corrected.

My profound gratitude goes to Professor Joseph Abiodun Balogun who painstakingly read the manuscript and made valuable suggestions for improvements as he wrote a foreword to the book. I cannot forget to mention his moral and financial support plus several calls to check on my well-being. He also shared six of his scholarly published books with me. I am very grateful to him and his wife, Olori, Dr. Adetutu. They are awesome family.

I am indebted to all the people who wrote their perceptions of me in the appendix of this book. I am amused with different names and titles given to me, which I cannot mention all but two of them are stunning. My former Vice-Chancellor, Professor Femi Mimiko called me the Oracle of Yemoja and Irunmole and the renowned world African Historian Professor Toyin Falola (TF) honored me with the title, The Irunmole of the World; that made me to burst to boisterous laughter. To those who don't know me well enough; they will probably believe that I worship the Yoruba religious deities. I don't belong to any religions, but I respect Yoruba deities because they are part of the Yoruba cultural and noetic values. I am an agnostic/skeptic on religious issues but fundamentally a Humanist, a lover of humanity. To the rest of you who contributed to the 'Perceptions of Segun Ogungbemi', I am humbled and honored for your inspiring perceptions and remarks.

Finally, my deepest appreciation goes to my friend, Dr. Muyiwa Sunday Ogunlade who accommodated us in his house for months and gave me a car to travel home and other places; and provided medical treatments in his hospital at no cost whenever any of us was sick. I am also indebted to all the individuals who have given moral and financial support to me on this project namely, Segun Ogungbemi Jr., Ademola and Temidayo Oridate, Sam and Toyin Iyelolu, Segun and Obiaderi Awo, Sonde and Idowu Omokore, Jide and

Angela Jones, Onaolapo and Elizabeth Okeniyi, Bolarin and Oludamilola Ijagbemi, Stephen Abiodun Abraham fondly called Gbera, Olusegun Oshaponle, Funsho Fatobi, my sister-in-law, Ayotunde Olaoba fondly called Big Mummy and Segun B. Ogungbemi's friends. Above all, my family has been very accommodating of the inconveniences while working on the book. I am grateful for their understanding and love.

PART ONE

THE ROOTS OF MY EXISTENCE

Chapter 1
GENEALOGY

Before my father joined his Ancestors about 1:30 a.m. on August 8, 2005 at his residence in Odeko ward, Idofin-Isanlu, Yagba East Local Government, Kogi State, Nigeria, he told me that he would not want me and my siblings to forget our roots because a man who does not know his historical background is lost. One of the most important natural gifts that my father had was longevity plus his ability to coherently narrate historical events with approximate exactitude. Such a rare natural talent is amazing to those of us who lived with or surrounded him.

My late parents Pa Afolami Ogungbemi and Mrs. Tinuke Agaja Ogungbemi had five of us in their marriage and we are: Luke, Joshua, Ibidun, Funmilayo and myself the first child although my father had two other children namely, Beji and Ajayi and my mother had a daughter in her previous marriage before marrying my father and her name is Mrs. Ebun Adedayo, Nee Ebun Awe and her children are: Olu, Yemisi, Omolara, Bolanle, Muyiwa and Bukola. We are all married men and women and blessed with many children and they are in this chronological order: my children, Segun Bidemi Ogungbemi Jr., Yetunde Bosede Ogungbemi, Temidayo Bimbola Ogungbemi and Tinuke Bisola Ogungbemi; Luke's children are, Moyinoluwa and Ekundayo, Joshua's children are, Iyabo, Ayokami, Tobi, Ibukun, Babajide and Oluwasemilore; Ibidun's children are, Toyin and Kemi; and Funmilayo's children are, Segun, Dayo and Dada.

My father had four immediate brothers and sisters. The younger brother was Igbe who died very young leaving only three sisters namely, Oni, Aremu, and Maroni. None of the three sisters is alive today but they have many siblings. Oni's children were Adebayo and a daughter both have passed away. Aremu had Ebun, Dele, Ajayi, Ranti, Tanmowo and Ibiye. Among the six children only Ebun has passed on. Maroni had the following children, Sunday, Friday, Ajayi, Tuesday, Tope, Ebun and Dupe. All of them are married with many children that form a great genealogy of beings.

I was fortunate to know my grandparents. My grandfather was Elder Joseph Ogungbemi fondly called Baba Alawo because of his entrepreneurial skills and trade in hides and skin ornament and all his descendants are called Kasinuawo because of the way he used to sit on the leather and creatively and ingeniously designed his state of the art. Pa Joseph Ogungbemi was one of the very few prominent individuals in his community and beyond. He was famous because of his art ornaments and characteristically known for his hard work, honesty, integrity, discipline, spontaneity and religiosity. My grandfather had another wife, Mrs. Igunnu Ogungbemi who had the following children, Frank, Moyeni, Esther, Isaiah and Rebecca. There are only two of her children still alive today and they are Esther and Isaiah. There are two major distinctive identities of this great chain of beings that we are noted for. The first one is Kasinuawo because many people find it too long to pronounce, they simply chose a convenient form of it, hence Kasi becomes a general name of identification with our great grandfather. The other name is Soko oligbo Edun, meaning, Soko who owns the forest where monkeys dwell, a description of a rich agricultural vegetation of palm trees and other cash crops. It is a traditional and cultural identity known as oriki-family chant name among Ere people of Yagba ethnic group in Yoruba land. My grandfather was very fond of me even though we did not live in the same town. He was at Odo-Ere and we were at Idofin. He used to visit very often and on one of his visits he asked my father to let me spend some weeks with him during the holiday. Of course, my father quickly obliged him. And during our long holiday I went to spend one month with him at Odo-Ere. I took knowledge of his craftsmanship. It was awesome! When the time came for me to go back home, I felt like staying back but then I had to go back to school. The last time we were together he was kind enough to give me some money and one of his needles. I did not understand the significance or the import of the needle until many years later.

My father's mother was Mrs. Sare Ogungbemi who was the only child of her mother Osayomi from Oge family, Odeko ward, Idofin-Isanlu. She was a younger sister to Pa. Iyee (Iyelolu) Eleonisi, the second King of Idofin. Some of his children were Elijah Iyelolu, Bodunde Iyelolu, Zacchaeus Iyelolu, Tayo Iyelolu and Boja Iyelolu. The nephew of Pa Iyee was Pa Samuel Oshadupin and some of his children were, Bosede Oshadupin, Dele Oshadupin, Hosea Oshadupin, Ezekiel Oshadupin, Dayo Oshadupin, Seti Oshadupin and Ola Oshadupin. Other family relations of Pa Iyee were Madam Oja Oshamo and Ayaba Olori Bejide Anjiku David, the mother of Prince Dele David etc.

My grandmother, Sare, took care of me in my early childhood. Initially, I thought she was my natural mother because of my closeness to her and the motherly care. But one day, there was a dramatic twist to my perception of my relationship with her. She called me and introduced my natural mother to me. I felt the old woman had technically disowned me and I gradually adjusted to the reality of her proposition. Even when I got to know my mother, I was never closed to her like my grandmother, Sare, until she passed on in October 1970. Although I had a premonition of her death and when I got the news of her demise, it was expected because of her age and poor health. In those days there were no adequate communication system of passing immediate information apart from postal services, which normally took several weeks or months before getting mails to their destinations. By the time I got the news of the death of my grandmother, she had been buried.

My grandmother from my mother's side was Molebambi who had three children namely, Oshalomo, Tinuke but fondly called Agaja and Ibironke who were younger sisters of Mark Oni Balogun popularly called Ejenti before he became the Owa of Ero, Odole in Odo-Eri, Yagba West Local Government Area, Kogi State. Pa Owa had several wives and many children but only two of them are very close to me and they are Femi and Tope. His mother was Saya, a very wealthy woman who married several wives for him. Madam Saya was the daughter of the family revered Matriarch Aoluke. My grandmother Molebambi passed away when I was not around in the 60s. All her children have also joined their Ancestors. On January 2, 2017, Pa Owa joined his ancestors.

Chapter 2
ANCESTRAL HOMES

My ancestors came from four different towns namely, Oke-Ere, Odo-Ere, Odo-Eri and Idofin-Isanlu respectively, in Yagbaland. It is therefore imperative to know that I am an embodiment of the four heritages. Let me give a brief synopsis of Yagba people because of its historical importance to our common cultural identity with Ile-Ife, the mythical ancestral home of all the Yoruba people in Nigeria and those in the diaspora. In a nutshell, the people of Yagbaland are Yoruba. The name, 'Yagba' is derived from Iya agba the acclaimed Queen who migrated from Ile-Ife and settled with her children a couple of centuries ago as Yagba in Kogi State.

Yagbaland area is divided into three local councils, and they are: Yagba West Local Government Area with a total land area of about 1280 Kilometers, Yagba East Local Government Area has a total land area of about 1400 Kilometers and

Mopa-Amuro Local Government Area which is the smallest has a total land area of over 800 Kilometers. Yagbaland area extends to some parts of Ekiti State namely, Irele, Oke-Ako, Itapagi, Ipao, Aiyede and Iye. There are also Yagba towns in the present Kwara State, and they are, Koro and Eruku. The common language of the people is Yagba although it has its variations that are understood not only by the Yagba speaking people but also by other Okun speaking people within Nigeria and in the diaspora. It is a trademark of identity and dignity.

The political dispensation in Nigeria has made it compelling for Yagba people to form a social political group together with their kith and kin in Ijumu, Kabba, Bunu and Oworo that now metamorphosed as Okunland, a dominant force for political equation, worthy of recognition and relevance in the current social, political, economic and cultural dispensation in Nigeria. It needs to be emphasized that the fact that we are Okun people does not make us lose our original Yagba identity and background.

Oke-Ere

My port of entry of this existential voyage, according to my father was Oke-Ere, which traditionally has three main wards, and they are Igbede, Iloe and Okete. Igbede is made of eight groups, and they are: Oke-Gbede, Odo-Gbede,

Ilae, Ogbarun, Akogun, Ogbose, Ogboje and Igbosalu respectively. Okete has three groups namely, Okedigba, Okete and Ayinagbede. Iloe has four groups, and they are: Okedorun, Idiagun, Atogun and Odosedo. Igbede is the first among the three wards that constitute Oke-Ere and by virtue of that position it is the eldest. Therefore, in the order of traditional hierarchy, Igbede must choose first among the three groups.

Olorun Olodumare, the Supreme Being who gave human beings freedom to choose among the deities to serve their personal and corporate interests metaphysically controls the dynamics of existence and its sustainability. The traditional deity worshipped by Igbede people is Igboojo. As a result of modernity most people at Oke-Ere have become religiously syncretic. In other words, many are Christians but in time of critical needs some of them, if not all, secretly seek help from the priests of the deities.

The Oke-Ere people were originally farmers although in each group there were hunters, blacksmiths and other trades but the predominant occupation was farming before the advent of missionaries and western civilization. As the emergence of modernity became a compelling force in the growth and development of any society Oke-Ere was not left alone. Some of its members moved southward and settled to continue their farming and other forms of living engagements for survival. The new farm settlement became Odo oko Ere and the short form of it is Odo-Ere.

My father married his wife Tinuke but fondly called Agaja from a neighboring town called Odo-Eri. Both lived together among the relations of my father in Oke-Gbede; looking forward to the fruit of the womb, which did not materialize.

Odo-Ere

As Odo-Ere began to breathe the air of modern civilization in the early 20th century, it became a center of attraction that made other clans from Oke-Ere and neighboring villages relocate there. My grandfather Joseph Alawo Ogungbemi was among the people who relocated to Odo-Ere around the early 20th century and continued his entrepreneurial skill in ornament using hides and skin. He also had his farmland within the immediate vicinity and in a far distant hinterland after Ofi River. The new settlement at Odo-Ere led to another family regrouping that formed lineage groups, clans, wards and compounds. My grandfather belonged to the Odomo/Asala family clan in Isaba ward. He was a prominent family figure known for his entrepreneurship, hard work, and discipline with sterling leadership qualities. He was the Olori-Ebi, Head of the clan, and an Elder in the Church, Sudan Interior Mission (SIM), Odo-Ere, and Community Leader etc. My father told me that the Odomo/Asala group did not have a family land at Odo-Ere except the land area given to them by the Ipa clan as a token of deep appreciation for making it possible for their women to bear children. The sons of the Ipa clan and their future descendants were warned not to take the land from the Odom/Asala family and descendants. To violate this traditional injunction has its irreversible consequences because it was a pact.

The fact that my grandfather relocated to Odo-Ere did not lead to a total family disconnect from Oke-Ere; my first ancestral home. As a matter of fact, Oke-Ere and Odo-Ere are regarded as one indivisible entity-Ere, which includes Akata. The Ere Welfare Association is a unique organization that fosters the common bond of unity among Ere people. Odo-Ere has become an emerging cosmopolitan town where modernity has given its express presence with aesthetic ambience. It is the Headquarters of Yagba West Local Government Area of Kogi State and home of people from far and near that has boosted the economic and commercial prosperity of the people.

Eri/ Odo-Eri

Eri land is a combination of Oke-Eri, (Igbaruku/Iyamerin), Odo-Eri, Okoto, and Odo-Ara. It has a boundary with Ejiba, Odo-Ere/Oke-Ere, Agboro and Idofin respectively. My mother Mrs. Tinuke Agaja Ogungbemi and her mother, Molebambi and their ancestors came from Odo-Eri, a town located on several hills in Yagba West Local Government Area. My grandmother had three daughters: Oshalomo, Tinuke Agaja and Ibironke. The family root of my mother in Odo-Eri is Opin/Idau clan and her mother's clan is Ansila. Odo-Eri is located on Ilorin-Kabba Trunk A Road of the Federal Government. Its immediate neighbors are, Odo-Ere, Odoara, Oke-Eri (Igbaruku, Iyamerin), Omi and Ejiba etc., all in Yagba West Local Government Area of Kogi State. One of the major occupations of the Eri people was and still is subsistence farming.

Idofin-Isanlu

Before their present location, there was no place called Idofin. There were 18 different clans that settled independently of one another. They were as follows: 1. Odeko 2. Isalubo 3. Okehanin (Okeyanrin) 4. Igboe 5. Etija 6. Idioro 7. Okele 8. Dogbe 9. Okara 10. Ifeaga 11. Inun-Oro 12. Okoko 13. Okegbo 14. Okelegun 15. Okofe (Akira) 16. Ogbadagun 17. Arigo 18. Idara. Each settlement had its own charismatic leader who governed according to traditions and his intuitive wit. When they moved to their present location, some settled in the north and others in the south hence the two divisions are called Oke-Dofin and Odo-Dofin respectively. Odeko is in Oke-Dofin, and it is the most populated among all the clans in the town.

Geographically, Idofin-Isanlu is located on the Ilorin-Kabba trunk A road of the Federal Republic of Nigeria. It has a common land area boundary with Ejiba and Eri in Yagba West Local Government Area of Kogi State and Iboro, Makutu-Isanlu, Itakete, Ogbom and Ogga in Yagba East Local Government Area in Kogi State. Idofin-Isanlu is one of the towns that has the largest land areas in the locality and shares ownership of the biggest River- Oyi River in both East and West Local Government Areas of Kogi State.

From time immemorial, Idofin-Isanlu people were and are still known as subsistence farmers. The expanse land area is good for cash crops namely, cocoa, coffee, palm produce, tobacco etc. There are several mineral resources such as tantalite, kaolin, limestone etc. Despite all these natural resources no industry has been built there to harness them.

It was in this town that my father's grandmother, Osayomi had as her ancestral home particularly, Odeko ward in Yagba East Local Government Area, Kogi State, Nigeria. She had only one daughter, Sare whose parents were from Ilae/ Oke-Gbede in Oke-Ere. It was her mother who made her come to Idofin-Isanlu to take care of her senior brother, Pa Iyelolo who subsequently became Oba, His Royal Highness (HRH) of Idofin-Isanlu at relatively old age. It was in this town that my mother conceived me in December 1945 and when the pregnancy was becoming noticeable my parents went to live with their family friend Bolaji at Ogbom in the same local council. My parents had to leave Idofin for Ogbom for fear of not losing the pregnancy and to protect my mother from unseen metaphysical forces with diabolical intentions. Whether the fears were real or not, my parents took precautionary measures and the wise counsel of 'prevention is better than cure'. My parents told me that they did not return to Idofin-Isanlu until after I was born.

Chapter 3
MY PARENTS

Father

My father, Pa Afolami Ogungbemi was born when there was no western form of written records. His date of birth was unknown, but he was able to associate himself with his peers of the same age group at Idofin-Isanlu and Ere where he came from. According to historical narratives of people at Idofin-Isanlu my father used to trek alone from Oke-Ere to the original settlement of Odeko clan before their relocation to the present site at Idofin. By the time my father joined his ancestors on August 8, 2005, Idofin-Isanlu was over 100 years old. Relations from Oke-Ere and Idofin-Isanlu told me that he was the oldest man in both communities at death.

The early adulthood of my father, according to him, was adventurous. In those days, there was no transport system and no good roads except pathways in most parts of the country. The general mode of transportation was on foot. He traveled to places seeking greener pastures. He used to trek from Oke-Ere to Lagos, a journey that probably took him and his friends several weeks and sometimes a month going from one village to another and from one small town to another. Sometimes they used kanako, a 'traditional supersonic device' to shorten the journey. He said that he rarely used it because of its negative effects. He knew so many villages and towns and when he narrated his experiences on the way, I hardly believed him. But one of the people who knew him very well, Pa Iyekolo Abe corroborated his stories and told me that my father used to trek to Ebutemeta, Lagos in those days.

As a result of the life expedition, my father did not marry on time. By the time he married my mother he was probably in his mid or late 40s. While seeking a better life at Ibadan he spent several years there and before leaving he impregnated a woman who gave him his first daughter and her name was Ebun; and on his return to Oke-Ere, he told me that he had another daughter from another woman at Ogbe in the same local area council with Oke-Ere. He was not married to either of the women who had two children for him. When it was time to get a wife, his father Pa Joseph Alawo Ogungbemi was part of the decision-making. His father was involved in the search for a suitable woman who would bear children for him. In those days, the primary reason for getting a wife was for procreation. The criteria for marriage were not based on the western concept of love and modern perception of physical attraction, richness, wealth etc., but primarily on commitment and care for the woman and respect of her parents and relations. There was another critical traditional element that had to be made in those days: the opinion of Ifa oracle had to be consulted. The oracle was the instrument used for the background check of both would-be couples and its approval for the authorization of both parents to give their children for marriage. After my parents passed the traditional scrutiny of the marriage test, they became husband and wife. They had five children: three boys and two girls. My father had penchant for more children and he got two from another woman although they were not married. Apart from the first two daughters he had in his voyage in the wilderness of life, the rest of us were born at Idofin-Isanlu. My father loved his children with great passion, and he demonstrated it in all ramifications. He was a disciplinarian, generous, transparent, honest, kind, trustworthy, industrious, intelligent, creative and religious. His opinions were always sought on critical issues for direction on social and religious matters in the community. Having been exposed to western education in his journeys to the defunct Western Region, he realized that to be successful in the emerging young Nigeria, his children would need western education. Through personal effort, he was able to read some Yoruba literature particularly

Bibeli Mimo, the Holy Bible. He also knew how to write in Yoruba and how to keep a written record. For instance, he had a small diary where he wrote important events in his life particularly, my date of birth. I found him to be a very organized person. He had passion for education and the little opportunity he had to learn Yoruba language he utilized it. He was my first teacher who taught me how to read Yoruba Bible at a very young age. I had to memorize certain parts of the New Testament for instance, (John 6:1-14) where Jesus fed his disciples with five loaves of bread and two pieces of fish. Looking back, I never liked his teaching method with the cane.

My father never forgot to share with me some aspects of his early life. According to him he learned subsistence farming at the feet of a man called Aro in Oke-Ere. Thereafter, he learned carpentry and later abandoned it and went to get involved in timber industry. He was a sawyer, but he did not get any satisfaction in the trade and subsequently returned to Idofin-Isanlu to start farming and hunting; using dogs, spears, traps and locally made firearms-guns. In his spare time, he was a local fisherman. He had his farmlands in different parts namely, Obagba, Kuku, Onjebo, Okehain, (Okeyanrin), Igbolodeko, Okedugbe etc. The farthest of the farm was Okeyanrin. It was about five miles away and during the rainy season we had to swim across the Oyi River. We occasionally slept in a locally made hut-house on the farm. It was a unique experience with fun but not the kind of fun I really wanted. In those days nobody used fertilizers at Idofin-Isanlu because the soils were naturally rich enough to produce good yields.

As a farmer, Pa Afolami grew crops like yam, cassava, corn, guinea-corn, pepper, beans, etc., for our daily consumption and cotton, coffee, tobacco that were considered cash crops, for commercial purposes. In his time, it was a general belief and practice that a farmer and hunter must have some knowledge of traditional medicines including incantations because human beings must learn how to co-exist with natural and evil forces; if they were to survive and have flourishing existence. He believed in ethics of human-nature-relatedness, which teaches that one should not take more from nature than what he needs to have a meaningful existence. He built a four-bedroom house with a detached kitchen, store and my mother's utility room in the mid-50s. When cocoa was a flourishing trade, he had a bumper harvest; and as a sign of social status, he bought a new Robin Hood bicycle. In the local community in those days, it was like owning a new car today. But the joy and happiness of my father over his 'material wealth' and social nobility status was short lived.

In those days under the defunct Northern Region government, social and economic development was slow and far between. Any community that wanted to accelerate its development had to bear the cost. Idofin-Isanlu being in the then Northern Region, the people could not wait for government to determine its present and future destiny. The people believed in self-community development like market projects and its maintenance, building of school development projects, health and environmental projects among others. Some individuals like my father and his friends in the Baptist Church, Thomas Komolafe, Tunde Oshamo, Joshua Obiyomi, Jack Kehinde Ogunbiwaje etc., had mooted the idea of having a school in Idofin but their powerful Oba, His Royal Highness, Ogunbiwaje, was against the move. He would not want any of his children to go to school because there would be nobody to help him on the farm. There were no concerted efforts to build a school until after his death in 1953. In 1954, members of the Baptist Church at Idofin wanted to build a mission primary school but elders in the town wanted a joint effort in the project. There was a consensus that the primary school should be a community project to be taken over by the Native Authority and not by the mission. In the same year a new Oba, His Royal Highness Anjiku David ascended the throne. He was favorably disposed to western education and being a staunch member of the Baptist Church, he supported the move to have a community elementary school.

Between 1954 and 1956 the preparation to build a two-classroom block by the community began with zeal and enthusiasm. All able-bodied men and women were out to make their contributions towards achieving their goal on time. As progress went on at the school site in the dry season of 1956, there was an outbreak of wildfire at Igbolodeko where my father had his cocoa plantation. The ravaging Harmattan wind aided the velocity of the burning fire and by the time people got to the farm to put out the fire my father, his cousin, Elijah Iyelolu and their neighbor Pa Bello Omo Ake had lost almost everything on the cocoa farm. It was the worst day my father never forgot because it affected his economic fortunes. It was a permanent setback because the farmland could not grow cocoa anymore. The only cash crop that my father depended on was tobacco, which could not fetch him enough money to take care of his family and extended families.

The destruction of the cocoa farm of my father and his cousin and neighbor did not stop him from participating in the community school project. While work was in progress at the site of the school, the Baptist Church facilities were used until the community completed the first block of two classrooms with an office for the headmaster and his staff towards the end of 1956. By January 1957 the two classrooms for primary one and two were occupied and teaching and learning began progressively.

Pa Afolami was a social man. He had a couple of friends

he socialized with particularly, Thomas Komolafe, Tunde Oshamo, Afolami Eniamo, etc. As a sign of their social status, they used smoke pipes with fancy. They used to fill their pipes with dried tobacco and then put naked fire on it and then puff the smoke. In those days, there were no warnings about the danger of smoking tobacco. They would smoke their tobacco with glee, and nobody dared to challenge them. They also enjoyed themselves with several kegs of palm wine.

My father used to participate in several social functions like traditional weddings, religious festivals, and new yam festivals. He was a good traditional singer and dancer. He was fondly called Folami *Onigbogun*, that is, Folami who sings and dances g*bogun*. He was popular with this music and any occasion that he had to sing and dance generally attracted a large crowd. Both men and women liked him for his artistic dance steps and melody. He never danced alone. Several of his friends and younger ones joined him namely, Pa Tunde Oshamo, Ajayi Ogun, Philip Oshamo and a few women of his age and younger ones. On several occasions, I became emotionally moved to dance like him especially, when his cousin, Bodunde Iyelolu played his locally made flute called *fere* in Yoruba to chant my father's name while singing and dancing skilfully. Some of the spectators were fond of spraying money on my father and his cousin, Bodunde. I admired the way he socialized because it was with moderation.

The social life of my father did rob him of his commitment to his fundamental religious beliefs more so in the face of modernity. He grew up knowing two basic religious faiths: Indigenous religion and Christianity. In his inherited traditional belief like other Yoruba ethnic nationality, Olodumare is the Supreme Being who created everything that is. He however has uncountable messengers called divinities from which anyone can choose to consult for their daily needs. Among such deities are Obatala otherwise called Orisanla, Ogun, Sango, Orunmila, Osanyin, Esu among others. In his ancestral family they are worshippers of Ogun, the deity of war, peace and justice. My father was also a devotee of Osanyin, the deity of leaves and herbal medicine. In his closeness to this deity and its other worshipers, my father had the knowledge of treating some diseases that affected children and he was able to treat infertility among men and women. In modern terms, he was a traditional intellectual in pediatrics and gynecology. His beliefs in Ogun and Osanyin also influenced his interest in Ifa, the oracle of Orunmila, the deity of knowledge, foretelling and predictions. All these beliefs were to my father a means to enhance the well-being of his family and to a larger extent to be of beneficial instrument to his knowledge of humanity.

When my father became a Christian in the Baptist Church, he saw Christianity as a religion of modernity that could lead to a better standard of living. To him, Jesus was like one of the messengers of Olodumare and so both the traditional religion and Christianity simply complemented each other for the well-being of the followers of Jesus Christ. He believed that Jesus was the Son of God who was sent for human redemption and to gain entry to eternal life one must believe in him. He believed in fervent prayers and obedience to the two cardinal principles of Jesus Christ: love God and love your fellow human beings. As a Christian, he believed that death is not the end of life, there is resurrection and judgment and only those who believe in Jesus Christ will be given the grace to live eternally with God and those who do not have that faith will go to hell fire. Perhaps his worry about eternal damnation for those who do not believe in Jesus Christ made him to be in constant prayers for his children, particularly his first son whose belief had become at variant with orthodox Christianity.

Like his father who was an Elder in the Sudan Interior Mission Church (SIM) at Odo-Ere, he too was an Elder in the Baptist Church at Idofin-Isanlu until his death on August 8, 2005. The Baptist Church gave him a befitting Christian burial. We had the 10th year memorial service for him in August 2015 with some gifts to the Church.

My Mother

Nobody kept a record of my mother's date of birth when she was born at Odo-Eri because western literacy was nonexistent in her locality. Be that as it may, I can make a speculated year of her birth. By the time I was born on August 26, 1946, she would have been at least 22 years old because my older sister was probably six years older than me. Therefore, her year of birth could be approximately 1924. In her time, the society did not put any viable premium on a girl-child education. There was a pervasive ignorance of the advantages inherent in exposing a girl-child to western education. She was probably given out to early marriage with little or no knowledge of what the institution entailed apart from being a baby-producing factory. Her first child was former Miss. Ebun Awe now Mrs. Ebun Adedayo. Her early marriage was short lived because of some unexpected domestic circumstances. She divorced her husband and several years later decided to get married again. By the time she made up her mind to marry my father she was much more mature. In her new marriage she was blessed with five children, three boys namely, Segun formerly (Elijah), Luke and Joshua and two girls, Ibidun and Funmilayo. She loved and cared for us to the best of her ability and resources. I was, however, not very close to her because my grandmother, Sare, offered to take care of me. She found me to be a spoilt child of grandmother and of course very lazy. I was shielded away from her discipline but whenever my grandmother was not around, I became very vulnerable. I saw her as an unwanted intruder to the relationship between my grandmother and me. We became close after I finished my elementary education in 1962.

I found my mother to be very resourceful and highly skilled in three entrepreneurial areas: cloth making, locally brewed wine and traditional hair plaiting. She was also into local trading, selling her wares and other farm produce like cotton, beans, yams, oranges, tobacco mostly on market days within her vicinity etc. Her successes in her local industry, like others in her condition, were crippled by the British policies and the sales of manufacturing products from the United Kingdom. Local industries lost incentives, creativity and resourcefulness and gradually economic recession led to poverty in her local community. Despite the economic downturn, she remained undaunted; domestic demand instilled resilience and determination in her to forge ahead using her natural economic survival instinct to pursue the principle of investment in her talent. She believed in the economic principle that stipulates 'three pence invested is better than one pound that is lying fallow'. At that time, Nigeria was using British currency of three basic denominations: pounds, shillings and pence. Although my mother invested the little savings, she had in local business it did not yield marginal profit to keep her in business because of British capitalism. After Nigeria Independence she wanted to continue with her petty trading, which kept her busy until her death in December 1978.

The religious disposition of my mother could be described as ambivalent. She did not embrace any religion at the expense of others. She saw religions as a means of adding values to her existence and that of her children and families. Having said that, it is important to mention that her indigenous religious background had a more profound influence on her than any other religions. When she attended church services and made her widows mite donation during the offering service, she simply did so like others without a deep Christian conviction because she did not know about the significance of the redemption plan of Jesus the Christ. I noticed on several occasions during the holidays when I was a student at Igbaja Bible College she would make some sacrifice on behalf of her children because she believed in *Olorun ko ko iranlowo*: God welcomed human assistance to always enhance protection. She was an incredible defender of indigenous religious practices that would add moral and economic values to her life without reservation. She was a very kind and generous woman known by all her people around her. She was known for her constant visits to her relations with the intention to solve their problems. For instance, one of her cousins Mrs. Bukola Akolo had been married without children and when she visited her the woman told my mother what she had been going through and yet no success. According to the woman, my mother went away to find a solution to her infertility. The woman came to Idofin-Isanlu with a gift of big roasted fish and some kola nuts to express her profound appreciation to my mother even though she had been deceased, but her children deserved to know her good deed. My mother's senior brother, late Pa Oni Mark Owa at Odo-Eri told me, when all hopes were lost, how my mother went on her way to get some money for his son to buy a pair of tennis shoes for his graduation ceremony in primary school. It was not the case that my mother was rich; rather it was a mark of her commitment to the needs of her people.

Madam Tinuke Agaja Ogungbemi had a great concern for harmonious relationships among her six children. She personally made the concern known to me towards the end of the 50s. She told me of her daughter Ebun who was living in Ibadan, and she would want me to relate to her as my other siblings. In 1959 my sister came from Ibadan on a visit to her mother at Idofin-Isanlu and she was introduced to me. I greeted her warmly and after some entreaties I went to join my friends on the football field. To my mother, that first step made a lasting impression to her and the rest of us. It really made it a bond between my sister and me, which has extended to her children and all members of our family till today. Her children, Olu, Yemisi, Lara, Bolanle, Muyiwa, Bukola and most of the grandchildren relate to the rest of my siblings relatively very well.

In 1976-1978 when I was teaching at Abdul Aziz Atta Memorial College (AAAMCO) Okene my mother gave me a surprise visit. I never thought she could travel on her own to Okene. When I saw her, I thought she came for her monthly stipends, but it was not long since I gave her previous stipend and I was wondering what could warrant her taking a risk to Okene? Did she come to see her last daughter, Funmilayo, that I put in school? But something told me that she wouldn't have come to see me unless it was important. I was, however, delighted to see her and to know about her state of health and the general well-being of the people at home. After her super, she asked if we could have a private discussion before going to bed. I obliged her request and told Funmilayo to go to her room. After pouring her encomium on me, I knew a bombshell was coming. I waited patiently to hear her narratives of our social fabrics and the expectations of parents to see their children succeeding in their daily endeavors. Now the bombshell, all my friends, Joseph Molemodile, Prince Dele David, Isaac Abegunde etc., have made their mothers proud of them because each of them has got married and has children, except me. She then wondered whether I was not impotent because she had not seen me with any girlfriend. All she wanted from me was to get a wife and have children. According to her, she could not wait to see her grandchildren and I should do something about it. I thanked her for the concern, but my focus was on how to further my education, and nothing should be a priority over it. She said that I have been one of the most educated in the community and the next stage of progress was to get married and have children. She broke down, as my idea to further my education was antithesis to her interest. The following morning, she decided to go back home, and I followed her to the Motor Park and bid her journey mercies. I went back to the college quarters where I lived and for several days I thought of how to make her happy. Before Christmas of that year, I went to introduce to her a lady I planned to marry. She was so excited and delighted in having her as my fiancee. When I told my mother the parental background of my fiancée, she intuitively approved our getting married without any further delay. In December 1977 the traditional arrangements were made, and our wedding was consummated and sealed. My wife was about five months pregnant in 1978 when I left for the United States for further studies at the Southern Methodist University (S.M.U.) Dallas, Texas. Sadly, my mother was not alive to see the long-awaited grandson before death snatched her away in December 1978. It was about a month before the child was born when she passed away in December 1978. It was devastating because she did not live to see the child, Segun Bidemi Ogungbemi Jr. she had wanted very badly. Did she have a premonition of her imminent death? Was it the reason why she impressed on me to have a wife and have a child before her departure on the planet earth? It may be difficult to answer the question rightly or wrongly because it could be either yes or no. The import of the message as far as I am concerned is that children should listen to the voice of reason of their parents.

My mother would have been the happiest grandmother today had she lived to see all her grandchildren, Segun, Yetunde, Temidayo, Tinuke: great-grandchildren, Segun Cristian Ogungbemi 111 and Gracie the children of Segun Jr. and Yetunde respectively. She would also have been most delighted to see the grandchildren of my younger brothers and sisters, Iyabo, Ayokanmi, Tobi, Ibukun, Moyinoluwa, Ekundayo, Toyin, Kemi, Segun, Dayo and Dada respectively.

Her good deeds, however, and all her children, grandchildren and great-grandchildren and many more of this great chain of beings will continue to immortalize Madam Tinuke Agaja Ogungbemi. She has also left a genetic trait of hair plaiting as a trademark among her female descendants namely, Ebun, Yemisi, Funmilayo, Bolanle, Yewande, Gift, Dada, Kemi, Tinuke etc.

She did not want to be remembered alone without her two sisters: senior sister Mrs. Oshalomo Oloke and younger sister Ibironke who was married to Mr. Adebayo at Igbaruku. She had four children namely, Josiah Oluwole, Joseph Olusegun, Florence Olutayo and Simeon Olutedo. My mother visited her sister Mrs. Ibironke Adebayo at Igbaruku many times, but unfortunately, I never went with her because it was a long distance and no means of comfortable transportation in those days. My mother enjoyed trekking long distances visiting her relatives. Years after the death of my mother, one of the children of Mrs. Ibironke Adebayo, Florence heard that I was in the country, and she decided to visit me. She got me on the phone when her mother passed away to inform me of the sad news. I wished I could have met her before her death. As destiny would have it, Florence and her husband came to Idofin-Isanlu for the funeral and burial ceremony of Ms. Oni Omodara, my former schoolmate in the 50s who rose to local recognition as a talented popular personality. Florence and her husband needed accommodation and their host Mr. Gbenga Omodara brought them to my house and introduced them to me as Mr. and Mrs. Ogungbemi. It was a thrilling moment of joy and happiness to meet Florence and her husband. Since then we have remained in constant contact. The family has changed their surname from Ogungbemi to Adebayo. My mother would have been the happiest had it been she was alive to see us together!

PART TWO

FORMATIVE YEARS

Chapter 4
LIVING IN A PLURALISTIC RELIGIOUS SOCIETY

The only paradise universe I knew as I was growing up was Idofin-Isanlu. It exposed the polarities of existence that would become my cultural identity and foundation on which to define my being-in-existence. I could not remember the circumstance that separated me from my mother and made me to be so glued very strongly to my grandmother, Madam Sare who I mistakenly considered my natural mother. Madam Sare had a friend fondly called *Iye pupa*, an old light complexioned woman whose name I got to know after her death as Madam Igununbiunre, the mother of Pa Benjamin Abegunde, a bricklayer who was a friend of my father. My grandmother and *Iye pupa* were so close to the extent that she would make me to sleep in their house together with other children who were much older than myself namely, Oni, Ola,

Flori and their mother Madam Aseja. The youngest amongst them in that house was Femi the son of Pa Abegunde. I was mostly very close to Flori because she used to play with me. She used to take care of Femi Abegunde when his mother was busy doing some house chores or domestic tasks. Femi was their baby of the house. I realized later that my father had no house of his own, so we were scouting with relations, a typical African communal lifestyle. The most memorable relatives that I grew up with were the family members of Pa Samuel Oshadupin- Dele, Ole, who became Hosea after being born again and baptized in the Sudan Interior Mission Church at Idofin, Bosede who became Mrs. Omobola, Esike (Ezekiel), Dayo, Seti (Seth), and Ola, the last born in the family. All these people have deceased except Ola Oshadupin who is now called Popular Photo, but I still have fond memories of them all. There were two other friends in Odeko that up till now we remained very close friends and they are Prince Dele David, who is my cousin: and late Honorable/Attorney Joseph Noah Molemodile. We grew together and shared the fear, anxiety and dread of the nights as we joined the caravan of human existence. The cloud of the present as we perceived it then was foggy and the future very dim because we did not know any other world than the community.

My knowledge of the environment that was an agrarian community was extremely limited but as I grew in everyday experience and intuition, the cognitive intellect was computerizing and storing the data of its daily activities for expository, analytical, creative and critical thinking. The location of Odeko within the forests, streams and Oyi River at Idofin-Isanlu, in my view, explained the basis of the religiosity of the people. There were/are three prominent religious groups at Idofin-Isanlu that formed part of my knowledge of life: Imole, Origba and Christianity. The first two are indigenous religious and cultural beliefs; and the third that is a byproduct of western modernity was Christianity. I will explain each one of them as it contributed to the perception of my place in the human cosmos. But first, let me say that when it comes to indigenous religious beliefs, the Yoruba are unique in the sense that there are common features that cut across different sub-ethnic groups. Therefore, the traditional religious beliefs as practiced at Idofin-Isanlu are not essentially different from the rest of the Yoruba ethnic groups. It is possible to find some indigenous religious variables as a result of environmental adaptations, which is normal in a large population that is scattered within the Yoruba geographical locations or spaces in Nigeria. Idofin people fall within this category.

IMOLE

According to Yoruba oral traditions, *Imole* or *Imale* is another name given to Orisa; multitudes of primordial divinities created by Olodumare, the Supreme Deity. In Idofin-Isanlu, *Imole* is prominently used rather than *Imale* to designate the generic name of Orisa. Its shrine at Igboe is called *ipara*, which is a stone throw from our place in Odeko.

I grew up in my early life to witness the seriousness the devotees attached to the worship of the divinity and its intents to ward off evil machinations in the community. Sometimes the worship was an expression of a metaphysical warfare against a perceived Dread that surrounded the community. But unknown to us then, it could be a characteristic nature of the deity. E Bolaji Idowu's conception of *imale* captures vividly the existential possibilities of my life in the community in those days when he says, "*imale*, was the designation for the dreadful ones whose habitations were the thick, dark groves and unusual places; those who walk the world of men at night and prowl the place at noonday; the very thought of whom was hair-raising; to pass by whose groves was blood-curdling; with whom man feels compelled to make terms for his own safety; more propitiated out of fear than worshiped in reverence." In those days it was dreadful going out when it was dark because stories about witches holding their nocturnal meetings in the night made it imperative for children to be silent and remain indoors. I remembered several of us urinated on our mat spread on the floor because we had no courage to go out at night to ease ourselves. We, however, on several nights when we were so pressed by nature woke up our parents to lead us out to ease ourselves. But it was not something an individual would like to do frequently because we did not want to disturb their sound sleep, having worked so hard in the daytime. There were also instances when our parents would wake us up and accompany us even when we were not that pressed by nature to ease ourselves. It was not expected that any of us would wet his mat. When my father had his own house, he most often allowed me to share with him his mud bed to save me from perennial dread of the night sometimes caused by the worshippers or devotees of the *Imole*.

The worship of *Imole* at Idofin-Isanlu was not always with dread and fear. On the day of their festival, it was with gale and fun. The worshippers would dress in white apparels and dance with gleeful body movements and steps. Their religious song was an expression of devotion and commitment. It goes thus in Yagba language:

Imole yinmse (2x)
Ibo ba gbemde mai oo
The rhythm of the drum sounds like this:
Ku ku ngbu, Ku ku ngbu

The song is an explicit and implicit belief in the tenacity of the deity they worship, and the acceptance of his directives. However, in the real life of the worshippers, there is a proviso that it all depends on the proportionate benefits derived from the deity. If the deity fails to meet their expectations, the worshippers will abandon him for another one that can satisfy their needs. It seems to me that the worshippers of Imole were satisfied with the deity and that was why they sang and danced gleefully to the rhythm of the drum. Both the sound of their drum and dancing steps served as aesthetic amusements. As children, in those days, we enjoyed the festival because we would not go to farm and there were plenty of food with goat meats, bush meats and chicken to serve visitors from neighboring towns and cities: religious dignitaries, elders and community leaders. The leftovers were for children who would struggle over it and sometimes fought one another to have a better share of the remnant food. On an occasion like this, it was the survival of the fittest.

We used to remember the beauty of the Imole festival for several weeks when the occasion had ended. We would relive the rendition of their song and emulate their dance steps even though we did not understand its meaning.

ORIGBA

This deity to my knowledge is only worshiped at Idofin-Isanlu in Yagba/Yorubaland in Nigeria. It is probably one of the multitudes of deities that are very obscured, which became relevant to the people of Idofin-Isanlu. A friend of mine, Prince Dele David said that Origba has its origin at Oyo, an old Yoruba town, in Oyo State. According to oral traditions about the deity, it was brought to Idofin-Isanlu by a stranger with the intention to ward off evil, increase human welfare, prevent bareness, reduce infant mortality rate, expose evildoers and foretell the future and encourage peace and unity in the community. Initially, it was a clan deity of the Igboe people at Odo-Dofin that metamorphosed to a community divinity. Its paraphernalia are of simple materials except its oblong-head that is made with beautiful ornaments with different colors. The drum is made of local materials, and it is beaten once in a year. The masquerade attire is made of guinea corn leaves when they turn brownish, and they are harvested at night by the youth. When it is woven together, it should be of the size of the person whose turn in the family clan to be the masquerade of the year. There is a grove called *igbo oro* that is prohibited to the uninitiated to trespass including women and children.

The eve of the Origba festival is significant because it is always observed after supper at the arena designated to the event. It is an occasion to expose; abuse and insult individuals who have secretly committed societal abominations or immoral deeds and thought they were unseen from the glaring eyes of mortals. An individual who has the information of the immoral acts will come out and first sing the Origba satire song before mentioning the name of the individual he wants to abuse and tell what he has done in secret. They usually take their turns one after the other. There are no individuals that cannot be exposed, abused and insulted with impunity on the night of this festival, no matter how highly paced in the community. It is the night of what the Yoruba call 'olo fofo', busy bodies. One is not permitted to carry on the abuse and insult with impunity after the eve of the Origba festival. I won't be surprised if individuals who suspected they would be targeted and exposed on the eve of Origba would absent themselves during the occasion to avoid the embarrassment. In other words, those who have skeleton in their cupboards will utilize the option of seeking a haven elsewhere during the occasion. Whether one is at home or not for the event it does not matter. What matters are the imports of the religious practice, which are: the deity does not tolerate indiscipline and hypocrisy; no matter whom the person is in the community.

On the morning of the masquerade's appearance in the public, the community is agog with preparations to participate in its parade, song and dance. The masquerade must dance from one place to another in the town to felicitate with people and those who have gifts to give him voluntarily do so with fun. As he goes round the town, children and young adults throng out to follow him and join to sing Origba's song. Its song is in Idofin-Isanlu dialect that was remembered by many of us then and probably even now. It goes like this:

Ori o, Origbo (2x) It is a song of invocation of Origba

that begins with Ori o.

O Origbo o	It is truly your song of invocation.
Omgbo, omgbo	It re-echoes the song of invocation.
O Origbo o	It is truly your song of invocation.
Omon'bati sobo re	He has come to tell his lies, which is satirical.
O Origbo o	It is truly your song of invocation.
A bagbon gaga mon'ga	This describes it's ugly costume chin.
O Origbo o	It is truly your song of invocation.
Ori o, Origbo (2x)	
O Origbo o	
Ogga sokoto	It tells the story of each deity in its neighborhood, Ogga worships sokoto.
O Origbo o	It is truly your song of invocation.
Ejiba sagbe	Ejiba is a neighborhood which is known for its dancers.
O Origbo o	It is truly your song of invocation.
Isanlu sore	Isanlu is a neighborhood known for sore.
O Origbo o	It is truly your song of invocation.
Amuro sapata	Amuro is a neighborhood known for sapata.
O Origbo o	It is truly your song of invocation.
Ibon sasunm	The Ibon, Nupe people

	are known for sasunm.
O Origbo o	It is truly your song of invocation.
Idofin so'rigba	Idofin is known for Origba,
O Origbo o	It is truly your song of invocation.

There is a particular spot at the marketplace designated for Origba masquerade to dance round it every year during its festival. In fact, it is his final dance event before going back to the grove. While at the marketplace, all the leaders both men and women would come out to pay homage to the deity and listen to his priest, the mouthpiece of the deity, for his message of admonition, warnings and predictions. Therefore, everyone would want to be present and hear the message without being told.

There is no religious festival that pulled a lot of crowds to Idofin-Isanlu when I was growing up, like Origba. The annual festival parade was fun to watch and celebrate. As children, it was a time for a lot of fun because most people would be back from their farm to participate one way or the other in the activities of Origba festival and more importantly it was held, and it is still being held, during the harmattan season with its cold weather between end of November and early December each year. Bush burning, fighting, and beating of drums are generally prohibited during the week of Origba festival and any violations of the injunctions come with specific penalties. This deity does not compromise indiscipline, for instance, stealing of the costumes of the masquerade will always receive spontaneous justice. Every adult in the community is conscious of the wrath of Origba on issues bordering on immorality or social injustice that will not enhance harmonious relationships in the community.

The two indigenous religious beliefs and practices, *Imole* and Origba at Idofin-Isanlu explicate vividly in a nutshell the facticity of my existence and the possibilities that I must unravel in my adulthood. How to accomplish it could not be found in the two religious beliefs because it requires some higher level of epistemological and scientific methodologies of modernity, a new renaissance and enlightenment, which Christianity was its prelude.

CHRISTIANITY

There were two small churches at Idofin-Isanlu when I was growing up, namely, the Baptist located in Odo-Dofin and the Sudan Interior Mission located in Oke-Dofin. There was, however, information that the first church in the community was African Church but it did not have strong followers to withstand the persecution from members of the indigenous religion, *Imole* and *Origba* unlike the two churches mentioned above that came later.

My father was one of the founding members of the Baptist Church. Some of the prominent founding fathers of the Baptist church were, Pa David Anjiku, who became Shabba and subsequently the Oba, His Royal Highness, of Idofin-Isanlu, Elder Owoeye, Ibitoye Moses, Joshua Obiyomi, Tunde Oshamo, Thomas Komolafe, Malachi Ogunbiwaje etc. In a nutshell, I was born into Christian faith and nurtured by my father and Pastor Theophilus of the Baptist Church. That explained the biblical name Elijah given to me at birth, which of course, I politely rejected as I grew up as an adult and took a Yoruba name Segun that has a cultural meaning, significance and identity. I also later discovered that being born into the household of Christians did not necessarily mean being born again. All the households of *Iye pupa*, Madam Igununbiunre, my grandmother, Madam Sare, Flori, Pa, Thomas Komolafe, the closest friend of my father, all the household of Pa Anjiku David were members of the Baptist Church.

It was customary for everybody to put on good clothes and look neat because we were going to be in the presence of God in the church, a holy place. Going to Church every Sunday was to me a social gathering, for our parents to interact with their friends and the children to associate freely with their peers in the Sunday school and to sing Christian songs even though we did not know their meaning. In the Sunday school we were told biblical stories but the most fascinating to me were the miracles of Jesus where he used five loaves of bread and two pieces of fish to feed thousands of people. We were made to memorize biblical passages and since they were the words of God, we did not ask questions. Every Sunday was a special day because we would eat pounded yam with delicious soup before going to church and in the afternoon, after the church service. Nobody went to work on the farm on Sundays, so we had the full day as children to play and run around with our friends and relations.

My association with the Baptist Church was short lived because my grandfather Pa Joseph Ogungbemi told my father that he wanted me to be a member of Sudan Interior Mission (S.I.M), which was formerly Africa Industrial Mission, for a reason not known to me. So, I stopped going to the Baptist Church. I later got to know that my grandfather was an elder in his Church at Odo-Ere and he wanted all his children and grandchildren to be members of S.I.M wherever they were. My father released me, and I became a member of S.I.M Church. Some of the founding and strong members of the Church were Pa Peter, Pa Molemodile Noah, Pa Ezra Abegunde, Pa Elijah Iyelolu, Pa Michael Dada, and Pa Titus Omokore, Pa Ezra Odu Balogun among others. All the households of these founding and strong members of the church became members of the church. So, when I joined the church I was able to make new friends among my peers namely, Alice Peter, Nellie Owa, Isaac Abegunde, Benjamin Abegunde, Ibiye Mokanjuola etc. Other members who were much older than me were David Owa, Kola Awogbenja, Zacchaeus Ope, Daniel Awogbenja, Elijah Biodun Daramola and several others. I became more fascinated with the church because some white missionaries used to come from S.I.M Hospital Egbe and Titcombe College Egbe to attend the Sunday Service with us. Having missionaries with some of our people dressed in European uniform was like a new dawn of western civilization in our locality. More importantly, there was Henry Daniel Osaniyi from Ejiba who was our Sunday school and Kindergarten teacher from 1952-1953. He used to teach us on Sundays from 4-6 pm. It was not just the Sunday school lessons that we learned from his class but western literacy, which made a lot of difference between the Sunday school lessons in the Baptist Church. Upon hindsight, I believe my grandfather made the right decision for me to become a member of the S.I.M Church.

The Church had weekly activities, which included early morning prayers before the farmers set out for their farms to ward off human machinations, overcome the persecutions from non-Christian believers, protection over natural and evil forces that were perceived to be dwelling in the thick forests that surrounded the town and their farmlands, witches that flew day and night etc. The reading of Psalm 23 before the prayer session was a usual practice to instill confidence in the mind of the people of God's caring for their needs and he was watching over each one of them as he did for King David of old. The evening prayer service after dinner and before night rest was meant for their well-being at night. I still remember their usual service song in Yoruba:

The translation is mine:

Wa bami gbe ale fere le tan	Abide with me the evening tide is almost over
Okunkun su Oluwa bamigbe	Nightfall is looming, Lord abide with me
Bi oluran lo wo mi ran baye	When there is no guardian
Iranwo alaini wa ba mi gbe.	The guardian of the needy, abide with me

To encourage literacy, the church had weekly Yoruba Bible class for both men and women. That enabled elderly people in the church who could not have western education to; at least read and understand the Bible in their own language; and to be crusaders for Christ. The teaching of morals and the infusion of discipline amongst church members had the backing of biblical authority that readers of the Bible could refer to while teaching their children some basic biblical moral injunctions, otherwise called the Ten Commandments in Exodus 20: 3-17. We were constantly reminded our obligation to obey and respect our parents because the Bible said so in Exodus 20: 12, "Honour thy father and thy mother: that thy days may be long upon the land which the LORD thy God giveth thee." Of course, we wanted to live long on the planet earth and so the moral training given to us as they were reading the Bible gave credence to the seriousness of being submissive to them. For those of us who were restless, troublesome and stubborn, our parents found another favorable biblical passage in the book of Proverbs 13: 24 that says, "He that spareth his rod hateth his son: but he that loveth him chasteneth him betimes." It became a popular mantra, 'spare the rod and spoil the child' to justify parents' use of cane as a corrective measure on disobedient children.

The road infrastructure that took place in the Yagbaland was a big boost to the wide spreading of Christianity and stoppage of persecution of Christians. The new religion encouraged boldness, steadfastness and perseverance that spread like wildfire that made them to sing a song of jubilation in Yoruba. It goes like this:

Igbagbo ma'gbile (3x)
Sa sa ngolo
Sa go lo.

As a young lad, I watched members dancing with frenzy

whenever they sang the song as if they were spiritually possessed. Those of us who were very young imitated the dance steps of old women and the leaders of the Church out of curiosity but not to the level of being spiritually possessed. The Church hymnal was full of spiritual songs and praises. At Idofin-Isanlu, members of S.I.M Church choir were known for their spiritual choruses and songs that encouraged young members to join the choir and to participate very actively in other church activities.

There were two Christian festivals that attracted me to Christianity: Christmas/New Year and Easter.

1.   Christmas/New Year

Christmas eve and New Year's Eve were special nights that got boys and girls actively busy. It was always the dry season with cold harmattan wind when bushes were very dry and almost nothing really engaging on the farm. So, the boys would go for fishing and hunting and would bring their catch to their girlfriends to cook for the night. Cooking then was basically by firewood. Our parents generally relaxed their disciplinarian attitude towards us for being seen around the girls because we were in one open location where cooking was taking place. They, however, kept their eagle eyes on us so that nothing abnormal happened. We knew we had to behave ourselves as disciplined children and members of the Christian Church.

Like other children, the euphoria of Christmas usually gripped my mind because it was a time our parents would buy new clothes for us, and it was a time many children whose clothes have not been sewn by their tailors to keep night vigil in the houses of the tailors. Wearing new clothes on Christmas day was a big and memorable thing to us. Those who could not get their clothes sewn for Christmas events were sad and they hardly came out to participate in the celebration of the festival. Dancing round the town to wish everyone Merry Christmas by Christians and members of the community was more than getting a gift from Santa Claus or Father Christmas as it was and still a common practice in modern time. In those days we never knew anything about Santa Claus or Father Christmas. It was a western idea and practice. What was important to me was to wear new clothes and enjoy the fun and happiness of the season.

2. Easter

The decoration of the Church building with palm fronds and flowers during the Easter has left a very lasting impression on me. I used to join other children to assist the youth and some elders in the beautification of the Church in those days. I had passion for the drama of the persecution and crucifixion of Jesus Christ on the cross that was reenacted every year. The resurrection event and the call on all Christians to wake up very early on Monday morning and go to a symbolic Mount Galilee, in the vicinity, to catch the glimpse of resurrected Christ was like an Olympic competition. The hope and excitement of seeing Jesus on 'Mount Galilee' after his resurrection wouldn't let me have the morning sound sleep. On several occasions all my efforts at home to see Jesus on our local 'Mount Galilee' on Monday after the resurrection was met with dazzling failure. Despite the failure to see Jesus on 'Mount Galilee' all hope was not lost. The faith of his return next year was very reassuring.

Members of the then two Churches: the Baptist and S.I.M would sing and dance from one end of the road to the other in jubilation of the resurrection of Jesus the Christ. The event gave the churches the boldness to preach the good news of God intervening in human history to save sinners from eternal damnation. I did not know the true meaning of those events apart from being a period that made us to be at home for celebration and to play with my friends. And above all, the church environment, as I understood it then, was a good venue for social interaction and exposure to modernity. The modernity that was gradually beaming its light on our community and its significant impact was futuristic. The mission churches were, in my view, the forerunners of modernity and modernization. Of course, all depends on the readiness of our community, if they want to remove the yoke of ignorance and embrace the forward march of intellectual progression to enhance their individual and corporate existence.

It is imperative to mention that as I was growing up, I saw some institutions established by the Sudan Interior Mission in some towns and villages in Yagbaland. In 1932 there were three Central Schools established by the Sudan Interior Mission at Egbe, Isanlu and Mopa to encourage neighboring villages to send their children and wards to them. In 1939 the Mission established a primary school at Ponyan. Furthermore in 1943 the Mission established new primary schools at Odo-Ere, Odo-Egbe, Ejiba and Koro respectively. There were several health infrastructures put in place namely, Egbe hospital, Maternity and Dispensary Isanlu, Orphanage at Mopa and Medical Leprosarium Oyi in 1945 that is on Idofin-Isanlu land. These institutions built by the Sudan Interior Mission set the pace for the new renaissance to gradually demystify the folklores of horror and dread the people had been living with.

It is apparent, as I now reflect on the past events at Idofin-Isanlu, that in these religions: Indigenous religion and Christianity have a common thread of fear manifesting from natural phenomena that human beings must subdue to be able to flourish. The solutions proffered by each religion were, to the best of the believers, a channel of pragmatic deliverance. But the progressive approach to overcome fear, it seems to me, is to remove it from human psyche through philosophical and scientific knowledge of the nature of human existence and its relationship to the environment. The theological proposition of relationship between man and his Creator is a metaphysical abstraction that makes religious beliefs relevant to human existence, which was beyond my comprehension during my early development.

Chapter 5
WESTERN EDUCATION

Idofin-Isanlu has been one of the most naturally blessed communities in Isanlu with abundant human potentials to make the town become one of the emerging modern and vibrant societies but, unfortunately, the awakening of the people to western education did not materialize until the middle 50s. Before that time there were no basic infrastructures like transportation, school, healthcare center, electricity, pipe borne water, tarred road etc. As a matter of fact, most communities in Yagbaland were almost in the same condition of Idofin community except a few communities like Egbe, Makutu, Mopa, etc., that have had some remarkable presence of the Sudan Interior Mission activities that I have espoused in the preceding Chapter. Due to lack of transportation, accommodation and feeding arrangements, it was difficult for young ones like me to go to Isanlu Central School at Makutu-Isanlu, which was about six miles from Idofin-Isanlu. Unfortunately, the Sudan Interior Mission did not build a primary school at Idofin unlike Ejiba that was about five miles away from my town. In 1953 some prominent members of the Baptist Church at Idofin muted the idea that the Baptist Mission should come to their aid to build a primary school at Idofin-Isanlu but the community thought otherwise. They decided to have Yagba Native Authority primary school and not a mission institution. In the interim, they decided to use the Baptist Church and its premises as takeoff site. But before then my cousin, Dele David and I were the very first generation of pupils that began an informal kindergarten in 1952 under Pastor Theophilus of the Baptist Church as a preparatory to formal primary education at Idofin in 1954.

We desired to stay with the Pastor who was to the community a teacher not because of learning anything from him but because we hated going to farm with our parents. We were troublesome, playful, and restless. We used to sustain injuries on the playing grounds and when they were not treated on time, they became painful wounds. My grandmother was an expert in treating my wounds and when they became sores, she would use traditional herbs that had burning sensation to hasten the healing. For two good years when we should have made progress in a formal institution like Isanlu Central

School at Makutu, we were playing an Ostrich game of ignorance with contentment. At that time, we did not know the value of western education.

As I have earlier stated that the primary school did not formally begin until 1954 and when it did, it was at a very low pace because most parents did not want to enroll their children in school for the fear of losing their labor force on the farm. However, a few parents like my father, amongst others, were ready to release their lazy children like me and, of course, my cousin, Dele. I was enrolled as Elijah Afolami, now Segun Ogungbemi and Dele was enrolled as Bamidele Shaba, now Prince Dele David because his father became Oba of Idofin after the demise of Oba Ogunbiwaje. There were other pupils who enrolled with us in 1954/1955 namely, Ajayi Bello, Boy Sani who later became Omosowon Sani, Aina Owa, who later became Daniel Awofenka Awogbenja, so also Zacchaeus Moses, changed his name to Zacchaeus Ope, Ola Komolafe, now Stephen Olu, Akintoye Ayeni who later changed his name to Akintoye Daodu and his sister, Rhoda Ayeni the only female, joined us in Primary 1. Our first teacher Headmaster in 1954 was Mr. Adeniyi, popularly called Baba Tunu, the father of Tunu and in 1955 Mr. Peter Orisei taught us. He was the first Ibo man to teach in the school. My mother and some parents feared his presence in our school because it was believed that the Ibos were cannibals, *jeni jeni*. But he was not a cannibal rather; he was a very friendly teacher and a magician who entertained us in class when he perceived that we were tired of his teaching. He would then use magic to provide biscuits and cubes of sugar for us to share with intention to arouse our interest and keep us awake in class.

It was not until 1956/1957 that we had better enrolments in the school with Benjamin Abegunde, Isaac Abegunde, Ola Isaiah, Michael Elisha, Ige Odu, Joseph Modu now Joseph Noah Molemodile, Sunday Mark, Abayomi Samuel, Ibitoye Agbana, Boja Elijah, now Boja Iyelolu, Luke Afolami, now Luke Omo Afolami Ogungbemi, Sunday Titus now Samuel Sunday Omokore and some girls namely, Toria Balogun, Oni Omodara, Omolayo Abe, Bosesde Malachi, Bosede Sani, Rafa Ayeni, etc. As the population of pupils increased in 1956/1957 there was demand for more teachers. Some of the new teachers that I remembered were Messrs. Adewale, George Elewa, Ige, the Headmaster in 1957, popularly called Baba Olu from Omi and Miss. Comfort Tunde Balogun, (now Mrs. Comfort Tunde Sheidu) was the only first female teacher from Makutu-Isanlu, but an indigene of Idofin-Isanlu.

The school ran a calendar of four quarters from January to December each year. It was a seven-year Primary School system under the defunct Northern Region. The Headmaster ran the affairs of the school under the supervision of the

Divisional Superintendent of Education. The running affairs of the school also had a local supervising content that served as first School Manager; Mr. Joshua Obiyomi in our time performed that function. The community shouldered the responsibility of building the classroom we used in 1957. That showed the seriousness and commitment of the people towards western education. The school was not free. Our parents/guardians and self-sponsored pupils had to pay school fees while all the pupils had to take care of their new classroom and the school premises in addition to the Baptist Church facilities they were using.

The school uniform was made from local fabrics in accordance with specific designs and quality. The tailor had to sew it according to the specification of the school. I didn't have any problem to get one made for me on time because my mother was an expert of the local loom. The school uniform could last between two to three years if it was washed and dyed regularly. It was economical and comfortable to wear but not easy to wash by young ones like me in those days.

The school was not always an interesting learning environment because of the high handedness of some of the teachers. Flogging of pupils for minor offences and other forms of severe punishment like cutting grasses and hoeing a large portion of school garden. But generally, I enjoyed the school environment better than going to farm with my parents.

When we started in 1954, we thought there wouldn't be any need for us to go to Isanlu Central School at Makutu to complete our First School-leaving Certificate because of lack of transportation and other learning social problems. I had to repeat the same class several years because there was no approval from the government for expansion. Those who were big boys namely, Aina Owa, Zacchaeus Moses and Ola Thomas who sponsored themselves went to Makutu in 1956 and 1957 respectively to continue from Primary 3. Between 1956 and 1958 Aina Owa who changed his name to Daniel Awofenka Awogbenja, and Zacchaeus Moses changed his name to Zacchaeus Ope had proven worthy of being good ambassadors of Idofin Community in character and academic performances. Idofin Community, which was conceived by the emerging Makutu elite, as an obscured place became known as 'Idofin City' with proper recognition and respect.

It was not until 1958 that several of us namely, Benjamin Abegunde, Isaac Abegunde, Joseph Noah, Dele David and I went to continue from Primary 3 at Isanlu Central School, Makutu under the headmastership of Mr. J.L. Osho, a charismatic teacher, a seasoned administrator and resourceful leader. Under his administration the mission school was quite a new environment with many new faces to interact with and to learn the basic school rules and discipline. Mr. J. L. Osho used to call those of us from Idofin, 'City' by virtue of our excellent performances in our respective classes. A name he did not forget when I met him in 1975 and asked for a favor, which he gladly obliged. By 1960, he was transferred to another school and Mr. Leslie Bello Obielodan; an indigene of Isanlu took over the headship of the mission school in 1961. But during the time of J.L. Osho the school was one of the best in academic, athletics and sports particularly, soccer. The school band was very organized. One of the songs that I still love to sing once a while is:

We are the boys of S.I.M

S.I.M Isanlu Central School

We are the boys of S.I.M

Oh! S.I.M

When singing the song, the girls would sing: We are the girls of S.I.M and when the boys and girls sang the song together as they filed in line and marching to their different classrooms, the thrilling melody of the song re-echoed the pride of being one of them.

The significance of this song was its identity mantra.

Everyone wanted to be a pupil of the school for the quality of teaching, discipline, sports, environmental cleanliness and sophistication.

There were many school pupils who were already adults coming from neighboring villages like Iye, Odogbe, Ilafin, Ilotin, Itedo, Mopo etc. to Isanlu Central School at Makutu. Bringing pupils young and old to converge at Isanlu Central School, exposed me to a new world order of academic competitiveness. Being in a new environment I soon learned that it required a change of attitude and focus to the academic reality. I was not intimidated by the huge challenges of the new environment because my father had taught me not to be afraid of anyone whose intention was to frustrate me wherever I found myself because it could lead to discouragement and failure; in my pursuit of life engagements. It was customary in those days for big boys to bully those of us with small statures but with my boldness to dare anyone, I rebuffed their bullying tendencies.

The style of leadership of Mr. L. B. Obielodan was slightly different from that of his predecessor, J. L. Osho. He never for once called those of us from Idofin our usual nickname: 'City'. In those days teachers were revered. They were like semi gods. The fear of some terrible teachers then was the beginning of wisdom. The good ones were those you could approach without fear of intimidation and ask for a favor and in most cases, you were assured of getting it.

Upon hindsight, some of the teachers that I considered to be terribly unfriendly to us were performing their duty to inculcate discipline and obey the school rules and regulations. Lateness to school was prohibited and any pupil that violated the rule would be severely punished. We were taught that 'punctuality is the soul of business' and the early we learned its truism the better. To attend a mission school in my time was to experience an admixture of morality and education. The good was the aesthetic ambience of the institution; the quality of teaching for future leadership and national integration, moral teachings and discipline and above all one should be Christ-like. The bad side of the school was the uncritical issues before judgments were made with severe punishment without hesitation. There were two scenarios that I believe those of us who were involved would find very difficult to forget. The first was the allegation that we were involved without investigation before we were punished had to do with three girls who offended us at home, and we felt we should beat them on our way to school. On our way to Makutu, we decided to place a sign of roadblock to entrap them and as soon as they saw our antics, they avoided our notorious plan and walked away from the objects of intrigue. One of the girls Ropo Oshaponle was a younger sister of one of our teachers from Idofin, late Mr. Bolaji Oshaponle and apparently, she went to tell her brother. Her brother didn't call any of us to find out what happened and why we harassed his sister and colleagues. Several weeks after the incident had happened outside the school premises, we had forgotten about it. However, during one of the morning devotions in 1961, the headmaster reported a case of road banditry and described the perpetrators of the act in Yoruba as, 'awon omo dana dana' and then began to call their names. The moment he began to call Dele Anjiku and Joseph Noah, I knew I was going to be the next person. So, he called me among the culprits and invited us to come up to face the whole congregation of school pupils. We were given six strokes of the cane each and we were told to go to the Headmaster's Office where our names would enter the *Black Book* and not the *White Book*! That was the most terrifying aspect of the punishment because names of terribly behaved pupils were recorded in it. The three of us decided to leave the school because of two basic reasons: the high handedness of some teachers and the hash economic condition that made the learning environment not conducive. I had to go to bed several times without adequate food or nothing at all in my stomach. But my condition was not an isolated case among those of us from Idofin. Some of the senior ones among us had to absent themselves from school during the week in order to seek some means for survival. Working on the farm, most of the time as a daily paid worker, was the easiest means for some of us to make ends meet.

We had to find a better environment where we could pursue our academic interest. We heard that in a small community called Idera in Igbomina Ekiti; there was free education that included feeding and accommodation. After we thoroughly investigated the veracity of the information and found out it to be true, we decided to take the risk; as people say: no ventures no gain. We planned how to escape without being caught by our landladies and friends. We set out for the adventure and luckily; we escaped from the eagle eyes within the vicinity. We were lucky to get a vehicle going to Egbe, but we couldn't stretch our luck to a level of complete success without being caught until we passed through Idofin. So, we prayed the driver did not stop at Idofin but unfortunately, he stopped, and our hearts nearly jumped from our mouths. We, however, composed ourselves very well until the driver started moving slowly and finally sped off. As soon as we got to Egbe we knew we were going to get a vehicle going to Omuaran in Igbomina Ekiti. On getting to Egbe we met a vehicle ready to go to Omuaran and we boarded it. The type of vehicle used for transportation then was a wooden truck and the seats were heavy planks meant for six or more people in a row. It was called in Yoruba, *Bole ka ja*, meaning, let us get down and fight because that was the attitude of their apprentice/conductors. If you didn't pay the transport fare, they were ready to pull you down for a fight. The roads were not tarred so the journey was very bumpy and dusty. We got to Omuaran late afternoon, and we headed straight to the house of our host, Mr. Buraimoh who was a prominent member of the S.I.M and an indigene of Idera. He welcomed us very warmly and treated us very well. We slept in his house and the following morning we thought he was going to take us to Idera, which to us was probably a short distance from Omuaran. After our breakfast he took his pen and drew on a piece of paper how we would continue our journey because Idera was quite a distance. So, we had to go to Oke-Onigbin and from there we would get a vehicle going to Idera. We thanked him and followed his directive. On getting to Oke-Onigbin we asked for a vehicle that would be going to Idera. We were told that no vehicles were available, and we inquired the road to Idera and the distance from Oke-Onigbin. They told us that it was 19 miles. So, we determined to trek to Idera that day. It was really a risky venture for three small boys without any elderly person with us. We were not afraid or deterred by what we saw on the way. We finally got to Idera in the evening. We were so tired but full of hope. We were invited to attend the evening service and from there we thought we were going to be introduced to our individual host. We were given food and accommodation for the night. The following morning, we met the Headmaster, welcomed us very warmly and asked for our transferred certificates from our school. We told him we didn't come with any transferred certificates. He then told us that since it was the same mission that governed the schools, he could not admit us without them. We were very sad, and we had to think of different options. So, we trekked back to Oke-Onigbin and from there I headed to Idofin without my two friends who thought there could be a magic wand somewhere to make their dream come true. Given the position of the Headmaster at Idera, I was convinced no school would admit them without the transferred certificates. They returned to Idofin without success and since we had no alternatives; our parents told us to go back to our school at Isanlu.

On Monday we reported to school and as usual, we had to attend the morning devotion like all other pupils. The Headmaster Pa Obielodan was sarcastic about our journey to Idera and back without success. In a sarcastic manner he, welcomed the travelers from Accra to Liverpool. Honestly, we did not know that we were the ones he was talking about until he mentioned our names: Joseph Noah, Dele Anjiku and Elijah Afolami. He then invited us up and told us to face the rest of the congregation. He then gave us six strokes of the cane each and told one of the teachers to give us some portions of the school area to hoe. And that was not all; our names were to be written the second time in the *Black Book*. Some weeks after our return to school, the Headmaster Pa Obielodan met some of us invited for an interview at

Saint Augustine Secondary School Kabba and praised us for the feat while in Primary 6. I knew I was not going for the interview since my parents could not afford to pay for my transportation from Isanlu to Kabba let alone the school fees. All that I was looking forward to was my graduation in 1962 and looking for something else to do and later further my education. In December 1962 I graduated with the First School Leaving Certificate, a journey that would have taken me seven years from 1952-1959 if I had started in 1952 and not 1954. But my future academic expedition was really shrouded in the wilderness of paradoxical uncertainty.

STUDENTSHIP AT UNIVERSITY OF IBADAN

YAGBA TEACHING STAFF AT ABDUL AZIZ ATTA MEMORIAL COLLEGE, OKENE

SMU, DALLAS

MY PH.D. AT UNIVERSITY OF TEXAS, DALLAS

UNIVERSITY OF TEXAS - DALLAS
Commencement
January 5, 1985

PART THREE

WAITING ON THE PROVIDENCE

Chapter 6
CAREER PATH TRAJECTORY

After the new year celebration in January 1963, I discovered that my friends in Idofin that we graduated together in December 1962 had left to pursue their different goals in life: Joseph Noah Molemodile had resumed at Titcombe College Egbe in the present Yagba West Local Government, Kogi State, Nigeria. My cousin, Dele Anjiku David had gone to Lagos to be with his mother. I had no idea where others had gone to pursue their future careers. My father decided that I should join my cousin, Adebayo, on the farm until he could figure out what was to be my next line of action. I could understand the dilemma my father was in since his cocoa farm had been burnt in 1956 and there were no major cash crops to fetch him sufficient liquid cash to send me to a secondary school or any other higher institution like my friend. My case was a big burden and embarrassment to him but what could he do other than patiently wait on Providence to intervene? I thought if I stayed at home and studied very hard for the next common entrance examination to a government secondary school, it could be a better choice to help myself and save my father the burden of looking for money from different sources to send me to a higher institution. But my mother had a different thought because she was not comfortable seeing me with a cutlass and a basket on my head every morning heading to farm and to come back home after sunset. One day she came to awake the cognitive consciousness of my father with her economic theory, which says: 'A three pence that is invested is better than one pound that is lying fallow.' She was being philosophical with her economic theory. Frankly speaking, I did not understand the metaphorical import of her dialogue with my father until many years later. Did my mother's economic speech-act theory have any effect on her husband? Yes, it did because within a week my father found a solution to my being a potential farming apprentice under him. He and his youngest sister, Maroni made a contact with Mr. Jacob Ige, their neighbor in Odeko ward who was working at Queen's Secondary School Ilorin, if he could get a job for me in Ilorin. Mr. Jacob Ige who was popularly called Bereke was delighted to inform my father that he should send me to him as soon as possible because one of his friends was looking for a young clerk for his shop. My father called his sister Maroni and broke the good news that Bereke, Jacob Ige had found me a job and I should resume as soon as possible. That was the good news, but the bad news was my parents had no money at hand for my transportation fare to Ilorin. When my father's sister, Maroni heard that my parents had no money at hand for my transport fare she went to take a loan of ten shillings to ease their burden. I was impressed with the spontaneous response of 'sister' Maroni for the loan even though my father later paid her the loan. It was like a dream come true. My parents also went to source for additional money for me to spend on the way and for other expenses before I earned my first salary.

I was told to get ready for Mr. Afolabi, the only driver that plied Ilorin-Kabba Road at that time and once I missed boarding the wooden truck, *Bole ka ja,* on the scheduled date, I had to wait for another week. To miss the vehicle on the scheduled date, I thought, would have been conceived as a bad omen. I was so excited about the journey, and I found it difficult to sleep as I was counting the number of days left for me to be in Ilorin, a town I was made to believe; where their people bear a popular name, Bello than anywhere in Yorubaland. A story I would later learn to be untrue. It was one of those myth tales in our community. In preparation for the journey, I had to wash my clothes and cut my hair to look more handsome. I was told to get ready for the last weekend of January 1963 when Afolabi, the driver of the truck, would be going to Ilorin. I hardly slept that night and before dawn my parents and sister Maroni came to wake me up and I told them that I was already awake and quickly brought out my wooden box where I had packed all my things and went to wait for the vehicle. It was not long when the vehicle came, and I boarded it. I was excited to leave and at the same time I was having a nostalgic feeling of missing my parents, relations and friends particularly, brother Adebayo who would be going alone with my father to work on the farm. My younger siblings, Luke and Joshua, were in primary school. Anyway, that is the nature of human destiny. I had to move on. The road was narrow, lonely, bumpy and dusty. The driver normally stopped on the way to pick passengers until there were no more spaces to be occupied. Mr. Afolabi was known as a good driver but sometimes very reckless and rude. His apprentice was probably nurtured and trained in the school of rudeness; and all forms of bad mannerism. If the transport fare was not paid on time, he could abuse the passengers and even threaten to beat them up or force them out of the vehicle without giving them their luggage.

The journey on the rough road ended abruptly when we got to a town called Ajasepo. There were passengers who alighted from the vehicle at Ajasepo and those who had not paid their transport fares should begin to pay. If for any reason some passengers could not pay the arbitrary charges, the driver would collect whatever they had and drop them at Ajasepo;

a town the driver was aware would not grant strangers accommodation. With that in mind those who could not pay had to take loans from their co-travelers. When the driver had collected all his money from the passengers, we were told to enter the vehicle one after the other to make sure all passengers going to Ilorin were given the first bench to seat. When everyone had sat down in the vehicle the driver took off on a very smooth road without dust. It was my first time on a tarred road. It wasn't long before we got to the motor park at Ilorin, and everyone had to come down and pick his or her luggage. As soon as I got my box and walked out of the area, I had a problem locating the address of my host at Idi-ape Jegede. It took several hours before a kindhearted person led me to his house. It was a big relief for me because I did not know any person apart from my host in Ilorin. I was welcomed to the house, and I narrated some of my travel ordeals, particularly, what happened at Ajasepo. They told me that strangers normally avoided being stranded there because they would not be accommodated even at night. I believe the practice still subsists till today.

I met Daniel Noah Molemodile, the younger brother of my friend, Joseph Noah Molemodile who was an apprentice under Mr. Jacob Ige in Ilorin. He went to fetch some water for me to take my bath even though I was already very tired and needed sleep. As soon as I had my bath, I went to bed. The next morning, I went to greet my host and his wife and to know when he would take me to my employer. He told me to follow his apprentice, Daniel, to Queen School where he had his workshop and on Saturday, February 2, 1963, he would take me to my employer, Baba Mulika. On that Saturday evening he and I went to Baba Mulika. It is not in Yoruba culture to call married couples by their names once they have children. The husband is called *Bab*a; father of his first child, for instance, *Baba Segun* and the wife is called *Iya* or M*omo Segun*. So, my boss was called Baba Mulika. He asked about my experience as a sales clerk, and I told him that I had no work experience apart from farming. He then told me that he would place me on a monthly salary of £1:5: its equivalent in the Nigeria current exchange is about N1000 today, April 20, 2023. He then gave me the conditions of service, which were: (1) the shop was also my bedroom at night, (2) I have to sweep the shop every morning, (3) keep the daily records of sales and close late every evening and work on Sunday after Church service. He told my uncle that he trusted his recommendation that I would be of good character and at the same time perform my duty creditably well without stealing anything in the shop. He also told me that he would provide feeding three times daily at his own expense. I thanked him and my uncle for the job and promised to do my job very well. I didn't like the idea of working on Sunday because my faith was to keep Sunday free and to devote it to serve my Christian God as demanded in the Scriptures. I kept the idea to myself because a bird at hand is better than hundreds in the bush. And my mother's economic theory that stipulates that 'three pence that is invested is better than one pound that is lying fallow' was a wise counsel that I could not reasonably ignore. So, I reported for work early February 1963 with enthusiasm and high hopes as I relied on Providence for a better future. As I reported for duty, my boss introduced me to his neighbors, and we exchanged pleasantries, and I started my work. In the evening he told me to follow him to his second shop and I did. He then introduced me to his first shop clerk/salesclerk, Ishola. He greeted me warmly and from there I went back to my shop. I did not see my position in the real term of a Shop Clerk/Salesclerk rather; I was a shop sales apprentice with monthly stipend in charge of bicycle parts, hurricane lantern and other assorted materials. It was a unique experience for me, but my mind was not taken away from going to a secondary school or at least a teacher training college. When customers were not around, I would begin to read for the common entrance examination. On two different occasions my boss caught me reading for exams and he was angry with me for using his office time to read. He told me not to turn my working hours to a self-tutorial period. I apologized to him and then followed his instruction. I, thereafter, started reading after closing hours around 10 pm when he had gone home leaving me alone in the shop where I slept every night. Having worked so hard in the daytime and closing at 10 pm, my body needed rest. I couldn't read sufficiently to adequately prepare well for the common entrance. I also needed other friends we could study together in order to perform very well in the common entrance. I discussed my dilemma with my uncle who got the job for me, and he told me to endure it until another available opportunity. I agreed with him and continued with my job. After a couple of weeks my uncle showed up and told me that a friend of his was about to open a shop and he would like me to work for him because he was a Christian. I was delighted with the good news, but I had to keep it to myself until he had time to discuss it with my boss.

My uncle got time to discuss with Baba Mulika, my boss, that I would like to discontinue my service in his shop. I did not know how he convinced the man because of the confidence he has built in me over the six months that I have stayed in his shop and attracted many customers who patronized his business. He was not happy that I was leaving but he accepted my resignation. At the end of July 1963, he paid my salary without any deduction.

I resumed work early August 1963 in the shop of Mr. Noah, a native of Ogga in the present Yagba West Local Government in Kogi State, who had been a longtime friend of my uncle. I was appointed a Shop Clerk with a salary of one pound (£1)= N748 in Nigerian currency exchange rate a month but the man promised to buy me clothes and some of my basic needs. The conditions of service included sleeping in the shop and keeping the shop clean and tidy, the shop would not open on Sundays and I could go to church and worship with my friends and relations. I also had time to study for my common entrance examinations. I felt at home with Mr. Noah because he was friendly, kind, generous and committed to improving my knowledge and education. Interestingly both of us came from Yagba so we discussed mostly in Yagba, a variant of Yoruba language. I was delighted to have my freedom of worship, association and freedom to pursue my interest to pursue my education.

The business was thriving, and each time Mr. Noah traveled and came back he was very pleased with me and on several occasions, he gave me surprise gifts. But our mutual work and moral ethics did not last long because of his social and business conflicts with State Security. He had criminal records. One day I summoned courage to find out from my uncle what he knew about the man. He was honest with me and after his narratives of all that he knew about my boss, I told him that I could not work for him anymore and I left for an unknown future that gave me more freedom with existential responsibilities. I was a newspaper vendor. I was at the same time looking for a better job.

In 1963 Ilorin was not a reading society. The rate of literacy was low, and the economy was not buoyant; and that explained why most workers trekked to their offices. The lucky civil servants and workers in the two major industries: Match Company and Tobacco Industry had bicycles and very few of them had motorcycles or cars. There were very few post-primary institutions and no tertiary institutions or Universities.

I became a vendor of newspapers in Ilorin with some rascally-minded teenagers. At that time, there were few newspapers in circulation and most buyers were government civil servants and workers in industries. Some of the newspapers in circulation were: *Daily Times, Tribune, Morning Post, Sketch, Iwe Iroy*in for the Yoruba speaking people etc. There were also some Magazines in circulation namely, *Drum* and *Spear*. The newspapers were sold three pence each and each vendor had a penny commission on each newspaper sold. The Magazines were more expensive but each copy that I sold gave me a better commission than that of the newspapers. I think each Magazine was sold for six pence and each vendor had two or three pence on each copy sold. I used to sell six copies of the newspapers daily and about ten Magazines monthly. So, my daily income from the newspapers was six pence an equivalent of five kobo in the early 70s when Nigerians began to use Naira. Some customers were fond of calling us without any intention of buying but only to browsing the headlines. Some people called us to know from us what was in each of the newspapers and after telling them they would not buy. So, in such instances, my friends and

I were ready to insult such customers for wasting our time because they knew they were not ready to buy. On several occasions some of them could not tolerate our insults and when we perceived they were ready to beat us we would curse them and run away. Before I stopped being a vendor, I had become addicted to reading newspapers and got familiar with local and foreign events in the world.

My uncle did not believe I could make any headway in life by being a vendor so he decided to send me back home. I asked one of my friends, Elijah Daniel to accompany me to appeal to my uncle not to send me back home. He obliged and when both of us met him and pleaded to allow me look for a job for two weeks; and if I failed to get one, he could send me back to Idofin-Isanlu. He accepted our appeal, and I stopped being a vendor. I began to look for a menial job and luckily; I got one at S.I.M Guest House, Ilorin in October 1963. I was employed as a gardener by Rev. and Mrs. Giesbrecht with a weekly salary of sixteen and six (16/6) British currency. I was so happy with the appointment and when my uncle came from work, I told him. He congratulated me and advised me to be of good behavior and be committed to my work because the missionaries could be of help to me in terms of furthering my education. Where I was living was about one and half miles from S.I.M Guest House and I had to be at work at 6:30 am; with a break at 12:30 pm, then resumed at 4 pm and closed at 6 pm. Given the stress of trekking very early in the morning and going back in the evening, I requested Mrs. Giesbrecht to allow me to be living in one of the rooms in the boy's quarters and she warmly granted it. I told my uncle, and he allowed me to go and live there. It was a big relief. The boy's quarters were overgrown with wild grasses that made it very bushy and lonely, but I was determined to live there. I cut down the wild grasses and cleaned up one of the rooms and moved in alone. When my father came to pay me a surprise visit; in order to know about my well-being and saw that I was living in such a lonely place, he did not make his impression known until one evening in 2005 when he was relating his experience to his friends and several children around him of his visit to me in 1963. He told them that if he had money, he would have asked me to leave the place. I told him that I was happy he did not have the means! I soon learned how to cook for myself and adjusted to the new existential reality of being-in-existence. When the Management of the Guest House needed additional workers, I got two of my friends, Elijah Daniel and Sule Akande appointed, and I stopped living alone as they moved to occupy the rest of the space in the building. In all these events, I did not know that the Providence was at work: guiding and protecting me for future prosperity. In 1964, the two missionaries went on furlough and did not return because of their age and perhaps the ill health of Rev. Giesbrecht. Rev. and Mrs. Blake were posted to man the affairs of the Guest House. They were a young couple full of high spirit and energy with Christian love of missionary zeal. They were friendly with everyone around them as they started learning Yoruba language to enhance their missionary activities.

Mrs. Blake appointed me as a Guest Housekeeper with an increment of six pence on my salary a week. My new salary was seventeen Shillings a week, which was better than what I was earning in each of my two previous appointments as a Shop Clerk. As a teenager, I was comfortable being independent and responsible for whatever I did. I knew I had some responsibilities to my parents and siblings. I made sure I sent money regularly through people going home to my parents. I had time to read for the annual common entrance examination but unfortunately the missionaries were not ready to sponsor anyone, and my meager salary could not support my pursuit of education in any High School.

It was not long before Rev. and Mrs. Blake went on furlough and Rev. and Mrs. Laird took over the management of the Guest House. They were missionaries in Sudan and when the political and religious crises endangered their lives they were redeployed to Nigeria. Mrs. Laird was a hard working woman and she decided to have me work as a steward with a little increment on my weekly salary. I was encouraged with the elevation but the manner she was treating those of us working for her was dehumanizing. When we requested her to give us permission to go for the annual common entrance examination at Baboko Primary School Ilorin; she bluntly refused and told us to resign should we decided to go for the exam. I suggested to my friends that we should talk to the husband and ask for his intervention. It worked and she allowed us to go. We did not come back on time because the venue of the examination was very far away from our place of work. When we returned, she fired me. I pleaded with her, but she did not accept my appeal perhaps because I was the mouthpiece of my friends. Her action put an end to my aspiration and hopes that someday one of the missionaries would be a source of my academic success. I was reminded the adage that says, 'if one road is not closed another one will not open.' I accepted my fate in good faith that my Providence would lead me to a better destiny.

I did not get another job until September 1964 when my uncle, Mr. Jacob Ige told me that some American Peace Corps were coming to Queen Elizabeth School in Ilorin. And before their arrival, Ms. Davies, the newly appointed Principal of the school from England needed a house help and I should go and see her if she could hire me as one of her domestic workers. I agreed to meet Ms. Davies and she hired me with a better salary. She placed me on a salary of four Pounds (£4) a month. There was one Ms. Elizabeth Hull, a British Council volunteer deployed to Queen Elizabeth School Ilorin who was given a temporary accommodation by Ms. Davies in her quarters. I took advantage of working for the Principal, Ms. Davies to interact with her with the intention for her to employ one of my friends whenever she moved to her own quarters. Elizabeth Hull agreed and when she moved to her new quarters she hired my friend, Francis Tunbosun Ikudaiyenu. Ms. Hull became an instrument to his academic success in life before his demise. When the Peace Corps resumed, they asked me to get them domestic workers. Several of my Isanlu friends were hired and later I joined them to work for Ms. Sally Levin. Between 1965-66 I started being more serious with the annual common entrance with the hope that one of these Peace Corps would be kind enough to give me a helping hand. In 1966 I was called for interviews at St. John's College Kaduna as one of the best candidates, Igbaja Teacher's College, Igbaja Bible College, Commercial Secondary School Edidi, among others. I got sponsorship from Ms. Ruth Bowden and Ms. Rosalie Peterson to go to Igbaja Bible College. Initially I did not want to go to Igbaja Bible College or any of the above schools apart from St. John's College Kaduna, but the institution denied my choice because I belonged to the Sudan Interior Mission. Without any financial resources to depend on Mr. Daniel Awofenka Awogbenja, persuaded me to go to where I had the slightest opportunity to succeed in life. His view was the convincing voice that made me go to Igbaja Bible College in October 1966.

The day before resumption at Igbaja Bible College he came to remind me to go to the two American Peace Corps who had indicated interest to sponsor me. I immediately went to meet Ms. Ruth Bowden to inform her that we were to resume the next day. She told me to come tomorrow at 7: a.m. I got there before 6:30 a.m. Before 7: a.m. she and her friend Ms. Rosalie Peterson were already up and Ruth came out and told me that Rosalie herself gave me nine pounds, British Sterling and that I should go to Ms. Peggy, my employer who would give me my salary for the week to complete the school fees. It seemed to me that they had already discussed my admission and how to get the fees paid behind the scene because as I got to Ms. Peggy and told her that I was going to my school; she gave me my salary for the week and congratulated me. I also told her that one of my friends would be working for her and she asked him to start work that day.

I resumed at Igbaja Bible College, Igbaja without any knowledge of the people and topography of the city. Igbaja has undulating hills and valleys that are good for farming. The people are mostly Muslims and that probably explained why the missionaries established the two post-primary institutions there: Igbaja Bible College; primarily for the training of pastors and mission workers; and Igbaja Teacher's College popularly called Igbaojule for the training of teachers in their mission schools. The two institutions were established in a large area of land with a demarcation to separate them.

Entering the premises of Igbaja Bible College and Seminary was like visiting a ghost town. Its serenity was conducive to academic life and religious discipline; a new life that I had to adapt if I really wanted to be successful.

The second day we resumed was for registration and payment of tuition and fees. The cost was twenty Pounds (£20) per year and each student was mandated to pay ten Pounds (£10) and worked for ten Pounds (£10) in the school. Each student had to work for the balance of ten Pounds each even if he had the capacity to pay the full fees. For those of us who came from a poor background, it was a generous arrangement and probably the best we could hope for. After most of us had registered, we were given an orientation with rules and regulations of the institution; and a visit to the Library, Dining room, the ELWA Recording Studios under Ms. Joyce Flint; and the Chapel.

There were 25 students in my class, all male and no female. Most of our teachers were white missionaries with some Africans. The Principal of the institution was Rev. Norman Waldo Lorenz and the Vice-Principal was Rev. Nathaniel Olutimayin. We were lucky to have some African teachers whose teaching and dedication gave us a solid foundation and they were Rev. Olutimayin, Mr. Bryan Kato, Mr. Elisha Abiodun Ajayi, Mr. Isaac Olaofe, Rev. Moses Durojaiye and Mr. Ezekiel Bolaji Iyekolo, a vocational teacher in 1967 from

Ahmadu Bello University, Zaria. When Rev. Lorenz went on Furlough, Rev. Larry Fehl became the Principal of the college. Some of our best teachers amongst the missionaries were Rev. Larry and Mrs. Shirley Fehl, Rev. Jack and Mrs. Jean Teachout, Rev. and Mrs. Rogers, Ms. Vivian Laird and Mr. Paul and Ms. Evie Bowers. Rev. Fehl, the Principal was magnanimous to pay attention to our argument that in a modern society, learning biblical subjects alone without liberal subjects like English Language, Literature in English, History, Geography etc. would make pastoral work not responding to the spiritual and intellectual needs of the time. That was probably why Isaac Olaofe, Mr. Elisha Abiodun Ajayi, Mrs. Fehl and Mr. Ezekiel Bolaji Iyekolo became veritable tools that boosted our motivation for academic excellence. Mr. Olaofe organized a debating contest between our students and the Igbaojule students and our students won the contest. We were proud of the performance of our students as it continued to boost our intellectual and academic morale. It also removed the myth of academic superiority of Igbaojule students over those of us at Bible College. We were all academically determined to compete at all levels with both Secondary Schools and Teacher Training institutions around us.

I was aware that what could make Ruth and Rosalie to continue my sponsorship at Igbaja Bible College was my academic performance. I was very lucky to have a senior roommate, Mr. Rowland Sunday Babatunde, a bookworm student who infected me with his midnight reading habit. I got used to it and the result was a resounding success. I was the best student in my class and when my sponsors saw my result each semester it probably gave them the encouragement to continue to assist me; and when they were leaving, Rosalie introduced me to another Peace Corps member, Mr. Kenneth Koosman who was also very helpful. He gave me financial and academic assistance for the short period that I knew him until he went back home.

I was a very playful student and I loved sports. I used to perform very well in sports particularly, football (soccer). I was made Assistant Captain of the School Team. Because of my youthful exuberance most of my classmates initially thought I was an average student including my best friends, Benjamin Olusola Adetiba, Moses Kayode Oshagbemi, Mr. Jethro Akobe and Elisha Tunde Oshagbemi. They were surprised when in 1970 I was the class Valedictorian. It was a remarkable feat in my early pursuit of post-primary education. While it was worthwhile celebrating our modest achievements, I remembered that out of 25 students that began the heroic academic journey only 13 of us graduated. The 13 heroes were already aware that the foundation received at Igbaja Bible College was a mere steppingstone, hence we had to continue to burn our academic candles at both ends because we were participants in a competitive world. I wrote my benefactors Ruth and Rosalie and expressed my profound gratitude to them. I did not close the line of correspondence from time to time with them because I knew there might be occasions that would warrant their further assistance.

I have to note that for those four-years, it was a tragic and most turbulent moment in the annals of Nigerian political space. It was the year of the first Military coup that led to the massacre of thousands of Igbo ethnic group in the North. It also subsequently resulted to a civil war from July 1967- January 1970. Because of the insecurity, no Igbo student was admitted at Igbaja Bible College until after our graduation in June 1970. It was as if the Providence decided to bring something awesome out of the chaos, which later in life unfolded existential realities of our individual and corporate existence with meaning and purpose.

Before we left for our different destinations most of us were lucky to have jobs awaiting us. I was given a job at Challenge Bookshop Mushin, Lagos as a Sales promoter of a religious Magazine called *African Challenge*. So, I had to travel home before resuming in July 1970. My parents and relations were very happy that I had successfully finished my course at Igbaja Bible College; and more importantly I was given a job. I did not stay long before going to Lagos to resume at Challenge Bookshop, Mushin Lagos. I needed money to take care of my parents, siblings, relations and myself. Before leaving home for Lagos, I had to think of accommodation, feeding and transportation. I wasn't sure if the Management of Challenge Bookshop would grant me a temporary accommodation for two or three months before I was able to be on my own. I contacted my cousin, Prince Bamidele David if he could accommodate me for a short period. He agreed to give me temporary accommodation if my employer could not. When I got assurance of a place to stay, I told my parents that I was ready to go to Lagos. They offered their prayers and wished me journey mercies and I left. My cousin welcomed me to his residence and congratulated me for the job.

PART FOUR

FORGING AHEAD

Chapter 7
BLUE COLLAR WORK EXPERIENCE

I resumed in early August 1970 at Challenge Bookshop Mushin under the administration of Mr. Mason, a missionary with business acumen per excellence. He told me that I would be an African Challenge Representative in Kaduna under their S.I.M Bookshop Branch; selling *African Challenge Magazine* to schools, tertiary institutions, Ahmadu Bello University Zaria, Bookshops and any religious organizations. There was a new Honda 175 motorcycle that was bought for the job; meanwhile, he assigned Pa James to give me a two-week orientation on how to use it. Secondly, he assigned me to Rev. Ijatuyi who had been doing the same job in Lagos to give me a two-to-three-week induction/training. I thanked him and asked if I could be given a temporary accommodation within the Challenge Building. He told me to look for a friend who could give me accommodations for a short period of several weeks before going to my base in Kaduna. I thanked him for the job and promised to be a conscientious, honest and hard working sales representative. Without a self-reflection on the offer, I was enthusiastic for the job with a motorcycle: Honda 175. It was a big achievement at that time. Besides, I was thinking of taking courses in Salesmanship to enhance my knowledge in business productivity and management. I was not sure the direction to pursue in the world of the unknown. I, however, had to forge ahead. I made up my mind to follow the directive of my boss, an astute missionary businessman, Mr. Mason.

Pa James taught me how to ride the big motorcycle and also arranged for my driver's license. He was directed to get vehicle insurance coverage for the motorcycle. He bought a helmet for me with a warning that I should never ride the motorcycle without wearing the helmet for my safety. It was a safety instruction that I never failed to obey.

I went to meet my second instructor, Rev. Ijatuyi, and he was glad to have me as a sales trainee. I went with him to almost all institutions in Lagos where he was selling African Challenge Magazine, a monthly publication. The job was hectic because of terrible traffic congestion in Lagos but it was also fun as well because it was exciting for me to know many places and meet new faces in Lagos. After three weeks of tutelage under Rev. Ijatuyi, I told him that it was time for me to leave for Kaduna. He was sad to hear that I was leaving so soon, apparently, he had probably forgotten that I had been with him for three weeks. He prayed for my protection and success in life and both of us departed to our places of residence and never for us to meet again as he joined his Lord after I left for Kaduna.

The Challenge Bookshop paid for my transportation from Lagos to Kaduna including the cost for shipping the motorcycle by rail. That was the first time I would travel in the second-class coach of a train. Before I left Lagos for Kaduna by rail, I had informed my friend, Elijah Daniel, to meet me at KDJ Terminus and he did. It was a great reunion since the mid-60s that we departed. He offered me accommodation in his place for a couple of months before I moved to my own rented single-room space in the same apartment complex.

I went to report for duty at S.I.M Bookshop headed by a missionary, Mr. Bradley. He welcomed me to his office and thereafter introduced me to the rest of his staff. He informed me that the waybill of the motorcycle had been received and when the clearance was completed it would be brought to the office within two days. In the meantime, he told me to join the rest of the staff in the bookselling section. I was impressed with a variety of books on religion and academics.

As I was attending to customers, I made sure my interest to read relevant materials that could enhance my preparation for advancement in my future business and academic pursuit was paramount.

It wasn't long when the motorcycle was delivered, and I started my primary assignment as a Challenge Magazine Sales Representative in Kaduna and Zaria axis. In the meantime, I realized that it was imperative for me to learn Hausa for social interaction and the promotion of my business interest because in the defunct Northern Region the elites were fond of speaking Hausa even though they understood English Language, which was and still is the lingua franca in Nigeria. With a little understanding of Hausa Language, I noticed that some of my colleagues in the Bookshop particularly, the Hausas, were not happy that a Yoruba from the South was given preferentials treatment by giving me a Honda 175 to use for a job some of them were capable of doing. I told one of them that I came from Kabba Province, which was part of the defunct Northern Region. My argument was not convincing to him because those of us from the then Kabba Province are Yoruba people and being in the same geographical and political Region wouldn't remove my cultural affinity with the Yoruba in the southwest. Therefore, being in the same region was for political expediency and convenience. What my colleague at work said did not resonate well with me but that was the reality. I became more careful in my dealings and conversations with all my non-Yoruba speaking staff of the S.I.M Bookshop because they were the majority. The best way to interact and associate freely with them was to learn their Hausa Language. I began to learn the language at work and within my neighborhood. When they realized how I gradually became fluent in Hausa language whenever they wanted to discuss anything about me, they would quickly change the subject-matter, and everyone would walk away one after the other from the scene of the discussion.

The magazine became widely received by Christians in Kaduna, the political and economic hub of the defunct northern region. A few bookshops, for instance, CSS Bookshop Kaduna Branch, S.I.M/ECWA Churches contributed to the promotion of the sales of *African Challenge*. I became a member of two S.I.M/ECWA Churches, namely Hausa/English Service and Yoruba Service at two distant locations in Kaduna to enhance the promotion and sales of the Christian magazine. When Rev. Olatunji Onikeku became the Pastor of Yoruba S.I.M/ECWA Church, he wanted me to serve as a temporary Church service leader. I could not reject the offer because we were former students at Igbaja Bible College and Seminary. He was a very nice person to work with and the wife was a pleasant and dedicated woman. She was the first person to advise me not to ride the Honda 175 motorcycle without a sweater in the cold harmattan and she made arrangement and got me a very thick and beautiful one. Several members of the Church became regular readers of *African Challenge* and they assisted to promote it at their places of work.

After several weeks of marketing African Challenge monthly Magazine in Kaduna, I decided to go to Zaria, the center of academic and intellectual environment in the defunct Northern Region. The establishment of learning institutions such as Ahmadu Bello University, School of Aviation, Advanced College of Education, Military Secondary School and Mission schools among others were the most glaring features of modernization in the Region. There were also several bookshops in Zaria but the best stocked of current books and teaching aid was CSS Bookshop Zaria, which was the Headquarters of all CSS Bookshops in the then Northern Region and the Regional Manager was Mr. Ezekiel Bolaji Iyekolo. His house in Zaria was my first place of call and he was kind enough to give me accommodation each time I went on sales trip. He was pleased to have me around him and he went through the memory lane of his early life and narrated how my grandfather was of immense help to him when he needed a scholarship for his education at Igbaja Teacher's College. On several occasions he took me to the house of Dr. Ezekiel Adeniyi Bangudu who was a Senior Lecturer in the Department of Mathematics at ABU, Samaru main campus Zaria. He was from Odo-Ere and I was surprised how he came about a surname of Hausa, but upon investigation

Mr. Iyekolo told me that his original surname was Aiyedun, a great warrior who never deserted his post and the Nupe soldiers nicknamed him b*agudu,* which he subsequently adopted but christened Bangudu as surname. When I was introduced to him and his wife, he welcomed me and we sat down to exchange pleasantries. We did not stay long before we left there and went to visit one of his friends, Mr. Joseph Aina who was previously unknown to me as a brother-in-law. He was living in Kachia within the metropolis of Zaria. Mr. Aina was pleasant, jovial and appeared very religious. Mr. Iyekolo narrated our family history and the unique character traits I have exhibited since he knew me when I was a student at Igbaja Bible College. I cast my mind to the time he taught my class in 1967 *European Renaissance,* which he simplified as 'when people began to think for themselves'. We did not stay long with Mr. Aina before we went back to Zaria in order to get ready for the next day activities. I asked myself why did Mr. Iyekolo have penchant for historical narratives of Ere people and wondered why he did not study History rather than Business Administration?

With the background knowledge of Zaria and its environs, I was confident of making a lot of sales there. My first sales trip to Zaria gave me confidence that I would make contacts with many people, particularly students in institutions where they had Fellowship of Christian Students because I was a former member at Igbaja Bible College and Seminary. I spent three days of hard work in Zaria and covered all the places I needed to reach and introduced a monthly *African Challenge* Magazine. I distributed all the copies I took to my agents in Zaria and went back to my boss, Mr. Bradley with good news of how people were receptive to the religious Magazine. I was encouraged by the receptive attitude of people to the magazine because it was not about its evangelistic intentions alone but also its education on family relationships on the one hand and youth moral responsibility to society on the other. Therefore, *the African Challenge* was for everyone irrespective of his social cultural and religious leaning.

The joy of making good sales in Kaduna/Zaria zone was abruptly cut short. The Management of the *African Challenge* increased its cover price as a result of cost increase of material production. My annual projection of sales suffered and I felt it was time to think on a better option. I met a couple of old friends in Kaduna who advised me to go and pursue my higher education at University of Ibadan when the opportunity of being admitted was open to candidates of my qualification. The wise counsel of my friends encouraged me, but I decided to stay on my job so that I could take care of my parents.

By the middle of 1971 I decided it was time to leave Kaduna for Ilorin where Mr. Blake was the Branch Manager of S.I.M Challenge Bookshop Ilorin. I contacted him and he was interested in having me as one of his staff. In September 1971 I requested Mr. Bradley to transfer me to Ilorin and he did. My main hidden agenda was to go to University of Ibadan and Ilorin being closer to Ibadan than Kaduna I felt I could make immediate contact on how to be admitted into the Diploma program in the Department of Religious Studies. I got to Ilorin in October 1971 and went to meet Mr. Blake and his wife. They had a recollection when I was working for them in the S.I.M Guesthouse. It was a great moment to be with them because they had been very nice to me in the past. I joined the staff of the Bookshop as an Assistant Storekeeper in charge of the Kalamazoo device system for stocktaking. I went to University of Ibadan early 1972. The aesthetic ambience of the campus welcomed me to its environment and a challenge of making it an institution of my dreams. I went straight to the Department of Religious Studies to inquire if I was qualified for the Diploma in Religious Studies and after they looked at my academic documents, I was told to go and apply because I was eminently qualified. I went to the admission office to get the application forms and other relevant information that I needed to complete the application for admission.

I went back to Ilorin and fortunately my former Vice-Principal came to the Bookshop, and I told him my plan to further my education at University of Ibadan. I told him the official copy of my transcript was needed to consummate the admission process and I would appreciate it if he could give the school Registrar the money for the transaction. He warmly accepted to assist me, and I gave him the money. Some weeks later I got a letter of acknowledgement of receipt for the money. I was full of expectation that I would be one of the students at my dream University. Unfortunately, I was not admitted that year and I went to the Head of Department of Religious Studies, Professor E. Bolaji Idowu to find out why I was not admitted. I gave him copies of my results from my former school and he gave me a note to the Assistant Registrar in the admission office. I was given prompt attention and the man said that my former school did not send my transcript and if they could send it on time there was a probability of being considered for a supplementary admission provided some of the candidates admitted failed to accept the offer. I wasn't sure if any candidate would turn down his or her offer of admission.

At work I was told that the Management of the Bookshop and my former school frown on my penchant for liberal study under Professor Idowu whose theological proposition could mislead an evangelical trained person like me. That explained in a nutshell why my transcript was not sent to the University of Ibadan! From the foregoing, I made up my mind that nothing could douse my aspiration and hope to pursue liberal education at University of Ibadan. There were some other religious issues that my stance on them did not go down well with the Management of the Bookshop at Ilorin and one morning after I led the usual morning prayer; the Manager invited me to his office and fired me and all my savings and the monthly salary were paid. I thanked him and left. My colleagues in the office were furious and they wanted to meet the Manager on my behalf but I objected to their plan. I, however, appreciated their spirit of solidarity and support. I determined to forge ahead regardless of the difficulties, challenges and obstacles on my way. My resilience and perseverance were anchored on the belief in my talent and ability to grab any opportunities that opened to me at any material time. So, I rationalized that my departure from S.I.M Bookshop was a good omen to take me to a higher plane of success.

It needs to be mentioned that I was a member of the S.I.M/ECWA Church Ilorin since 1963 when it was struggling for growth and development. So, when I came back from Kaduna to Ilorin in 1971 the Church had grown and flourished. There was, however, tension within the Church among some strong members from Yagba group because the Igbomina group had dominated exclusively the control of the Church revenue. The feelings of disunity began to forcefully rear its ugly head. Efforts were made to resolve the conflict, but it became very apparently clear that the solution was to have a polite brotherly love of schism, a new ECWA Church. There were some trained pastors who were members of the movement namely, Rev. Ariye of the Gospel Light Ministry Pastor, Odofin, Pastor Henry Falope and me. The logistic committee was to handle the venue where the first service would commence. The Management of Palace Cinema granted us the permission to use the venue for the First Sunday Service. We had to get the service program, which included the order of service and the Pastor to preach the sermon. We prayed for the guidance of the Holy Spirit and after our prayer, we unanimously asked Pastor Falope to preach on the first Sunday Service that later became the beginning of the 2nd ECWA Church located at Amilegbe, Ilorin. Most members of what became 1st ECWA Church Ilorin could not believe what they saw when they entered their church without faces of Yagba people who were members of the church. There were concerted efforts made to stop the schism but it was too late. The people had resolved to take their cross with determination. They decided like the Old Testament Israelite heroes who said, 'to your tents O ye Israel'. I was glad to be part of that revolution because it showed the true nature of Yagba people in the face of religious adversity.

Meanwhile, I was optimistic of getting another job elsewhere. In November 1972 I went to meet Mr. Bolaji Iyekolo the Regional Manager of CSS Bookshop Zaria and narrated my ordeal with the S.I.M Bookshop Ilorin. I told him that I had already registered for GCE with a view to using the result to give me additional advantage because of the competitiveness of admission at University of Ibadan each year. I thought having the minimum admission requirement would probably not give me a guarantee of admission. Mr. Iyekolo expressed optimism in my ability to achieve my goal. Being a product of S.I.M himself, he understood my plight at S.I.M Bookshop Ilorin and my desire to go for further education at University of Ibadan. He gave me accommodation with feeding without charges and above all a job with a mandate to resume in January 1973. Nothing could be so soothing to my bruised ego than a job guaranteed with a mandate to take up the offer in January 1973. I left Zaria with my head high up and the good news of a better offer to tell my younger sister, Ibidun who was living with me and several of my friends who were concerned about my welfare and future since I lost my job.

On getting back to Ilorin, I broke the good news to my relations and friends and began to plan my exit. First my younger sister had to go back to our parents at home pending the time I settled down in Zaria for her to join me. I spent the rest of my time studying for the GCE papers in November and December 1972. I was going to miss my friends particularly, Joseph N. Molemodile, brother Daniel A. Awofenka Awogbenja and my sister Ibidun. I had to go home with my sister to explain to our parents why she had to be at home for a while and to give them some money to take care of their basic needs and for the school fees of my sister in the primary school at home. My parents prayed for my safety and good luck in all my endeavors. I assured them of my financial support from time to time. I left home for Ilorin to get prepared for Zaria.

I left Ilorin early 1973 by rail for Zaria. It was a long journey with several stopovers on the way before arriving at my destination. I alighted from the train; I went to stay with Mr. Iyekolo, Regional Manager of CSS Bookshop. Despite the 'crowd' in his house, he offered me temporary accommodation. On January 9, 1973, I joined the staff of CSS Bookshop as an Assistant Storekeeper. To reduce congestion in my host's house, I went to stay with my brother-in-law, Mr. Joseph Aina. His wife, Rebecca, was my younger sister. Within a month of my stay with them I got my own accommodation and thereafter sent for Ibidun to come and stay with me to continue her education. She came and my friend Mr. Titus Biodun Amjo, a teacher in the Army Primary School Zaria, enrolled there. While in Zaria, I had a good number of friends from Odo-Ere, Isanlu etc. I also made friends among the staff of CSS Bookshop. Mr. Iyekolo made sure that the staff members in the bookshop were mixed in terms of gender, ethnicity and religious affiliations. The CSS Bookshop Zaria was a center for academic material resources for teaching and learning in the city and its environ. I remember an occasion when one Alhaji from Yola came to buy primary school books worth thousands of Naira and he didn't have the money on him, and he discussed with the Regional Manager to send a reliable staff to follow him with the materials to Yola. I was assigned the job. It was a risk I was delighted to take regardless of distance and crossing River Benue on a ferry, but it was also an adventure worth exploring. We got to Yola later in the evening and when it was time to sleep, I chose a hotel in Jimeta Yola, the commercial Centre of Yola. The next morning, I dressed up to meet Alhaji at Barclays Bank Nigeria Limited, Jemita, and now Union Bank Plc. I was instructed by Mr. Iyekolo, Regional Manager Zaria to make the payment to CSS Bookshop Headquarters in Lagos. I made the transaction and got a teller as proof of payment. I left Yola the same day but couldn't make it to Zaria. The Regional Manager told me to meet the Pastor of S.I.M/ECWA Church in Gombe who probably was a well-known person to give me accommodation for the night and the man obliged. The following morning, I left Gombe for Zaria. It was a unique experience that combined the job of a Storekeeper with that of a Sales Representative. In 1974, I was also sent to go on a similar errand to follow Alhaji Yuguda the owner of Yuguda Bookshop, the biggest in Sokoto and its environs to deliver primary school books and stationery worth thousands of Naira; and to make payment to the Bookshop in Zaria, which I did. The Regional Manager commended me for the professional performance on the two journeys made to Yola and Sokoto respectively. That was a time when some members of staff in the Bookshop were engaged in business sharp practices that could cause a loss of revenues to the Bookshop.

I was a very active member of S.I.M/ECWA Church Zaria when Rev. Adeyanju was the minister and Mr. Iyekolo was the Superintendent of the Sunday school. I was one of the teachers in Sunday school. Apart from being active in the Sunday school, I was involved in the YMCA Sport activities particularly, Football (Soccer) and Volleyball. Mr. Biodun Amjo and I played table tennis together at the premises of CSS Bookshop and Railway Staff Club, Zaria. All these religious and social activities were necessary for me to keep me mentally, physically and spiritually fit. I also spent some time reading and meditating, but my mind was often on how to gain admission to University of Ibadan (UI).

I reapplied for admission to UI in 1974 and luckily got admitted to the Department of Religious Studies. I was very happy but where was I going to get a sponsor? My income from the Bookshop was meager; it could hardly sustain my monthly expenses and the care of my parents at home. I told Mr. Iyekolo the Regional Manager of CSS Bookshop about my admission to UI, but the source of financial support was my major concern. He congratulated me for the admission but felt it was better to stay back and register for GCE Advanced Level because he knew I could pass it and then reapply to UI with a possibility of a Federal Government scholarship. I thanked him for the suggestion, but I felt otherwise. I decided to follow my mind because my destiny depended on whatever choice I made. I resigned from my appointment.

As I was leaving Zaria there was a moment of nostalgic feeling and memory of my association with the family of Mr. Iyekolo particularly, his wife who had been nice to me, her sister Taye and my cousin, Abayomi. I could not but laugh momentarily when I remember Mr. Briggs, the Storekeeper who was my boss in the Store Department, a 'comedian' fluent in English, Hausa and Igbo languages but very unpredictable in wit and character; Timothy an errand boy of Ayodeji a 'Maradona', Mr. Awo Bello an ambivalent character, Sunmbo, Florence, Mrs. Asuquo, Mr. Adeyeri, a young lady called Segun, Mr. Audu in the Audit Department who smoked like chimney, Mr. Olu Gbadebo, Mr. Ada, a very quiet and easy-going Salesman, etc. Before I left, we had a group photograph as one member of the CSS Bookshop family. I don't know where I have kept the photograph, but I still have a vivid memory of each one of them. Perhaps some of them might have been deceased by now but their memory of oneness as members of staff at CSS Bookshop Zaria continues to resonate in my mind as if the events happened yesterday.

PART FIVE

THE PURSUIT OF HIGHER EDUCATION

Chapter 8
UNIVERSITY OF IBADAN (UI)

When I resumed at UI on October 2, 1974 there were only two Federal Universities in Nigeria: University Ibadan (UI) and University of Lagos, Akoka, (UNILAG) respectively and the rest were Regional Universities; University of Ife, (UNIFE) now Obafemi Awolowo University, (OAU), Ahmadu Bello University (ABU) Zaria, University of Nigeria Nsukka (UNN) and University of Benin (UNIBEN). All these Regional Universities have been taken over by the Federal Government of Nigeria and new ones established. Currently there are at least 40 Federal Universities in Nigeria. There are 47 States Universities and not less than 75 Private Universities in the country and it is most likely the number will continue to increase as the need arises.

University of Ibadan had been my ideal institution in Nigeria and when I was admitted in 1974 nothing could be better described as a fulfillment of a long-desired goal. But where was I going to get financial assistance for tuition, books, accommodation, and feeding including sundry expenses? I wrote a letter to Rosalie Peterson; now Rosalie Peterson-Bhatnagar in Dublin and she contacted her mother Mrs. Ann Peterson in Bridgeport Kansas, USA and to my surprise the response was positive. The mother sent some money to me before I left Zaria that covered all my expenses for the first year. Mrs. Peterson also sent a scholarship form from the World Council of Churches to me with an instruction that after I have filled it, I should take it to a signatory living in Osogbo to sign it and then mail it back to her. It was like a dream come true. I went to meet the man and after telling him my mission to his house he greeted me with a congratulatory good intention. He then asked what I had brought for him to sign the scholarship form? I was stunned because I did not expect a man of God to demand a bribe from an indigent student like me. I politely told him as an indigent student, I had nothing to give him in terms of gratification. He refused to sign it because I did not give him a gratification. I wrote to Mrs. Peterson that the man did not sign it because I failed to offer him a bribe. After two months, I got a letter of approval of the scholarship and the man ceased to be one of the signatories. I also got the Kwara State Bursary Award for two years. Mrs. Ann Peterson was also sending me some stipends on a regular basis. With all these financial support, while at UI, I was able to support my parents, siblings including my senior sister Mrs. Ebun Adedayo is fondly called Iya Badan and other relatives.

The freshmen, as they called new students then, resumed a week before the stale students. The first week that we resumed as freshmen was for registration and orientation. It was then that I met several new students from Isanlu, Odo-Ere and Egbe. The registration was slightly rigorous, but the orientation was well organized because all the procedures were already packaged in a folder of each student. I was assigned a bed space in Block A, Independence Hall. I felt lonely because I was the first student admitted and registered at UI from Idofin-Isanlu until Biodun Balogun came from ABU where he was admitted for Pharmacy but on getting there his name appeared under the list of students admitted for Geology. He left for UI where he was admitted in the Department of Physiotherapy with a Federal Government Scholarship. I was delighted to see him, and we were hoping that Bamidele Ogbe Solomon from Idofin-Isanlu would join us, having been admitted in the Department of Petroleum engineering. Rather than joining us at UI he decided to utilize the Federal Government Scholarship given to him to study Chemical Engineering in an American university. Only Biodun and I from Idofin registered at UI in 1974.

I was curious to know many places on campus particularly, the existing Cafeterias in Zik, Kuti and Sultan Bello Halls before the new Central Cafeteria was built, Faculty of Arts Class Lecture Rooms, University Library, Bookshop, Jaja Clinic, Sports Arena, Gymnasium Hall, UI Zoological Garden, Chapel of Resurrection, etc. The imposing architectural structure, the beautiful lawns and the serenity of the University of Ibadan in the 70s made the Ivory Tower an enviable public institution for academic discipline and pursuit of knowledge acquisition towards self and national development.

When lectures began for all students, we had the opportunity to know our classmates and lecturers one after the other. Most of my classmates were teachers in secondary schools; while some were Catholic nuns, Church trained Ministers and the rest were High School graduates. From my recollection we were 25 in class and out of that number seven were women. Some of our Lecturers who actually impressed me were Rev. (Dr.) J. Omosade Awolalu, who taught us African Traditional Religion (ATR), S. Oyin Abogunrin, New Testament Theology, Olushola Olukunle, Philosophy of Religion and Old Testament History, Dr. Tasie and Mercy Oduyoye, taught Church History, but the courses that triggered my curiosity most were African Traditional Religion, Philosophy of Religion and New Testament Theology particularly, Rudolf Bultmann New Testament

Theology, a very radical departure from my background of S.I.M/ECWA Conservative theology. I used to empathize with my Lecturers, Dr. Olukunle and Dr. Abogunrin; who rose to the rank of Professor several years after my graduation in 1976; but at that time, he differed from my theological disposition because, in my view, if they died at the material time, they were teaching us, I was very 'certain' that they would go to hellfire! I received their lectures as challenges that demanded on my part the need to investigate and interrogate their liberal propositions for a 'healthy' academic understanding. On several occasions I made appointment with the Head of Department of Religious Studies, Prof. E. Bolaji Idowu to clarify some issues on his concepts of ATR and Olodumare that he espoused in his books *African Traditional Religion: A Definition*, and *Olodumare God in Yoruba Belief*. He later invited me to his house for further interactive discussions. But there was an unresolved issue in my mind, which was the existence of God, be it in Yoruba belief or in Christian faith. Does God exist? It is a million-dollar question.

I also had several appointments with Dr. Awolalu who later became a professor to discuss some pertinent issues in ATR. My interrogation on an aspect of his lecture on ATR made him have a good impression about me. He used to call me 'this boy from Kwara', which was before Kogi State was carved out of Kwara and Benue States: the defunct Kabba

Province in Northern Region. I later realized that Professor Awolalu did not remember my name but only my former state of origin.

The University Library became my second classroom, and the books became my best teachers but the more I read the more I realized my ignorance and the more I wanted to overcome it through rigorous research and participation in class discussions. When I became frequent in the library the workers there became my friends so they allowed me to spend more hours reading in the postgraduate Library section. I used to be one of those who closed last with the Library Staff. I used to get to my Hall of residence very late but students at Independence Hall and Zik Hall hardly sleep because of their large population. In the midnight, for some reason of boredom, you could suddenly hear some individuals in Zik Hall roaring like lions and some students from Independence Hall would respond by calling them 'Zooties' not only because they roared like lions but also their Hall was and still close to the Zoological Garden. It was real fun in those days!! The narratives of the events in our Independence Hall are still vivid in my memory as if they happened yesterday.

Being involved in sport activities had its reward at UI. I generally like sports and athletic events. I believed they were naturally part of my untapped potential because I did not have a rapid growth like my age group. Before getting to UI, I had developed my skill in boxing, table tennis, football (soccer), volleyball and badminton. At UI, I spent a few weeks at my leisure time swimming but I soon realized that swimming in a river was different from swimming in a swimming pool. I reacted to the chlorine in the swimming pool and hence stopped swimming. I participated in the yearly marathon race at UI and other athletic events including football for my Hall. So, in my second year when all second-year students were to live off campus I was given accommodation in my Hall; but before I resumed in my second year Biodun Balogun had decided to remain in Tedder Hall in order to share his bed space with me rather than going to Alexander Brown Hall that was reserved for medical students at University College Hospital (UCH) Ibadan. I appreciated his kind gesture and since I got accommodation at Independence Hall, he left for Alex Brown Hall. Biodun has remained very close to me even though he is much younger in age but highly matured in character and discipline with high sense of responsibility to his relations, friends and colleagues.

In my days at UI there were no dull moments because we always had scholarly and intellectual engagements apart from lectures. There were public lectures, seminars, workshops, etc. Among the radical scholars on campus was Comrade Ola Oni who was a 'Man of the people' as far as members of Student Union were concerned. There were also the Kegites for amusements and the Pyrates Confraternity that created momentary awe and fear when holding their meetings at night.

There were two social and religious responsibilities I held very dear to my heart at UI: teaching in the Sunday school and giving the little I had to charity. I was one of the students from the Department of Religious Studies that taught in the children Sunday school at Abadina UI every Sunday whenever we were in session. At the end of the year, we used the offering collected to buy gifts for the less privileged in Ibadan, particularly orphanages. We also visited those places to encourage them and prayed for the children and their caretakers. All these academic, social and religious activities contributed to a better way to understand education in its holistic nature. Up till now I still have soft spots for poor children, and I consider it a moral obligation to assist in the best way I can.

It is no surprise that university education in my time was for adults. There were, however, some instances when adults at UI demonstrated unsavory behavior that became dangerously uncivil. For instance, in the middle 70s the Management of the University decided to increase the number of beds in the wooden blocks on several locations without adequate consideration of the health hazards involved to students. The students living in those blocks made their objections known through appropriate procedures to the University Management of the Vice-Chancellor, Professor Oritshejolomi Thomas but nothing concrete was done. One evening at about 10 pm, a few students moved to the Student Union Building for a solidarity protest to the VC's Lodge. I was among the students that went to his Lodge to let him know our grievances. We met resistance at the gate but eventually we got through to his compound and we sat down on the lawn and when our songs of protest could not let him sleep, he came down in his pajamas to listen to us. We presented our grievances to him, and he pleaded with us to go back to our halls of residence and promised that the double bunk beds in those wooden block buildings would be removed. We were pleased with his response, and we dispersed about 1 a.m. and planned another protest in case he reneged on his promise. Later in the day, there was a circular on immediate removal of all the double bunk beds from those buildings. On February 13, 1975, the Military coup that brought General Muritala Mohammed to power brought a change in the leadership of the University Administration. The Vice-Chancellor was removed and there were insinuations that the students' protest probably led to his removal. The veracity of the insinuations could not be verified because we were not privy to all the facts that informed the Military to remove him. A new Vice-Chancellor was appointed amongst the ranks of Professors in the institution. He was Professor Tekena Tamuno from the Department of History and former Dean Faculty of Arts. He was the first alumnus of UI to be appointed as Vice-Chancellor. His appointment was received with wild jubilation on campus because students believed that being an alumnus of the institution, he would be able to address the urgent needs of the students. He did address some of the challenges of the students but that could not stop them from peaceful and sometimes violent protests. It wasn't long before he realized that being an alumnus VC of UI was one thing, ability to prevent students from unnecessary protests was another. The cause of the second students' protest in the mid-70s began in his faculty. It had to do with the refusal of the Department of History to register Mr. Banji Adegboro, the Students' Union President for the final year exams in the Faculty of Arts. The case went to the Senate and the position of the Department of History and Faculty of Arts was upheld. The Students' Union President, Mr. Adegboro had infracted on the rules and regulations for registration and so he technically was not really a bona fide student even though the University authority recognized him as the leader of the Students' Union. The issue was not amicably resolved, and it sparked off a violent protest. Some students were alleged to have rough handled the Warden of Kuti Hall and they were to face the disciplinary committee and they were found guilty and hence summarily dismissed from the institution when we were on a compulsory recess. During the compulsory recess I could not go home so I had to stay with a friend, Mr. Frank Aliu, a brilliant Chemistry teacher at School of Basic Studies, University of Ilorin. We enjoyed being together. When the long recess was called off; it was a big relief because we were tired being away from the university. On resumption, the examination timetable had been pasted everywhere and being the end of the session; nobody was ready for a solidarity protest. All final year students were interested in completing their program and face the future that appeared bright for them. The immediate bright angle of the future after graduation was abundant job opportunities. Kwara State Civil Service Commission, Ilorin had interviewed me for a position in the Ministry of Education. I was asked to report at their office to know my placement. When I finished my exams, I went to report with a letter from the University that I had successfully completed my program but the appointment like others were still under consideration. I had to go home to meet my parents to thank them for their moral support.

I was eager to be at home to supervise my small house project that was nearing completion. With the little money on me at that time I spent it on my house project and by June 1976 I had completed it and then moved in. It was and still a cozy place that marked part of my rising higher in life as an upstart. My parents were very proud of what they considered my 'huge achievements' but not knowing it was a beginning of greater things to come. As I was at home; a friend of mine came to tell me that my letter of appointment was ready in the Ministry of Education, Ilorin and waiting for collection. I was very happy with the information; and I quickly went to get my things together for the journey to Ilorin to collect the letter and report for duty. In my letter of appointment I was seconded to the Governor's Office. I reported there but there wasn't anything for me to do. After a week, I went back to the Ministry of Education, Secondary school division under Mrs. Shaba and told her my area of interest. Initially my first choice was Queen Elizabeth Secondary School Ilorin. She talked me out of my choice because I was still a bachelor and secondly the susceptibility to sudden transfer was higher. She advised me to accept a deployment to Abdul Aziz Atta Memorial College Okene (AAAMCO), formerly Provincial Secondary School Okene, in the defunct Northern Region. I accepted the offer and went to report to the Principal of the school, Mr. R. B. Balogun who was delighted to have me. By the time I resumed at Okene, students were still on holidays, and I went with three of my relations namely Joshua Ogungbemi, Ajayi Titus Omokore and Ajayi Igununtoba with the intention to send them to school and reduce their dependence on their parents. Mr. Balogun understood my good intention for my relations and graciously gave me a temporary accommodation pending the time the resumption of students when I would be allocated a Junior Staff quarters. I met my former Headmaster at S.I.M Isanlu Central School, Mr. Leslie Bello Obielodan who was the 'Agric' teacher at AAAMCO. He still recognized me because hardly could teachers in those days lose memory of their most troublesome pupils, particularly those of us in the 'Black Book'. He became a father, friend and counselor who showed me the way to achieve academic progress abroad. I used to accompany him on several of his trips to Ilorin the capital of Kwara State. I also had a couple of very close friends namely, Mr. Fatulu, mathematics teacher, Mr. Kunle Alao, physics teacher and Mr. Agbana, Arabic and Islamic teacher. I was a Bible Knowledge (BK) teacher. The Principal gave me sports and administrative responsibilities: House Master of Sutton and Football coach.

1. House Master of Sutton

When I accepted the House mastership of Sutton, I did not know the inherent challenges involved until a few weeks afterward. It was my responsibility to look after the cleanliness of the house and its surroundings. It also involved going to the house at night and inspect if all the students were on bed and to report anyone that was not on bed to the Principal of the school. The general welfare of the students in each house was the intention of appointing House Masters. One night I went to inspect the students and found out how senior ones tortured their juniors at night. There were occasions that some students became ill at night, and they needed immediate healthcare assistance. Besides, Sutton had a peculiar problem. The students told me their frustrations about sleeping at night because some spirits came from a nearby tree and rocks to terrify them. They told me that it had been happening before I became their House Master, and nobody could stop them. I told them to come and call me anytime the spirits or whatever was scaring them at night. One night when I was sleeping some of them ran to my staff quarters to tell me that the spirits came again to scare them. I quickly got out of bed and dressed up and went with them to see those evil spirits that were tormenting my students at night. On getting there the students said that the evil spirits had disappeared. Since they knew I was coming, and they ran away it meant that they feared me and so they should go and sleep. I instructed them that if they ventured to come back, they should come and call me. There were no telephones or mobile phones unlike now. But I thought it was nothing but a hoax, but I did not tell them. For several months there was no disturbance from the evil spirit, so I thought the problem was over. It was not yet over. The students came again in the dead of night to tell me that the evil spirits were there again. So, I followed them and they pointed at the place where they were around the tree. I went to the tree and looked round it alone and I couldn't see anything. They were surprised I had the courage to go to that tree alone at such hours of the night without being hurt. I instructed them that in case they surfaced again they should tell them that their House Master would come and deal with them if they dare. And that put an end to their nightmares in a society infested with voodoo and superstitions.

2. Football Coach

As a new coach, I made sure that no student in the team used any energy-enhanced substance. I made the students realize that success is often based on hard work, constant practice to boost stamina and the psychology to defeat their opponents. It really worked in all their football engagements. In 1976/77 Football competition among Secondary schools in the State our team won the highest trophy, Davies/Soladoye Cup. It was one of the greatest achievements that made us proud at AAAMCO. The Principal, Mr. R. B. Balogun was happy that his school won the trophy that year. And coincidentally, that was toward the end of his term as principal of the college. It was a team work with a team spirit by my coaching team members and our indomitable students who made the college proud.

Chapter 9
UNITED STATES OF AMERICA

In one of our staff room felicitations at AAAMCO, Okene in 1977, Baba Leslie B. Obielodan asked why I had not applied to any universities in the USA, and I told him that I did not know anyone there. He then gave me the address of Rev. Nathaniel Olutimayin who was a Th.D. student at Dallas Theological Seminary. I told him that Baba Olutimayin was my Vice-Principal at Igbaja Bible College. I wrote to Baba Olutimayin and told him that his friend Baba Obielodan gave me his address to contact him for addresses of universities in the USA to further my education. He sent two addresses: one that he considered conservative and the other liberal. I applied to both and Perkins School of Theology, Southern Methodist University Dallas Texas, USA that he considered liberal sent application forms to me. I applied for admission and scholarship; and in April 1978 I got a letter of admission and scholarship. It took almost a month before I got a student visa form 1-120 and when I got it, I did not waste time to arrange to go to Lagos for the visa. In June 1978, I took permission from the Principal of the school that I was going to the American Embassy in Lagos for a visa interview and he granted it. I went to Lagos and stayed with my 'brother' Chief Iyekolo. He was delighted to see me and when I told him my mission to Lagos, he was pessimistic about the possibility of getting the visa. I assured him that I was going to get it. He congratulated me and wished me good luck at the interview. Meanwhile, he told me that he had a flight to Benin the following morning. As we had our breakfast after morning devotion he got ready and I bid him goodbye. I then went to the American Embassy in Victoria Island and met a large crowd so early in the morning. The place was well arranged and orderly and when the time came for all of us to be interviewed we were invited inside the building. When it was my turn, I was asked a few questions and I answered them. All my credentials were checked and the lady who did the interview seemed satisfied with my answers and she told me to go and have my seat. She came back with my passport and congratulated me. Others who were waiting to be interviewed asked why my case was like a priority case. I did not answer them because it was not an arena for conversation. That was how I got the visa on Wednesday, June 21, 1978, without any hassle. It was one of my happiest moments in life! I was convinced that my rising profile through education in the USA was guaranteed. When I left the US Embassy, I went to Chief Iyekolo's house at Mushin Olosha to pick my bag and left a note for him that I have gotten the visa and left for home. I got to Mopa when most of the neighborhood had gone to sleep except my pregnant wife who had been keeping vigil and when the vehicle stopped in front of their house, she ran out to see whether I was the one. She quickly came down from the upstairs to welcome me and her parents woke up to greet me. I told my wife that I was given a visa and she went to break the news to her parents. They congratulated me for the achievement and her father advised that I should arrange for my wife to join me in the US. I thanked him for the advice and told him that I would like to have her with me after the delivery of our first child. After I had a light meal, we went to bed. The following morning, we left for AAAMCO and I reported to the Principal of the school. He was glad I got the visa and wished me a successful academic pursuit in America. I went to break the good news to Baba Obielodan who was the architect of the achievement, and he congratulated me. I soon began to arrange for my disengagement from the State Ministry of Education, Ilorin and Okene to relocate to my hometown in full preparation for my exit from Nigeria. I went to Kwara State Hotel Ilorin to buy the air ticket. I got a round trip KLM air ticket for 430 Naira and my itinerary was Lagos-Chicago-Dallas, Texas on August 15-16, 1978 with a night stopover at Amsterdam without additional charges for hotel accommodation and transportation to the airport. It was probably the Golden Age of Nigeria!! I left Ilorin for home to spend some days with my parents and relatives. About a week to the day of my flight, I decided to leave home. The news that I was going to the United States of America on August 15, 1978, for further studies stunned my parents, particularly my mother who felt I have had enough of western education in Nigeria and why should I be going to the USA for further studies? Her only consolation was that I was already married, and my wife was pregnant. She would be expecting the arrival of her grandchild within a couple of months. That was her greatest hope and comforting solace!! I believed the first psychological battle had been won and the next was feeding and maintenance care that had to be properly addressed with empirical backup that was convincing because I was the breadwinner of the family; so, I understood their worries and concerns. In Nigeria, children with means are expected to take care of their needy and aged parents because no governments take responsibilities for them as Senior citizens. When they saw all the arrangements that I had made for their care; they expressed their satisfaction with prayers and blessings. If I could remember correctly, in about 9:00 a.m. on August 8, 1978, I told them that it was time for me to go and wait for transportation by the roadside that was going to Ibadan en route to Lagos. I bid them farewell. As I stepped out of my house with my traveling box and looked over my shoulder, I saw my mother following me. I stopped for her and pleaded with her to go back to the house because I did not want to give any impression that I was going on a long distance trip, and I did not want people to be asking her where I was going that warranted her escorting me. She went back and I looked over my shoulder and we both had emotional eye contacts but unfortunately I did not know that was going to be the last time I would see her.

I decided to go to Ibadan to inform my senior sister, Mrs. Ebun Adedayo and her husband that I was on my way to the United States of America for further studies. I got to Ibadan in the afternoon and met my sister and her family. When I told her my trip to the USA, she called her husband and broke the news to him. Before we went to bed her husband requested me to get a better school for their son, Olu before leaving for Lagos. It was a difficult decision for me to make because it would require traveling to Eruku and Omu-Aran in Kwara State!! It was a compelling 'missionary journey' I could not turndown. The following morning her husband and I set for the journey and luckily, we succeeded in getting their son transferred to Government Secondary School Omu-Aran.

I left Ibadan on Saturday, August 12, 1978, for Lagos to make sure I met my mentor, Chief Bolaji Iyekolo who had always welcomed me to his apartment in Mushin, Lagos. He had anticipated my arrival on the weekend and as soon he heard my voice, he sprang on his feet to open the door for me to come in. He was a spirited and an amazing man of good will. The second day, he wanted me to meet his friend, Chief Kola Jamodu and I said sure, and we did. Chief Kola Jamodu was delighted to see me for the first time. We had a nice time together.

On Tuesday, August 15,1978 at about 6:00 p.m. Chief Iyekolo and some members of the family escorted me to the airport on time to go through the security routines. When I was through with the security officers, I went to thank those who came to see me off and I went to wait for boarding time. We departed as scheduled and we got to Amsterdam where we had a stopover. I was lodged in a hotel with bed and breakfast and before I slept off, I put on the alarm to wake me up at 5 a.m. and I also told them in the reception to wake me up in case the alarm failed to wake me up. The arrangements worked, the alarm rang at exactly 5 a.m. and the receptionist called to wake me up and told me when breakfast would be ready. I got up and took my shower and before 6:30 a.m. I was downstairs and found my way to the restaurant. Our flight was 10 am and we had to be there on time. The KLM airport shuttle came for us, and everybody was in the bus and off to the airport. The airport was neat and orderly. At 10 a.m. we left Amsterdam for Chicago in the US. It was a long distance, but the serving crews reduced the boredom with intermittent menus and drinks. As we were approaching Chicago, the Pilot informed us. I couldn't wait to get down to see how an American city looked like. When we landed and came out of the plane, we had to go through the security checkpoint. It was a boring exercise. They found that I came with some *gari*, (a food substance made from cassava) in my box, and I told them it was one of my delights especially, when soaked in cold water, since I was not used to most of the food served in the plane. They allowed me to take it with me and advised me to hurry to the terminal of my flight to Dallas. I had about 15 minutes left to board. I ran to the terminal panting like a dog as the Pilot and crew were waiting for me to board the plane. As soon as got there I quickly boarded the plane and found my seat, sat down and fastened my seatbelt. As I adjusted myself properly in my seat, I requested a crew to give me some water to drink and she did. It wasn't long before I slept off. The plane touched down at Dallas/Fort Worth International airport in the evening. I joined others to the baggage claim section to get my luggage and when I got it, I went to ask from the information desk how to get transportation to Southern Methodist University. They got a taxi for me and off I went to the school.

On getting to the university, I was told that students had not resumed but being a foreign student, they were going to assist me with accommodation. I was given a room in Perkins Hall and when I got in, there were no bed sheets and pillowcases and when I told them they said it was my responsibility to come with those things. I told them that at the University of Ibadan in Nigeria, we were not treated that way. They told me, Segun, 'this is not Africa' and we laughed but they were going to help me out. David Crow went to get all the beddings for me. The next day, I found a means to reach Rev. Olutimayin at Dallas Theological Seminary. He came to see me. It was six years since we met and so many things had happened. I appreciated his interest in my education and thanked him for being very supportive. Pastor David Adamo, one of my junior students at Igbaja Bible College was among the students admitted with scholarship at Perkins School of theology. He came a week after my arrival. I was very happy to have another Nigerian who was well known to me in Nigeria. Rev. Olutimayin came again to see both of us because we were his former students and secondly, we came from the same locality and members of S.I.M/ECWA.

Dallas is generally hot in the summer especially in July and August each year but that of 1978 was exceptionally severe, but inside the buildings it was cool throughout. I could hardly go out because it was sunny, hot and dry. But I had to go out and source for money to eat because I had very little money on me. So, I went to meet Dr. John Holt, the Director of Admissions who had been very pleasant to approach. He contacted Mr. Black who arranged to get some money for my upkeep for a week. I was taken care of by members of the Perkins community. I made good friends among them and when Fall Semester began, I had many more friends namely, Campton Slyest, Keith Morgan, John Thornburg, Mary, Martha, Marty, Mark etc.

I registered for courses that would lead to better understanding of philosophical theology, philosophy, social ethics, moral theology, Wittgenstein philosophy of language, history etc. I was guided in my choice of courses to register for by my Course Advisor, Professor Joseph Allen. He was more than a course advisor but a friend who cared for my good health, family, education and prosperity. There were some Professors at SMU that deserved being mentioned in addition to Professor Allen namely, Schubert Ogden, Babcock, Charles Wood, Edwin Slyest, Hardin, John Holt, and Mark Kaplan, D.Z. Philip amongst others. In addition to these great teachers and friends of mine at Southern Methodist University, there were two Libraries that contributed significantly to my academic success: Bridwell and Fondren. The former closed at 10 p.m. while the latter closed at 2 a.m. One could be lost in the Fondren Library because of a collection of books, journals, periodicals, monographs etc. The archives section of the library was monumental in its collections. David Adamo and I used to close when the workers turned off the first warning light.

In my second year at Perkins, the majority of the students voted me as Senate Representative of foreign Students. It was a mark of good relationship among the student community. To earn extra pocket money, I was given a part-time job as cashier at Perkins Bookshop. I was able to save some money that I sent home for the care of my family, parents and relatives. Some members of the Perkins community were concerned about my family at home and decided to raise fund to bring them to join me. They succeeded in raising enough money for my wife and son, Segun Bidemi Ogungbemi Jr. to join me. It was a great moment I was looking forward to in life. I was exceedingly happy when they came to join me. Before their arrival, I had been given a room in Hawk Hall where married students lived with their spouses and children.

Before the end of 1979 and early 1980, I had applied to several universities for admission into their Ph.D. in philosophy programs. Professor Allen wanted me to go to Yale, his alma mater for another master's degree in Symbolic theology and he was going to recommend me for a scholarship. I was not interested in the course, and I told him my area of focus was philosophy. His concern was how to get a scholarship for me to pursue a Ph.D. program because of its financial cost. I applied to the department of philosophy at Harvard and its Chairman/HOD raised the issue of financial support especially as I was a foreign student with my spouse and child. The other consideration I had was the cold weather, which I detested with passion. I finally decided to apply to Emory University, Atlanta, Georgia and The University of Texas at Dallas, Richardson, Texas (UT-Dallas) where they have philosophy and humanities programs. It was an interdisciplinary program, which appealed to me. I applied to both institutions, and I was admitted. The Department of Philosophy at Emory University admitted me with advance standing while Postgraduate School of Humanities at UT-Dallas admitted me provisionally that for the first 24 credit hours, if I made any grade less than B, I would be asked to withdraw from the program. Which one should I choose? There were other compelling considerations to be examined before making any choice out of the two institutions. The first issue to deal with was: should I leave Dallas for Atlanta, an unknown destination, where I easily get support from friends and churches? Was the provisional admission given to me at UT-Dallas not a challenge and an opportunity to prove my academic worth? Or was it a discriminatory device to scare me from the program? On my first visit to the UT-Dallas, I met one professor who eventually became my mentor and friend, Professor Louis Pojman. He impressed me so much that I could not resist being one of his students. The profiles of the professors were a class of its own as they came from Ivy League institutions like Yale, Harvard, Oxford, Columbia, Cambridge etc. It was a psychological mindset. It does not mean that being a product of an Ivy League institution necessarily makes one a better teacher.

Someone can be a product of a non-Ivy League University and yet be an effective/productive teacher like John Rawls who taught at Harvard.

The tuition and other fees at UT-Dallas were moderate and affordable for most students. There was also a concession for students from friendly countries where Texas oil companies were exploring oil namely, Nigeria, Iran, Egypt etc. As moderate as the cost of going to UT-Dallas was, I could not afford it without financial support from friends and First United Methodist Church in Dallas. Meanwhile, I contacted the Chairman, Department of Philosophy at Emory University that I appreciated the offer of admission given to me but due to my limited financial resources I was not able to accept it.

After some consultations with friends and those who were willing to assist me at UT-Dallas, I decided to accept the offer of admission and registered for the Fall Semester courses. I was glad when Professor Pojman was appointed my course Adviser. The Fall Semester registration procedure and the orientation week were not cumbersome. As a foreign student, I had to register for 12 credit units to maintain the mandatory studentship. When registrations were over, academic lectures began. There were nine students in my class, and I was the only Black student. I was wondering why I was the only Black student in a class of nine students in the program. Before the semester ended, I went to meet the Dean of the Postgraduate School of Humanities to know why my admission was provisional with a caveat of threat. He promised to investigate it and after some weeks of lectures I got a letter that retracted the conditional provision of my admission. To sustain my studentship, I needed reliable financial support. So, I applied for Nigerian Federal Scholarship in 1981/82 and luckily I got it. It covered all my expenses for three years. With my improved financial condition, I was able to send more money to my parents at home and rendered some contingent services to friends and relations.

My Ph.D. program at UT-Dallas was by coursework and research. It required two years of coursework with a grade not less than B to qualify for the written and oral examinations. When I succeeded in both exams, the Ph.D. dissertation proposal had to be defended satisfactorily before I qualified as a Ph.D. Candidate and thereafter, writing of the dissertation and the final stage was the defense. At each level of the hurdles, Postgraduate School of Humanities rules stipulated that if any student failed the first and second times, the hope of continuing in the program became very slim. Before the successful completion of my coursework, it was mandatory for me to go to School of Oriental and African Studies, University of London, British Museum, Museum of Mankind, etc., for eight weeks of research because one of my major focuses was African Studies and African Philosophy. I first discussed the cost of going to University of London with Mrs. Gay Dahlstrom who had been like a mother to me and Rev. Ben Feemster the Head Pastor of First United Methodist Plano, Texas. Rev. Feemster made contact to a friend in London. His friend wrote to him that they could be of help to me, but he and the Church should bear the cost. The Church in Plano raised all the necessary funds for me, and I left Plano for London in the summer of 1982. It was a rewarding experience to be with my host at John Wesley's House. John Wesley was the founder of the Methodist Church. It was a privilege for me to be accommodated in his house. I was surprised to meet two of my former schoolmates at S.M.U there. In one of the evenings when we were in the mood to have leisure, my former schoolmates at S.M.U took me to a church converted to a beer parlor to relax. What an abomination, I chuckled! But that did not stop the enjoyment of my jug. A new age that undermined the church and its religious ideals.

Transportation to University of London was by underground train they called Tube. It was the most convenient to use for me. It was not difficult to get to University of London and immediately I got there. I went to the School of Oriental and African Studies to present a letter of introduction to the Librarian to enable me have access to their Library including the Senate Library. I was given a card that authorized me to use their facilities. One could not imagine how the institution had so much research work written on Africans and uniquely preserved in their academic treasury. I spent six weeks there and a week at the British Museum and visited other relevant places like Canterbury, Buckingham Palace, and Westminster Abbey. The wife of my host wanted to know what I had achieved before I left for Plano. I told her about African Philosophy, and she said such an idea of academic discipline did not exist. It was an exciting debate that revealed a western ignorance of African philosophy. I thanked her for the debate and reminded her and her husband that it was about time for me to go back to the US. I spent the last week to buy books and souvenirs in the Bookstores around the University of London. I also went to Liverpool market to shop for materials for my wife and friends.

I returned to Plano, Texas on August 4, 1982, and met my family in good health. I had lost some weight due to running up and down in London, but the good thing was that I came back safely. I went to Rev. Ben Feemster to thank him and on Sunday I was in the Church to thank the congregation for their financial and moral support. Before we resumed for the 1982/83 academic sessions, I had written my report to be submitted to the Dean of the Postgraduate School of Humanities. Professor Janis Mays was the first I met and gave her a report on her assignment. She welcomed me back and appreciated the report; but soon after she left the university. I met my Ph.D. advisers, Professors Pojman, Worsfold, Armstrong and Dennis Kratz on the dates for my Comprehensive written and oral Exams. I was told that the Dean of Postgraduate School would contact me when they were ready. It took me about six months to prepare for the exams and at the end of it all I succeeded. As part of the program, I had to go for at least six months of internship.

Completion of the dissertation took a longer period because of the illness of my son, departure of my Supervisor, Professor Pojman for University of Mississippi, death of Professor Armstrong, additional domestic responsibility and teaching at Bishop College Dallas amongst others; but finally, everything was completed at the end of Fall Semester, 1984 and the Commencement (Convocation) took place on January 5, 1985. Out of nine classmates in 1980, only two of us, Sam Storms and I got our Ph.Ds. in December 1984. It was at that time the greatest achievement that boosted my rising profile in academic and social status.

PART SIX

GOING BACK HOME

PART IV

GOING BACK HOME

Chapter 10
REASONS FOR GOING HOME

When I told my parents I was going to study abroad, it was cheering news to them but with a question: how long would it take you to come back home? I could not give them a definitive date, but I assured them of coming back to look after them and in the interim, I would be giving them some financial assistance. This promise was a commitment that must be fulfilled. Unfortunately, my mother passed away in December 1978 leaving my father and my siblings behind with challenges that remained my responsibility alone.

The scholarship given to me by Perkins School of Theology, Southern Methodist University Dallas was meant to contribute to African development and to encourage me to pursue my academic interest in any field of my choice.

So when I graduated there on May 18, 1980 it was not compelling for me to return home. So, I went to pursue a Ph.D. in Philosophy and Humanities at The University of Texas at Dallas, Richardson Texas (UT-Dallas) with Nigeria Federal Scholarship on a condition to return home to contribute to the development of the country. I graduated from UT-Dallas in December 1984. On January 1, 1985, I wrote in my diary "It is my plan to go back to Nigeria this year. My New Year resolution is to pursue knowledge by means of research and to use that knowledge for the betterment of humanity." That resolution began to be fulfilled in the US.

My teaching career in the university system began at Bishop College Dallas, Texas in 1983-1985. Having got my Ph.D. with a two-year teaching experience at Bishop College Dallas, Texas, I felt it was time to return home to help my people and country. Mrs. Gay Dahlstrom who was like a mother to me still wanted me to stay behind because Nigeria was not a stable country. She had given me a lot of financial support for over three years, and she wanted to continue. My wife did not want us to go back home because of different reasons. At work, Professor Mangham, my boss at Bishop College, wanted me to stay and promised to increase my salary. I appreciated his offer, but it was time for me to return home; and thereafter I submitted my resignation letter. My work authorization was renewed but I turned it down. The only support I had came from some of my sponsors in the

Methodist Church in Plano, Texas and my son; but his major concern was the beautiful Volvo 244 DL that he loved with passion. I told him I had bought a better car than Volvo 244 DL and the new car was a blue Mercedes Benz 200. He was probably not convinced because when I sold the Volvo, he wept bitterly. To me, nothing could convince me to stay back in the US because everything has its time; it was time to go back home and to be of help to my people and country. It was a calling with determination, commitment and passion to contribute to human capacity building of my country and with the view to accelerating its development and growth through education. Besides, the Yoruba adage says, *'Ajo ki dun konile ma re le,'* meaning no matter how nice and comfortable you are in a foreign country, it should not stop you from going back home.

In the meantime, Ogun State University Ago-Iwoye, Ogun State Nigeria had offered me a teaching position in the Department of Philosophy. It was a newly established university that needed scholars with Ph.Ds. and more importantly, the Vice-Chancellor; Professor J. Olubi Sodipo was a philosopher. I felt I could make some useful contributions to a young department and support the administration of the Vice-Chancellor who was interested in my service.

In addition to the foregoing, those of us from Yagba, Yoruba speaking people formerly in Kwara Sate but now in Kogi State: Dele Solomon, Biodun Balogun, David Adamo, Sunday Afolabi and I had a compelling ethos to go back home after the completion of our Ph.D. programs. Dr. Bamidele Ogbe Solomon became the forerunner to go home to serve the compulsory national service in the Department of Chemical Engineering at University of Ife Ile-Ife in 1983. As Federal Government scholars returning home, Dr. Balogun and I were to board Nigeria Airways free of charge. So, on July 27, 1985, I left Dallas Texas with my family for LaGuardia airport New York where Dr. Balogun joined us to board Nigeria Airways en route to Lagos. It was like a family reunion because I had not seen him for about two years since I visited him in Pittsburg, although we were constantly in contact on phone and by post. That was the first time he was meeting my wife and son. He, thereafter, relocated to University of Ife, Ile-Ife in 1986. Dr. Julius Sunday Afolabi and Dr. David Tuesday Adamo were the last batch that came back home in 1986. What a huge investment and academic dividends harvested by the then Federal Government of Nigeria!!

Chapter 11

EXPERIENCE ON RETURNING TO NIGERIA

As we got ready to go back to Nigeria on July 27, 1985, a few spirited friends and a relation namely, David Adamo, Emmanuel Babatunde and his wife, Thomas Bode Ogunrinu and his wife, Sunday Omokore, amongst others escorted us to Dallas/Fort Worth International Airport. Our departure elicited emotions as I watched some of them using handkerchiefs to wipe their tears. I couldn't talk to anyone or do more than to wave hands and hold the hand of my son to go through the security checks. We arrived in Lagos on July 28, 1985 and several of our relations Jide Omokore, Dr. Dele Solomon, Chief Bolaji Iyekolo, and Abayomi Ajayi amongst others came to meet us. As we were in the general lobby in the airport, my son, Segun Ogungbemi Jr. expressed his first cultural shock as he held my hand and tapped me on the back and said, 'Dad I have never seen a bunch of Black people like this in my life' and everyone busted to laughter!! He was surprised to see many Black people at the airport because we never lived among African Americans or many Nigerians in Dallas and Plano Texas. We had lived mostly in the white dominated areas. He did not know that thenceforth he was going to live with Nigerians, the most populous African nation in the world. And as we got to Chief Iyekolo's house, he asked, 'Dad where is your Mercedes Benz car?' I told him it was on the way coming by sea and not by air. I wasn't sure if he understood the implication of what I said because there were no follow up questions. We were tired and hungry. Mrs. Florence Biodun Iyekolo fondly called Iya Toyin had prepared delicious African food for us. We were made to feel at home. After our meal we were taken to our room with our luggage. Unfortunately, the luggage of Dr. Balogun did not come until several days later. It was a frustrating experience although he eventually got it and then traveled to Ilorin to visit his family before going for his interview at Obafemi Awolowo University (OAU) Ile-Ife and thereafter returned to the USA. He returned to OAU Ile-Ife as a faculty member in 1986.

We returned to Nigeria during the Military Government of Buhari when his administrative principle of War Against Indiscipline (WAI) was enforced. We thought Nigeria was going in the right direction with the genuine investment in moral discipline. After a few days of our arrival some hoodlums entered the yard where we were staying but luck ran against them as Chief Iyekolo came out and threatened to shoot the thieves and we woke up including our neighbors. Recognizing that their deed had failed they took to their heels. It was scary but it put us on our toes, as we never slept with our eyes closed. In the morning Chief Iyekolo got some people to fix the damaged part of the protecting sliding door burglarproof. The thieves never came back again.

While we were still awaiting the rest of our personal effects to arrive by sea, my wife Dupe and I went on a visit to Ogun State University Ago-Iwoye. The environment did not look like a university that my wife had projected in her mind. We had to sleep in the university Guest House, which to most people around was 'executive' in nature but nothing there made it so in the real sense of the normal or standard of aesthetic ambience. I told my wife that she should not expect the kind of institution in the US at Ago-Iwoye; a local community was in need of people like us to contribute in our small way to its modernization through education. We returned to Lagos the second day and by that time I suspected that my wife was not going to be a party to my idea of national sacrifice despite the fact of financial support for her education in Nigeria by First Methodist Church Plano, Texas. She was not convinced that her educational dream and achievement would be realized in Nigeria and when I was not around, she went back to her parents at Mopa and about a week later she called to inform me of her safe arrival back to the US; and I should take care of our son very well.

Barely a month of our return to Nigeria on August 27, 1985, another military coup ousted Buhari government and Ibrahim Badamasi Babangida took over as Military Head of State. It confirmed the premonition of Mrs. Dahlstrom that Nigeria was not stable and therefore, I should reconsider my resolve to go back home rather than remain in the US. As the Yoruba adage says: Oro agba bio se lowuro ope titi ase lojo ale; meaning, the word of wisdom of elders no matter how long it takes will come to fruition. It is an experience I will continue to live with for life.

The change of government was a routine in Nigeria political space, and it couldn't discourage us in the pursuit of our mission and determination even though my US visa was valid till 1987. The coup, however, had a negative impact on business activities in the country. It affected the clearing of my car on time at Tin Can Island, Lagos. The implication of it was that I had to pay demurrage daily on the car until it was finally cleared on October 21, 1985, and my cousin Prince Dele David drove the car to Chief Iyekolo's house late in the evening. The long wait to get the car by my son was assuaged. He was glad to see it parked where he could see it daily and more importantly to have a ride and get out of boredom.

Meanwhile, I still had to clear my personal effects at Roll on Roll off (also known as RORO), which was about a mile from Tin Can Island. The clearance of my personal effects took about a week even though all my documents were genuine; some Customs Officers still demanded some gratifications. I insisted that they were not going to get anything from me as a federal government scholar apart from the lawful percentage custom duty charges. I eventually got my things out of the place and paid the Clearing Agent who was also an accomplice of greedy customs officers. At that time WAI had begun to lose its grip on the social moral fabric of the society. It therefore raised doubt of sustainable moral discipline in the country the moment the government in power is removed. The Babangida government seemed to receive the blessing of the majority of Nigerians because many elites and intellectuals particularly, the media houses were uncomfortable with the draconic rule of Buhari administration. As I watched the direction the Babangida administration was going on the devaluation of the Nigeria currency because the International Monetary Fund (IMF) felt the Naira was overvalued. When our people asked of my opinion on the matter, I told them that Mexico did it and their peso became almost worthless, and Nigeria should tread gingerly the path of devaluation of its currency to avoid the economic calamity that befell Mexico.

The outcry of the Nigerian public on the issue was a total rejection of IMF and World Bank loan and its conditionality but the Babangida administration viewed it differently and introduced the Structural Adjustment Program (SAP) policies in 1986 knowing full well that "SAPs are based on a narrow economic model that perpetuates poverty, inequality, and environmental degradation." In 1986 Babangida administration yielded to the foreign voice of IMF/World bank on SAP with its economic consequences on national development and growth. Only time will tell when Nigeria's economy will ever recover from the poisonous fruit of the SAP.

PART SEVEN

ACADEMIC CAREER IN AFRICAN UNIVERSITIES

Chapter 12
OGUN STATE UNIVERSITY AGO-IWOYE, NOW OLABISI ONABANJO UNIVERSITY

"Raise the level of academic discipline and it will raise men who would strain every nerve to win it, and the more a man strains himself to be equal to the task, the tougher he becomes physically and mentally."

~Tai Solarin

Dr. Bamidele Ogbe Solomon (now a full Professor) told me in 1985 that Dr. Oladipo Fashina in the Department of Philosophy, University of Ile-Ife, Oyo State wanted me to join Ogun State University Ago-1woye, Ogun State. So, when Dr. Solomon went with me to Idofin and on our return to Lagos, my son and I spent two or three days with him at Ile-Ife. While at Ife he introduced me to Dr. Fashina. I was glad to meet him. He gave me a letter to Professor J. Olubi Sodipo, the Vice-Chancellor of the University. I had no knowledge of the geographical location of the place. He told me that it was a newly established institution where my expertise would be needed and my impact would be felt better than a well-established one like University of Ife, Ile-Ife, which was what I had wanted. I informed him that I was ready to be a part of its growth and development. I was aware that the institution would not have the kind of architectural and infrastructural development like any American colleges and universities that I was used to, but it wouldn't be a place that lacked a dignifying modest structure with good staff offices and classroom lectures. Whatever the condition of the level of development at Ogun State University, I was prepared to be one of its academics that would contribute meaningfully to its advancement.

Ogun State University was established in 1982 by the administration of Governor Olabisi Onabanjo, a seasoned journalist known for his popular column, *Aiyekooto*, a Yoruba name of a bird called parrot generally known in Yoruba folklore for telling authentic truth. The column, *Aiyekooto* used to appear in the Daily Service, Daily Express and the Nigerian Tribune in those days. I first went to visit the university on August 14, 1985 before I officially reported for duty in September 1985 when the institution was in the toddler year under the leadership of Professor John Olubi Sodipo, the first Vice-Chancellor who was the first Professor of African Philosophy. The principal officers: Vice-Chancellor, Registrar, Bursar and Librarian had their offices in the Mini Campus at Ago-Iwoye. Faculty of science and business offices; bank, restaurants, etc., were also in the Mini Campus. The Faculty of Arts was located at Ijebu-Igbo about two miles from the Mini Campus. It was a temporary location that lacked adequate infrastructure but both staff and students managed the situation and lived with the challenges. Having seen the young university grappling with development challenges, it would be a good idea to have a linkage with other institutions abroad, which the President of The University of Texas at Dallas was interested in but when I brought it to the attention of Ogun State University authority, it was not its priority. I then concentrated on the routine of assumption of duty.

It was customary for new staff to route all official instruments of his/her resumption for duty through the Head of Department or anyone appointed to play the headship role. In my own case the Department of Philosophy had a Coordinator, Dr. Oladipo Fashina who was assisted by Mr. John Ayotunde Bewaji whenever he was not around. When I came it was Mr. Bewaji I found on the ground and I routed my papers through him to the Dean of Arts, Professor Oyin Ogunba, from University of Ife (OAU) and from him to the

Registrar. The bureaucracy of getting things done on time was strange and cumbersome in a new institution; but at the end of it all, everything was efficiently and satisfactorily done. After I submitted all the resume paperwork, I requested the university Housing Officer to help me find a decent accommodation anywhere within the vicinity; and he agreed. When the university resumed in October 1985, I was still in Lagos until November 1985 when I got accommodation at Government Reservation Area (GRA) Ijebu-Ode and a private primary school called Sanni Luba at Ijebu-Ode for my children, Segun and Yetunde. Meanwhile, Chief Bolaji Iyekolo, Managing Director of Thomas Nelson and Pitman, Limited Ilupeju, Lagos helped me to keep my personal effects in their warehouse until the university secured accommodation for me.

RELOCATION TO IJEBU-ODE

When I moved to Ijebu-Ode in November 1985, there were no serious academic activities going on and it gave me the leverage to get myself well organized for my lectures and other official responsibilities in the university. The GRA was a serene environment, and the security was relatively tight. There were two immediate neighbors namely, Dr. and Mrs. Sola Kazeem and the Divisional Police Officer (DPO) and his family. Dr. Kazeem was an Economist Lecturer at Ogun State University. The first night was not pleasant for my son and me because mosquitoes had a free night to celebrate and feast on their victims. When we woke up and I saw layers of mosquitoes' bites on Segun's body, I knew he was going to have malaria soon. I had a sense of remorse because I should have used insecticide to kill the mosquitoes before we went to bed; but we were both tired and needed to sleep. On the second day I promised my son that before going to bed I would spray the rooms. We ate what we could lay our hands on before I started to clean up the rest of the house, even though it had been cleaned up before we moved in, but it did not meet my standard and expectations. We arranged our things in the rooms and got almost everything in their proper places and in the evening, we went to buy insecticides and sprayed everywhere mosquitoes could hibernate. When we went to bed it was a peaceful night for both of us. I was happy that Segun did not have any spot on his body from the mosquitoes' bite. About a week later my son began to show symptoms of malaria fever. He was immediately treated for it.

Segun was registered in primary one at Sanni Luba primary school, which was about five minutes' drive from where we were living in the GRA. He was well received by the Head of the school, Mrs. Oyesola. She became a family friend to my family. She instructed her daughters to help us with house chores pending the time I was able to get housemaids. I was not thinking of getting housemaids when I had my sisters, nieces, and cousins who could live with us and go to school.

It would be a financial relief to them and their parents. They would be able to focus on their education and move progressively towards achieving the level of empowerment to enhance integration into the social and economic 'club' of the elites in the society, which was part of my vision and mission for coming back home. I first brought my cousin, Tope Omokore (a.k.a Akuku, Strongman) to stay with me and I registered him at one of the best private Secondary Schools: Sanni Luba Secondary School, Ijebu-Ode. After a few weeks he returned home and thereafter I brought my nieces, Omolara Grace Adedayo, Yemisi Adedayo and my younger sister, Funmilayo Ogungbemi. Lara was registered at Sanni Luba Secondary School and Funmilayo was registered at Muslim Girls High School adjacent to Sanni Luba Secondary School, Ijebu-Ode. Yemisi was teaching in a private Nursery and Primary School, Ijebu-Ode. I wanted her to go to College of Education, Ijebu-Ode because she was qualified for admission and luckily I got her admitted to the institution. I felt my daughter Yetunde who was about three years old and living with her grandparents at Mopa should be living with us. So, on August 7, 1986, I went to her grandparents at Mopa and brought her to Ijebu-Ode and registered her at Sanni Luba nursery school.

My senior sister, Mrs. Ebun Adedayo in Ibadan and two of her other children, Olu and Bolanle occasionally visited us. Chief Bolaji Iyekolo, Dr. Dele Solomon, Dr. Biodun

Balogun, Dr. Sunday Afolabi, Friday Jide Omokore among others paid us regular visits and kept us company. When they visited, we felt awesome, and their departure left us with empty feelings; but it also made us look forward to their next visits. There were two scenarios during the visits of Dr. Balogun and my brother Jide Omokore I have not forgotten: Dr. Balogun found my son holding a newspaper that my vendor brought and thought that the boy was looking at the pictures inside it and I told him that the boy was actually reading it. He didn't believe that he could read it at his age. So, he told the boy to read it aloud to him and he did. He was amazed that he could read it very fluently. The second one was when Jide came to visit us and as he was leaving, he gave the children, Segun and Yetunde some money and as he left Yetunde brought her own for me to keep for her and I thought Segun was going to do the same but on the contrary. When I waited for him to bring his money and he didn't want me to keep it for him, I called him and asked why he had not given me his money like his sister did, he said, "Dad, Yetunde does not know the value of money." He then asked me where Jide was working because he couldn't fathom how someone could give him the amount of money he got from him. I told him that Jide was a businessman and he turned around and said, "Dad I want to be like him." And I asked why, he replied, "I want to be a businessman and have plenty of money like him." It was a good ambition but also prophetic! With all these relations and children with me;

plus, other relations coming to visit us from time to time, my mind was at ease; and I was able to focus properly on my teaching, research and administrative work in the university. There were essential things needed for a modest comfort in my house and office to enhance productivity:

Firstly, I had to make some bookshelves using the local carpenters at Ijebu-Ode. Everything had to be negotiated with the carpenters, the type of woods to use, nails to use, cost of transportation, etc. Most often I did not know when they were telling the truth on a few things, they needed to make beautiful and durable bookshelves. It took two weeks for them to get the bookshelves ready, but I was pleased with the quality of the materials used with finesse. It took me several days to arrange the books because I had a lot of books and when it was completed, it gave me some satisfaction. I believe teaching, aided with research materials, would add significant values to the delivery of lectures and meet the quality assurance to empower my students. I also believe that the library would be of mutual benefits to anyone who was interested in my aspiration of being a university teacher. My primary targets were my colleagues in the department and students although other colleagues and students from other departments were welcome.

Secondly, Office allocation in the university was a necessary condition for me to perform optimally as a university lecturer. As I have noted earlier that Ogun State University particularly, Ijebu-Igbo campus where I was, some of the basic infrastructural facilities were grossly inadequate, but we managed with what was available as pioneer Lecturers. I was given an office space that I shared with a female colleague in the Department of History. I had to make a lot of adjustments to accommodate their way and manner students were allowed to offices of Lecturers without appointments unlike what I was used to in colleges and universities in the United States of America.

Thirdly, I needed to know the lecturers and administrative staff in the Department of Philosophy and Faculty of Arts. Without introducing myself, I was surprised that most of them knew my name and some of them told me that I was the only Lecturer in the university with a new Mercedes Benz without being a full professor. To them, it was an unusual phenomenon! Therefore, the car had introduced me without being aware of it. In 1985/86 academic sessions, in the Department of Philosophy only Dr. Fashina, the Adjunct/Coordinator, and I, out of nine Lecturers, had Doctorates. Other members of the academic staff were Tunde Bewaji, Martin Onwegbusi, Ayo Fadahunsi, Ebun Womiloju, Akin Onigbinde, Nurudeen Olarinde and Mr. Gbadegesin. I admired their zeal and dedication most often but sometimes they were lackadaisical and their closeness to students amounted to cheap popularity and good friendship.

Their exposure to literature and books in philosophy was very limited but they were eager to acquire teaching materials in their areas of specializations. Several of my colleagues in the department registered for Ph.D. programs at University of Ibadan, University of Lagos, and University of Ife, now Obafemi Awolowo University. My library was an asset to them particularly, Ayo Fadahunsi and Ebun Womiloju. Several years later when the Department had more academic staff, Samuel Ade Ali and Dele Balogun frequently used the library. Reflecting on the impact of the library on their academic achievements, which they acknowledged, it has given me joy and happiness because, not only did all of them get their Doctorates, but also after several years of hard work and publications they became full professors.

The department program was adequate for undergraduate students in philosophy, and I was impressed with a few courses in African philosophy but generally speaking it was more of Western philosophy. As I looked at the program, I felt we needed more courses in African philosophy than Western philosophy; and more importantly, the interdisciplinary nature of philosophy should be implanted in the minds of the students. While my ideas were personal, I knew I could not introduce any of them until I became Head of the Department. There was a fundamental problem because all my colleagues had a stereotypical form of teaching philosophy courses; a few of them used the lecture notes of their undergraduate to teach their students. To introduce new courses and methods of teaching outside what they were used to would be met with stiff opposition. I was aware that new courses could not be introduced midway until when the department academic program was due for review after two or three years and that was not an easy exercise. In a nutshell, all department academic programs had to be approved by Ogun State University Senate after they had passed through their Departments and Faculties boards. Going through the procedures and processes is cumbersome to me due to my background of how it is done in colleges/universities in the United State of America.

Moral and academic disciplines are important both on the part of students and Lecturers if society is to benefit from the quality of education and training offered by Ogun State University now Olabisi Onabanjo University. As a matter of fact, the university, like other tertiary institutions in the country, awards students their certificates, diplomas and degrees based on moral discipline: 'character and learning'. During my time in the university, there was a firm commitment to moral and academic disciplines on the part of students and Lecturers. I remember a case of improper behavior by some lecturers in the Faculty of Arts and the matter was decisively dealt; five lecturers 2 in the Department of Philosophy, 2 in the Department of Religious Studies and 1 in the Department of English and Literature in English, respectively were dismissed during the 1986/87 academic year. I was impressed with the standard of moral and academic disciplines under the leadership of Professor J. Olubi Sodipo, the Vice Chancellor. I looked up to him as an academic and administrative role model.

I commenced teaching in January 1986 after I had organized all my teaching materials. I got my course outlines and textbooks for all my courses ready. Each student was given a copy of the course outline detailing the scope and objectives of the course with assignments/tests; and a list of reading chapters in books recommended for the semester on a weekly basis, among others. My method of teaching was to encourage textbook reading acquisition and to demonstrate the importance of creative reasoning, thinking and writing. It was essentially to discourage rote learning and restriction to class notes knowledge syndrome, which was prevalent then. I also had office hours on a weekly basis when students could come to see me with flexibility for occasional urgent matters to be discussed. Unless there was a compelling reason, as a matter of policy, I was opposed to students coming to my house.

There was and I believe still, a compulsory academic demand on all graduating students in the Nigerian university system to write a 'Long Essay' and without it no student will be allowed to graduate. In the 1985/86 academic year, Dr.

Fashina was the Co-Ordinator of the Department when I was to supervise the Long Essays of some final year students in the department. I, however, wondered how students assigned to me could write satisfactory Long Essay proposals without sufficient groundwork in research methodology. The danger, it seemed to me, was that if students were not adequately exposed to the rubrics of research methodology in Humanities there was a high probability of them plagiarizing works without realizing its academic implications. I also felt that the supervisors had very limited exposure to literature in philosophy and its branches for them to know sources plagiarized by the students they were supervising. There was a common knowledge within the university community that several students hired lecturers within and outside their departments to write their Long Essays for them. What was not made public was the price paid either in cash or in kind by the students. I had a premonition that plagiarism would become endemic, and the exploitation of students would become pandemic. Meanwhile, I wrote a research guide and methodology for my students to follow with the intention of making it compulsory for all the students in the department when eventually I become Head of the Department. It was common knowledge that without being Head of the Department, it was difficult to make any meaningful contributions for change more so if the leadership in the department was not favorable to it.

I considered the 1986/87 school year under the leadership of Dr. Joseph Omoregbe, Associate Professor of Philosophy at University of Lagos, a tutorial year to learn some of the politics in the university system. It was a year I became conversant with the intrigues, betrayals and outright persecutions in the system. I refused to join any caucus on campus because of my principle of openness and fair play. It was the first time the Department was having a Head of Department on Sabbatical who was always on ground to attend spontaneously to issues and challenges confronting the department. It was the time when information on sexual harassment and sex for grade broke out during the Faculty Board meeting that involved several young Lecturers in the department. It was a tough time for me to really know those who appreciated me from a mere cordial respect by virtue of being the only Lecturer on ground with Doctorate using a brand-new Mercedes Benz popularly conceived by Senior colleagues as 'Professorial car', which was a symbol of living very comfortably well.

I did not know who influenced my invitation to the Department of Philosophy, University of Ife, Ile-Ife that honored me on several occasions to their seminars where I presented several papers and each time I went, Mr. Akin Onigbinde in our department; most often accompanied me. My method of presentation was to read my papers and then listen to comments, remarks, criticisms and questions rather than summarizing the papers and then respond to comments and criticisms as they suggested because of limited time they had for seminar presentations. Of course, both methods are permissible at seminars, workshops and conferences depending on a few factors, for instance, time, number of presenters and space. I felt the planning should have accommodated full presentation of papers particularly when it was one invited guest. My papers were well received with robust discussions that ended in agreements and disagreements. One of my views on the powers of African Ancestors during the Atlantic slave trade that a handful of white slave traders came and took their descendants without rescue interventions raised doubts about the authenticity inherent in such African beliefs. Perhaps my criticism didn't go down well with some of our colleagues at that time because of the raging debate on whether there was anything called African Philosophy. Western intellectual bias against the rational capacity of Africans to conceptualize philosophy was behind the outright denial of the existence of African Philosophy. My criticism of African Ancestors who were not able to save their descendants from the onslaught attack by some white slave traders was seen as a Western influence that undermined one of the critical and cardinal metaphysical African beliefs. I was and still a fervent believer in the existence of African Philosophy because all human races have natural endowment of intellect, intelligence and the light of reason without exceptions.

The Faculty of Arts at Ogun State University under the Deanship of Professor Oyin Ogunba encouraged all members of academic Staff to present seminar papers in the faculty. I decided to present a paper entitled, 'A Philosophical Reflection on the Religiosity of Traditional Yoruba'. I submitted my paper to the Seminar Co-Ordinator of Faculty of Arts. The Faculty Board Room was the venue for Faculty seminar presentations. The Dean, Professor Oyin Ogunba was the Chairman on the day I presented the paper. The venue was full, and I was wondering why we had so many people attending my presentation. I was given 20 minutes to present the paper. There was a barrage of condemnation of the paper from junior colleagues because the paper was conceived as antagonism of Yoruba religious values, but the Dean assessed it differently and came to my rescue. He told the audience that Dr. Ogungbemi's presentation was one of the very best ever presented in the Faculty Seminar and he highlighted the merits of the paper. I was delighted with his comments. I later submitted the paper to Fr. Dr. Kenny, Editor of *Orita: Ibadan Journal of Religious Studies* for publication in the Department of Religious Studies, University of Ibadan. The paper was published in 1986 with the Editor's comment that elevated my intellectual spirit. Reflecting on that historic moment, the paper remains one of my best-published works. The article contributed to my promotion to Lecturer 1 under the Deanship of Professor Ade Kukoyi, from University of Lagos whose sabbatical was for a year. In 1987/88, the Vice-Chancellor, Professor J. Olubi Sodipo appointed me Acting Head of the Department of Philosophy.

ACADEMIC ADMINISTRATIVE ROLES

My appointment as Acting Head of Department of Philosophy was a surprise to members of the department because the outgoing 1986/87 Head of the Department Dr. Joseph Omoregbe had informed some colleagues that Mr. Bahl in the Department of Philosophy at University of Lagos was going to be the Head of the Department. What most of them did not know was that by the time Mr. Bahl applied for a sabbatical appointment, he was a Lecturer 1 without a Doctorate whereas I got my Ph.D. in 1984. The VC, Professor Sodipo felt it was necessary to appoint the most senior person who was on a permanent appointment amongst the academic staff on the ground for continuity and development instead of appointing people on sabbatical from different universities from time to time and whose leadership experiences could not provide the peculiarity of Ogun State University. More importantly the VC had confidence in me that I could do the job and if there was anything I needed he was ready to assist me. Dr. Omoregbe was displeased that his colleague Mr. Bahl who had been promoted to Senior Lecturer position was not made Head of the department. He made his displeasure known to the VC Professor Sodipo who had determined not to change his mind on his confidence in my leadership quality and service. I was later accused that I influenced the VC because of his interest in me. Dr. Omoregbe and his friend Dr. Bahl developed cold attitudes towards me. It was the beginning of my administrative experience in a university system in Nigeria. I made sure Dr. Bahl was carried along in my administration like other members of the department. It was a very difficult time for me because I had to cope with my domestic responsibility as a single parent looking after two children, Segun Ogungbemi Jr., Yetunde Bosede Ogungbemi, my old father, his children and extended family members. Living expenses were within limit because of the high value of Nigeria currency, the Naira. In spite of these difficulties, I was determined to build a department I was convinced was needed by my academic and administrative contributions just as I needed to expand my orientation of African knowledge production.

Professor Kola Folayan from the Department of History OAU Ile-Ife had two years sabbatical 1987-1989 and was appointed Dean of Faculty of Arts. He was an astute university administrator whose leadership and tutelage gave me the opportunity to carry out some of the reforms I wanted to implement in the department. At Faculty Board meetings he noticed I was always different in my response to issues, and he found out that I was the one telling the truth no matter what others felt. In one of the meetings of the Faculty Board, he told members that he had come to appreciate the courage of Dr. Ogungbemi for speaking out his mind always and without any doubt his integrity and approach to different issues had helped his administration. I was honored and humbled by his encomium, but I knew others were not happy with his remark as I could see on their countenance. Since then, the Dean, Professor Kola Folayan and I became very close friends. Perhaps my principle of integrity and courage to stand for truth drew me very close to the Dean, Faculty of Arts, Professor Folayan and the VC, Professor J. Olubi Sodipo.

Before I became Acting Head of the Department of Philosophy, I was working on some of the things my training and teaching experience in the United States of America could contribute to a better way of doing things in the system. Among things that I wanted to effect changes were:

i. Teaching method (Course Outline and Textbooks)

ii. Marking Scheme

iii. Student learning method/Creative reasoning

iv. Office Hours

v. Research mythology

vi. Long Essay Supervision/Long Essay Writing (Writing Manual: Turabian)

vii. Revision of Departmental program, (African Aesthetics and Philosophy of Human Nature)

viii. Course Allocation (Interdisciplinary Approach)

ix. Responsibilities and Accountability

I realized very early that unless one is Head of the Department, to reform accustomed practices, would meet with stiff opposition. I did not plan to achieve the above listed items at once because I knew they would resist innovation or change that demanded extra time and workload because all of them except Dr. Bahl who was on sabbatical were postgraduate students in neighboring universities.

On resumption as Acting Head of Department, I called a departmental meeting. The meeting was well attended, and I expressed my appreciation for coming and hereafter distributed the last minutes of the meeting chaired by the former Head of the Department, Dr. Joseph Omoregbe. After we had gone through the minutes and all the matters arising in it, we began to deliberate on the main agenda of my administration.

At the beginning of each semester, it was customary to allocate courses and other departmental responsibilities. I suggested that it was better to allocate courses to Lecturers for the two semesters at the beginning of each session so that everyone would be abreast of the courses to teach and get teaching materials for them. I then hinted that courses would not be based on the narrow concept of specialization because philosophy is interdisciplinary. I also told them that the departmental program would be revised. I introduced two courses namely, Introduction to African Aesthetics and Philosophy of Human Nature. I also suggested that each Lecturer should have Office Hours pasted on their doors and such hours should not be in the evening or late hours and it should not be on weekends given the peculiarity of the university system. Students had no accommodation on campus and many of them lived far away from the campus at Ijebu-Igbo. We also debated a uniformed method of writing a guide of Long Essay by the 400 Level students. I produced a standard writing guide that is sketched below.

INTRODUCTION

I have written this brief writing guide to assist undergraduate students who may have difficulties in writing a term paper or a long essay project particularly, in the humanities.

One of the difficult tasks in writing on any subject is choosing a **TOPIC.** Or how do I choose a good topic? Or how do I choose a good topic that someone has not written on it? How do I write on a topic that my professor has given us in class? These are some of the questions that become existential challenges you must deal with. Before you choose a topic, you have to think of where you will get relevant materials on the subject. You must be sure you are capable of writing on the topic. It is better you read relevant books or literature materials that will aid your understanding of the subject matter. Write down any topics that come to your mind on a piece of paper and reflect on each one of them. It is advisable the topic is not long and convoluted. For instance, "What is the Meaning of Life?" "Is abortion a moral issue?" "Racism is antisocial," etc., are good examples. After you have got a topic you want to write on, you have to begin on how to go about writing it. Below is a standard format to follow.

i. Statement of the Problem

ii. Statement of Purpose

iii. Literature Review

iv. Research Methodology

v. Thesis/Theses

vi. Sources

vii. Limitation of the Research

viii. Contribution to Knowledge

ix. Summary

x. Tentative Outline

xi. Endnotes

xii. Footnotes

xiii. References

xiv. Bibliography

Recommended Writing Handbooks: Kate Turabian, MLA, APA, and Chicago Manual.

Students taught to be mindful of the importance of authors' property rights so that they did not engage in plagiarism. The research writing guide was not meant for the students alone because paradoxically, the Lecturers were also students elsewhere and I thought it would be beneficial to them as well.

Other issues discussed were teaching method that would include a course outline that gave a brief introduction of the course, the requirements of the course: class attendance, quizzes, tests, reading assignments on a weekly basis and final examination. Each Lecturer was to submit his or her marking scheme to the Acting Head of the Department. Furthermore, Lecturers were to discourage rote learning because it would not give them creative reasoning or creative thinking. The hallmark of philosophy is argumentation based on logical reasoning.

The need to take departmental responsibilities seriously was emphasized because every Lecturer would be held accountable for his or her duties in the department. The departmental meetings were considered sacrosanct, and all members were expected to be present and if anyone was not going to be around, the Head of the Department should be informed directly or through a member or any other means that was convenient to the

Lecturer. The meeting ended well with expectations that the cooperation of all members in the department would enhance the quality of service I envisioned. I soon realized that everything was not always the way they appeared. There had been an underground plot undertaken by all members of academic staff in the department including those who I thought were very close to me. A letter of protest was surreptitiously written against my style of administration of the department through the Dean, Professor Kola Folayan and an advanced copy was hurriedly sent to the VC, Professor J. Olubi Sodipo. Normally, they should allow the Dean to handle the matter without bothering the VC but because they believed that the Dean was my friend, he would probably not report the case to the VC and their ultimate interest would have not been served. The Dean made an internal investigation of what precipitated the action of my colleagues in the department to write such a letter of protest against my administration of the department before he sent it to me. As I was with the Dean, the VC invited him to his office in the Mini Campus Ago-Iwoye. I went back to my office with conviction that the conspiracy theory would fail because every important proposal I intended to execute in the department had been discussed with him because he was a philosopher. I saw the conspiracy theory as a challenge to test the verves of truth and integrity.

The Dean came back from the VC and sent for me. He told me that he had written a memo to all members of the department for a meeting to resolve the issues raised in their protest letter. I went back to my office and got the memo for the scheduled meeting and the venue, Faculty of Arts Boardroom. On the date of the meeting everyone was present, and the Dean invited the cognate Dean of Social Sciences, Professor Layi Erinhoso and all the Heads of Departments in the Faculty of Arts including senior colleagues. The meeting was chaired by Professor Kola Folayan, Dean of Faculty of Arts with two of his administrative staff in attendance.

Normal administrative procedures were followed before the Dean gave the reason for the meeting. The letter of protest by my members in the department was read and each of them was asked if the letter emanated from them and they responded yes. The Dean asked them if they had any other things to add so that all the issues would be resolved. They said nothing more except stationery items that I collected for the department and refused to give out whenever they needed them. Upon a thorough interrogation, the truth manifested that all they did was a conspiracy. I brought out where everyone signed as they collected stationery items with dates. At the end of it all, I was exonerated of any wrongdoing, and they apologized for their action and promised to cooperate with me to move the department forward.

After the meeting, the Dean and I went to meet the VC to let him know the outcome of the meeting. The VC was happy that everything was resolved, and he encouraged me to continue with the good work I was doing in the department. The Dean told the VC that the decision of the meeting would be forwarded to him when it was ready, and I believed he did.

The peaceful resolution of the conspiracy against me in the department made me to become more conscious, circumspect and prudent in my dealings with colleagues in the department, Faculty and the entire university community. That said, it also emboldened my resolve to carry out new ideas and strategies to improve the standard and quality of academic service delivery in the department. My colleagues soon began to have confidence in my leadership and gradually began to key into the new changes I introduced because it evidently helped to improve their teaching methods with discipline and administrative experience in the university system.

As the academic year of 1987/1988 was getting to the midyear every staff was looking up to the Heads of the Departments for their annual assessments and recommendations for promotions/annual increments. It was a tedious academic exercise that I never had to experience until I became Head of the Department at Ogun State University. The exercise was in stages: Departments, Faculties and University Central Appointments and Promotions (AP&P) for all Lecturers below Reader (Associate Professor) and full Professor. The last two categories had to go to the University Governing Council for approval and ratification before the candidates could be pronounced either as Readers (Associate Professors) or as Professors. This was a time I noticed most academic and non-academic staff of the university curry favors or became good friends of their Heads of the Departments and Deans of their Faculties. I enjoyed the supports of my staff and I felt I should be fair to everybody using the criteria given to me to be strictly followed. I had to invite senior colleagues in the Department to be part of the review exercise. At the end of the exercise those who met the requirements were recommended for promotion and those who did not meet the requirements were recommended for annual increment. There was a member of the academic staff that I did not recommend for promotion who got furious and was unable to control his emotion and he told me that he was going to fight me physically, metaphysically and otherwise. I tried to explain to him why I could not recommend him unless he had other papers to support his case. I, however, told him to carry out his threat because I was fair to him and everyone. Some months later as I approached the door of my office, some students who were waiting to see me drew my attention to three little birds on the door and as I was about to open the door one of them wanted to hit my chest and I used my left hand to catch it and threw it on the floor and entered my office. The students were surprised that I was not afraid. I entered my office and attended to them. A couple of weeks later the man who threatened to fight me had an accident and killed a pedestrian. He was arrested and detained in the police station for several days but later discharged. He felt terribly disturbed and remorseful for the loss of life. His journey was not yet over. Some weeks later he was attacked by a group of armed robbers and his car was snatched away. We had a departmental meeting and discussed what we could do to help him. We expressed condolences to him and wish him quick recovery with the hope that the police would recover his car from the daredevil armed robbers. There were insinuations that nemesis caught up with him because of what he told me. I doubt if what he said out of anger that he was going to fight me had anything to do with the birds that hung on the door of my office and all that happened to him afterward. They could be a mere coincidence without any logical and scientific connection or inference. The positive review of his year of service for promotion was based on other evidence of his contribution to the university. Years after the event he reached out to me and expressed his regret for what happened in those days. We have been in constant contact that led to exchange of ideas and academic research publications.

At the end of the academic year my Acting Headship appointment was renewed for another year 1988/1989 and it would enable me to consolidate on my previous year's achievements and focus on new strands and challenges. What I focused on was mentoring all of them that were still pursuing their postgraduate programs in other universities. I made relevant books available to those who needed them and discussed areas that were not clear to them. My vision and mission for the future development of the department was to retain the best amongst our students who were from Ogun State and particularly, from Ijebu and Egba/Egbado respectively. The first graduates from the department that I recommended for appointment as Graduate Assistants were Samuel Ade Ali and Olayinka Opafola. They were interviewed and got appointed as Graduate assistants. I had a total number of four Graduate Assistants, three Assistant Lecturers and one Lecturer 1. So, in all, there were nine academics and three non-academic staff. We had to manage and accommodate ourselves within very limited office spaces and yet the jobs had to be done very well. I admired their sacrifice, devotion and commitment.

I had to devote more time to my research and knowledge

production to be able to make progress and in order to command respect among my peers. Leadership requires being in the forefront by good example. My contributions in the Faculty meetings, workshops, Seminars, etc., gave me additional responsibilities. So also, in the University Senate the VC took cognizance of my useful contributions and he appointed me as member of several sub-Senate Committees, for instance, Member of Library Committee, Member of Faculty of Arts Advisory Committee, Member of Faculty of Law Advisory Committee, etc.

There were no academics due for promotion in 1988/1989 in the department, but each had to be assessed nonetheless for annual increment. I assessed the non-academic members in the department and since I had no problem with them, every one of them who met the basic requirements was recommended for promotion. One of them was given commendation. The annual assessment papers were sent to the Dean's Office, Faculty of Arts for further action. Professor Kola Folayan, Dean of Arts informed members of the Faculty that his sabbatical was coming to an end and he had to go back to his department at University of Ife, Ile-Ife, (OAU) Ile-Ife. A committee was set up to arrange a modest sendoff party for him. A few weeks later the committee reported its report and after their deliberations, it was adopted, and a date was fixed for the occasion. He was given a befitting sendoff.

Before the end of the Rain Semester, the VC renewed my headship appointment for another year, 1989/1990. When the University resumed, Professor Abiodun Adetugbo from Department of Linguistics, Faculty of Arts, University of Lagos became the new Dean of Faculty of Arts. He was a very senior Professor with many years of university experience. A man of such university experience, in my view, would help the faculty to build on the exemplary academic and administrative quality of his predecessor. When the university resumed for the Harmattan Semester and I met him in his office, he appeared casual and responded to my greetings very warmly. I noticed he loved smoking in his office and being allergic to smoking, I politely excused myself from his office. And as time went on, I began to pay serious attention to his administrative strategy and how I could work with him as Acting Head of the Department of Philosophy.

My plan for the year was to continue perfecting the itemized agendas of last year and not to introduce new ones. We needed to intensify our effort by recognizing an interdisciplinary approach to the teaching of philosophy to enhance students' understanding of the wide spectrum of knowledge in the humanities. All my plans, I believed, could be achieved by the department through dialogue, persuasion and by holding regular departmental meetings.

Meanwhile, Departmental meetings were held regularly to

address different issues and challenges to be surmounted by working together as team players for the overall interest of both staff and students in the department. The results of students were computed manually and thoroughly scrutinized before presentation at the Faculty Board of Examiners before going to the Senate. It was the responsibility of the Dean or his representative to present the results of each department in his Faculty to Senate for approval. The Department of Philosophy was known for getting its results on time without errors in most cases and if there were any errors at all, they were minor ones that would not stop the Senate from approving them. The whole exercise was a tedious process that had to be repeated every semester to get the results of students to them. We made sure that our students got their results on time.

We introduced a roster for each member of the department to know when to present a departmental seminar. Given the busy schedules of our academic staff that were pursuing their doctoral studies in the neighboring universities, and the poor facilities we had, we could not accomplish all our goals as we had planned but we kept the spirit of academic scholarship going in terms of individual's research and publications. It was imperative to have published articles in reputable journals, chapters in books, evidence of research materials, etc., to be promoted. The department maintained its adherence to the rules and regulations as contained in the university handbook by making sure that philosophy students and staff obeyed them.

The Military Government of Ibrahim Gbadamosi Babangida introduced a monetary policy of the International Monetary Fund (IMF) called Structural Adjustment Programme (SAP) in July 1986 that had a negative impact on the economy and by 1989 it was biting very hard on workers. So, many Lecturers began to introduce sales of handouts to students to augment their meager income. The University Senate banned the sales of handouts to students and no lecturers should surreptitiously engage in it.

By the Rain semester of 1989/90, the Dean, Professor Abiodun Adetugbo and the Department of Philosophy were beginning to be at a loggerhead on the discipline of a female student who violated the mandatory 70 percent of class attendance in the semester before she could register and sit for her exams. The student abandoned her Long Essay without informing her supervisor and when the Lecturer could not find her around, she reported the case to the department. The department reported the case to the Dean and documented all the efforts made to reach the student who had gone to London without informing the department and the faculty. When she came back to register for exam, the department did not allow her to register, and the case was reported to the Dean and Faculty Board. The Faculty Board noticed that she had no genuine reason to abandon her studies without informing the department and faculty. So, she was advised to comply with the rules and regulations of university in the handbook. The department felt the case had been settled but surprisingly the Dean had taken the case to Committee of Provosts and Deans of the university with the intention to overrule the decision of the Faculty Board. How did the bubble burst?

There was a meeting of the Committee of Provosts and Deans, which Professor Adetugbo should attend, being the Dean of Faculty of Arts and more importantly the case he had taken to the committee was to be discussed. But unfortunately, he was ill and a senior person in the Faculty was to represent him since the Sub-Dean was not around either. So, I was asked to represent the Dean. At the meeting I quickly glanced through the minutes of the last meeting to keep abreast of what was there for the Faculty of Arts and surprisingly the case of the female student in the Department of Philosophy was there. The Dean, Professor Abiodun Adetugbo had put the blame on me that I was the one who did not want her to register for exams. I was stunned and I took courage to tell the truth about the case and the decision of the Faculty Board. The Chairman of the Committee was the VC, but the Deputy VC was acting for him. Both the Deputy VC and the Registrar were telling me to respect the decision of the Dean of the Faculty of Arts, but I disagreed with them. As the debate was going on the VC stepped in and as he settled down, he was briefed about the case and he said the case should go to the Senate. I was relieved because if the committee had approved the position of the Dean the Senate would simply have ratified it and that would have ended the case in favor of the student.

When the case got to the Senate, most members of the Senate were furious and mandated that the case be taken to the Faculty. When the case was brought to the Faculty Board; reactions from members indicated that the decision of Dean was morally counter intuitive. Recognizing the disapproval of his action, the Dean apologized for what he did, and the Faculty Board reaffirmed its earlier decision. The Department was victorious and the unity in the department waxed stronger. The department and its leadership became the heroes of truth. The fact that Professor Adetugbo apologized for what he did, did not mean that he would not take its pound of flesh on me. He waited patiently like a wounded lion for the time of my promotion to Senior Lecturer position. I knew what he could do to me, so I had applied to Moi University Eldoret, a Federal University in Kenya and by September 1990 I had been offered a Senior Lecturer position in the Department of Philosophy and Religious Studies. By October 1990 I was appointed substantive Head of Department of Philosophy, Ogun State University Ago-Iwoye, a position that infuriated Professor Adetugbo, who was already an outgoing Dean of Arts.

In December 1990, I told Professor J. Olubi Sodipo that it was time for me to leave the University having got a job in Kenya. He thought I was going to the University of Nairobi so that he could ask his friend, Professor H. Odera Oruka to defer my appointment by at least a year because my services were still needed at Ago-Iwoye. I felt it was time to leave their university more so that he was ending his second term in December 1990. Before I left, one of the best students, Dele Balogun in the Department of Philosophy wanted to be appointed a Graduate Assistant and I recommended him and took his case to the VC, and he subsequently got the job.

I informed the department of my plan to end my service at Ago-Iwoye. They could not believe that I was serious about it. When they got to know that it was true, they quickly had a sendoff party for me.

END OF MY SERVICE AT OGUN STATE UNIVERSITY

After the sendoff party, I asked one of my younger brothers, Joshua Ogungbemi to come to the GRA Ijebu-Ode where I was living to assist me with the transportation of my personal effects to my house at home, Idofin-Isanlu. He came and we packed everything into a big truck and he and the driver left for Idofin-Isanlu, and my children and I followed them in my car. My father and relatives were wondering why I came home with such a truckload of personal effects. I explained to them that I was going out of the country for a couple of years. I, however, told my father exactly where I was going and promised that his financial upkeep would not suffer. I made solid arrangements for him to keep him happy. I told my father that I would be leaving early in the morning on December 22,1990. His usual practice was early Morning Prayer for all his children, and he would not let me go without his prayer. When he finished his prayer and good wishes, we left for Ijebu-Ode. I had already booked a suite in the State-owned Hotel in Ijebu-Ode. My niece Lara Adedayo came to meet us from Ibadan and my fiancée, Iyabo Temidayo Adeyemi with my children spent the night together. I told my fiancée that I would arrange for her to join us in Kenya provided her uncle accepted the plan. The following morning, December 23, 1990, we began to checkout and set out for our flight at Murtala Muhammed International Airport Lagos. We left Ijebu-Ode and surprisingly there was heavy rainfall on the way, which did not stop even as we got to the airport. We quickly went to check-in at the stand of Ethiopia Airline and bid everyone farewell. I did not know that that would be the last time I would see my fiancée, Iyabo Temidayo Adeyemi.

REFLECTING ON MY ACCOMPLISHMENTS AT OGUN STATE UNIVERSITY

Looking back at my years of services at Ogun State University Ago-Iwoye, now Olabisi Onabanjo University, those that I mentored have made me very proud namely, Professors Tunde Bewaji, Ayo Fadahunsi and Professor/Mrs. Ebun Womiloju Oduwole who was former DVC at Olabisi Onabanjo University. Amongst the students retained, three of them also became Professors, the late Samuel Ade Ali, Dele Balogun and Olayinka Opafola. And finally, one of the oldest academics that I mentored, Dr. Martins Onwegbusi became a Senior Lecturer. They have collectively made the Department of Philosophy at Olabisi Onabanjo grow leaps and bounds.

Chapter 13

MOI UNIVERSITY ELDORET, KENYA

"I should wish to see a world in which education aimed at mental freedom rather than at imprisoning the minds of the young in a rigid armor of dogma calculated to protect them through life against the shafts of impartial evidence."

~Bertrand Russell

LEAVING FOR KENYA

The flight from Lagos to Nairobi airport was six hours. As we arrived on December 23, 1990, the cold weather stared us on the face. We got a place to stay while I covered the children with the heavy winter coat as we were waiting for a representative from Moi University to take us to where we were to stay for the night. After waiting for several hours in a helpless condition, a young man, Mr. Maina came to our rescue. He made all the contacts with the authority of Moi University, and he was told to lodge us at Sarova PanAfric Hotel Nairobi. It was a big relief to us. We enjoyed their hospitality services. The following morning, we were taken to Sirikwa Hotel Eldoret, Kenya, which was about three hours' drive on a very good road. We were lodged in the hotel, and we had our Christmas and New Year celebrations there. Professor Adeniran and the family were the first Nigerians to pay us a visit at Sirikwa Hotel. I had a couple of friends among workers of the hotel and academics from Moi University who came to relax and entertain their friends. When we discussed African political situations in other countries, they expressed their minds freely but when it was about Kenya, I noticed they would keep mute. I wondered why they were not enthusiastic to express their views on things that affected them. When I noticed that they did not want to talk about Kenya politics we ended our discussion. As I left for my room in the hotel, one of them followed me and told me why talking about Kenya politics in the open was a risky and dangerous academic exercise. He also advised me to be careful criticizing Kenya political officeholders, particularly President arap Moi. He told me that the kind of freedom we had in Nigeria was an academic luxury that did not exist in their country. I thanked him and decided to keep my mouth shut on Kenya politics. As political events unfolded in Nigeria, the Kenyan government was not comfortable with the radical union leaders and Civil Rights Advocates who were challenging the Babangida military administration. All the Nigerian Magazines and Newspapers circulated in Kenya suddenly disappeared from the stands of their vendors. Apart from the restrictive freedom, we enjoyed the hotel facilities and of course, the professional hospitality of the workers for about a month before I decided to relocate to the main campus because it was not convenient for my children to go to school by boarding the university bus daily. The university campus was about 35 miles from the hotel.

AT MOI UNIVERSITY

Moi University was established in 1984 by the administration of President Daniel arap Moi. It is in the serene Kesses community, Uasin Gishu County, Kenya. Eldoret is the commercial nerve where most of the staff of the institution was living. The Vice Chancellor was Professor Shellamiah Keya, a seasoned scholar and astute administrator. He had been a Visiting Professor at University of Ibadan an experience he proudly shared with Nigerian academics at Moi University. It was a privilege to know him and work under his administration. Professor Ole Karie was the Deputy VC; Dr. James Sang was the Chief Administrative Officer-Registrar. They were very pleasant university administrators. Mr. George Njuguna, Mr. Mike Singoei and others in the administrative sector of the university later became the first group of friends I had on campus.

Before I could settle down for academic activities on campus, I had to take care of the education of my children. Segun Ogungbemi Jr. had finished a year at Ijebu-Ode Grammar School but due to his age he was to go back to Standard 7 while Yeti started Standard 1 even though she had finished Primary 1 at Sanni Luba Ijebu-Ode in Nigeria. The university primary school on campus was set on the Kenya education system of 8-4-4 unlike the Nigerian system of 6-3-3-4. The school authority mandated the pupils to trek to school regardless of the status of their parents. I was given a befitting accommodation on campus although it was quite a distance from the primary school, but my children preferred it to going on bus from the hotel. They soon began to adjust to their environment and started learning Kiswahili the national language in Kenya, but English Language remained the official lingua franca used in their various institutions.

Professor Emmanuel Obeng was the Head of the Department of Philosophy and Religious Studies when I reported for duty. He introduced me to members of the department and the Dean, School of Social Cultural and Development Studies, Professor Joshua J. Akong'a. When we came back to the department, Dr. Obeng assigned me an office space and gave me a copy of the departmental program. He was also instrumental to my relocation to campus to make it easier for my children to go to school on campus. His wife and children became very close to us, and we shared many things in common because they were formerly at university of Ilorin with Dr. David Tuesday Adamo, a well-known colleague of mine who later came with his family to join us on April 7, 1991. There were several other academics from West and East Africa namely, Professor Michael Adeyemi, Professor Senanu, Mr. Ajai, Professor Adeniran, Professor Stephen Lubega, Dr. Abel Gibe, Dr. Afolabi, etc.

As students were about to resume for the semester in January 1991, the Head of the department, Professor Emmanuel Obeng called for a departmental meeting for the purpose of allocating courses and departmental responsibilities to all the academic staff. As the meeting began, I was introduced to members of the department and everyone was introduced to me namely, Professor Emmanuel Obeng, Fr. (Dr.) Njino, Mr. Adam Chepkwony, Ms. Hazel, Rev. Peter, Mr. Simon Chessesstto, etc. The department had both undergraduate and postgraduate programs; and I was assigned courses in both of them. I was most interested in teaching African philosophy, Ethics, Philosophy of religion, Existentialism, Philosophy of human nature and Metaphysics at undergraduate level and at the postgraduate level, I was interested in African world view, Metaphysics, Christian ethics and secular Ethics. I was assigned three postgraduate students to supervise; two of them were in the master's degree program and one in the D. Phil. I felt that it was necessary to create a Department of Philosophy separately from the unholy alliance with Religious Studies. The two departments were merged pending the time the university management made up its mind to separate them. My intention was to have a Philosophy Department. I spent my first year, 1991 academic year, working out the possibility of making it a reality in the 1992 academic year. That was my vision and mission for 1992 and I did a lot of consultations and made all the necessary preparations in terms of development of a departmental program. I believed in getting anything of that magnitude done, one should have the good will of the people, and to get the good will of the people; one must be friendly and show leadership traits. Another academic mission that I had in mind was how to amplify the importance of African philosophy to enhance African human capacity building. I was also mindful of improving my research and publications. I wrote two papers that I presented at the World Congress of Philosophy organized under the leadership of Professor H. Odera Oruka, a Kenyan foremost African Philosopher. It was held in Nairobi, Kenya, July 21-25, 1991. Dr. and Mrs. Adamo were kind enough to have my children stay with them as I prepared to attend the conference in Nairobi. I returned from Nairobi on July 25, 1991, and went to the house of Dr. Adamo and his family and thanked them for taking care of my children. The children were happy to see me back safely and we left for our house.

The World Congress of Philosophy held in Nairobi was the first I have ever attended and met many philosophers from Europe, America, Africa and other parts of the world. At the conference, I met some great African scholars and Philosophers namely, Professor J. Olubi Sodipo, Professor Ali Mazrui, Professor Paulin J. Houndtonji, and Professor Kwasi Wiredu, among others. The outcome of the conference and my anticipation for promotion in 1992 encouraged me to submit my application for a professorial position on August 29, 1991, to the Chairman of the Department of Philosophy and Religion. I believed that the positive outcome would complement my action plan for the 1992 academic year.

I was appointed Head of the Department of Philosophy, Moi University on January 9, 1992. I was delighted for the appointment because it was a vision and missions come to reality. I had only Mr. Chessetto as a permanent staff and whose specialization was in philosophy and Fr. (Dr.) Njino, a Catholic priest in the department of Religious Studies who had knowledge in some areas of philosophy who could be used on a temporary basis. I contacted Professor Oruka in the Department of Philosophy, University of Nairobi if he knew some of his staff that would like to join me in the young department. He introduced me to three of them who were ready for full-time employment at Moi University. I asked them to come with their credentials to meet the Dean, Professor Okumu and they did. The three were Mary,

Pamela and Michael and after their interactive session with the university authority they were told to expect their letters of invitation for an interview. When they got their invitation letters they came, and they were interviewed. They all did very well at the interview and I was glad they were appointed for the various positions they applied for. I started the Department of Philosophy with six academic staff members: Chessetto, Njino, Mary, Pamela, Michael and me. Professor J. Olubi Sodipo later came to join us while Professor Oruka was appointed External Examiner. I had two non-academic staff that made the administrative work in the department less cumbersome.

Meanwhile, Moi University advertised for professorial cadre and Department of Philosophy was included and I applied; and luckily was shortlisted amongst others to be interviewed on February 3, 1992. The interview was rigorous and tiring but I succeeded and was appointed as an Associate professor of philosophy; and hence addressed professor as it is done in Kenya and the United State of America. It appeared 1992 was my academic and research fortune: I was invited by the Editorial Board of *Journal of African Religion and Philosophy* to give a public lecture entitled, "A Critical Assessment of Religions in Africa" at Makerere University, Kampala on May 14, 1992; International Conference at National University, Lesotho Southern Africa on October 26-November 3,1992; paper entitled, "Conventional and Traditional Medicine: A

Philosophical View", Workshop on Ethno-medicine held at Lake Bogoria Hotel, Kenya, November 4-7, 1992 and several Seminars at Moi University.

The pursuit of human happiness is not found in academic progress alone but also in economic, political and social relations among others. This was true in my case in 1992 as I was making steady progress in research, teaching and publications without much income to complement my effort. The impact of the economic meltdown in Kenya made teachers to ask for upward review of their salary. President arap Moi did not want the university lecturers and professors to be part of the agitation. On July 3, 1992, the Vice-Chancellor, Professor Keya sent an invitation letter to me to join other professors to meet President Daniel arap Moi at the State House Nakuru on July 5, 1992. We were kept in the cloud because the President invited us to the State House. A university bus was provided for the trip, and we all went. There was no professor at Moi University who did not go because most of the professors were expatriates and we wanted to know him in person and to listen to his purpose for inviting us. Was he going to give us a march order to go back to our countries or what business did we have with his administration that warranted meeting us at the State House? So, we held our breath and waited for his political and administrative message. Nakuru is in the heart of the rift valley and the weather is generally cold all year round. We got to Nakuru and waited for the President and surprisingly he came at exactly the scheduled time. After observing all the protocols, he began to address us. He was eloquent and very polite. He told us that he invited us to let us know that he was first and foremost a teacher and he would make us comfortable within the resources of his administration and the Vice-Chancellor of each Federal university would deliver his package to us. He then asked if we had any questions? There were no questions and he thanked us and drove back to Nairobi. He lived up to his promise; our salaries were increased with some arrears paid. Yes, there was a raise in salary but so also a tax increase; however, overall we were still better off.

My schedule for the rest of the year was a very busy one. I was expecting the arrival of Professor Sodipo and when I got his date of arrival, Dr. Afolabi accompanied me to the airport in Nairobi on September 13, 1992. We came back to Eldoret the same day and he was lodged at Sirikwa Hotel. He came to the main campus on September 14, 1992 and I went to introduce him to the Dean, Professor John Joseph Okumu and he went to introduce him to the Vice-Chancellor, Professor Keya and his Senior Administrative Staff. We had a departmental meeting on September 18, 1992, and Professor Sodipo was introduced to members of the department. He was warmly received as the first Professor of Philosophy in Africa and former pioneer Vice-Chancellor of Ogun State University Ago-Iwoye, Ogun State, Nigeria to be a member of the young philosophy department. It was a rare privilege to have him with us. After attending several departmental meetings with us, Professor Sodipo expressed his satisfaction with the departmental program and the administration of the department. He appreciated our devotions to teaching and research that culminated in the monthly seminar paper presentations. He volunteered to present a seminar paper in December 1992 on issues dealing with University Management in Africa. After making all the necessary contacts with the Dean, Professor Okumu, the seminar was slated for 11-12^{30} p.m. on December 1, 1992. The information on the seminar was circulated to offices on campus and the mini campus of the university; and a formal invitation letter was sent to the University Administration. The departmental seminar organizers made sure that the arrangements were without flaws and copies of the seminar papers were enough for circulation after the presentation of the paper. The venue was spacious enough to accommodate a large audience that came for the seminar. The Dean, Professor John Joseph Okumu was the Chairman of the occasion. The seminar started on time without breaching the normal protocol.

Professor Sodipo's presentation was stimulating, entertaining and challenging. It also aroused many questions, but time could not allow him to answer them all. The University

Administration appreciated the outcome of the seminar and wished others to emulate the practice. The department had its last seminar for the year on December 7, 1992.

We ended the semester with an encouraging performance. I announced that one of our best graduating students, Francis Wairagu would be retained as a Graduate Assistant just as two of my students in the postgraduate program in the Department of Religious Studies: Mary Nyangweso and Eunice Karanja were retained as Assistant Lecturers. My research publications considerably improved due largely to the serene environment and the resourcefulness of my colleagues at Moi University. It is worthy to note that several years after Professor Sodipo delivered his presentation at Moi University the excerpt was included in *Philosophy and the African prospect: Selected essays of Professor J. Olubi Sodipo* edited by Ayo Fadahunsi and Olusegun Oladipo: Ibadan, Nigeria: Hope publications.

My 1993 academic plan for the department was first to review 1992 academic performance and know where we have done well and to encourage members not to rest on their oars; and where we have not performed good enough and needed to improve. One of the areas to focus on was staff development and recruitment of senior academics because Professor Sodipo was going to leave for the United Kingdom at end of the semester. As we resumed in January

1993, our academic and non-academic staff members were full of energy and optimism and ready for work. We had our departmental meeting to discuss the agendas and action roadmap for the year. Generally speaking, our departmental meetings were within one hour. All the results that were pending were given a priority, followed by course allocations and administrative assignment, staff welfare, student matters, Seminar presentations, international conferences among others were the major issues addressed at our meetings.

From the domestic front, I got the university to buy the air ticket for my wife, Mrs. Olayemi Busayo Ogungbemi to join us in February 1993. It was an exciting expectation with some additional responsibilities but in all, it was worth it. My son had finished in the primary school on campus and there was no Government or private Secondary schools nearby for him to continue his education. He had to stay at home to receive private tutoring in English Language and Mathematics. He started to demonstrate his literary talent by writing a 'Children's Story Book', which I thought was a hobby he created to while away his time due to loneliness. His sister Yetunde was still in primary school on campus and doing very well in all her classes including surprisingly Kiswahili Language.

I left campus on February 5, 1993, to meet my wife who was arriving at Jomo Kenyatta International Airport Nairobi at

7:30 a.m. on February 6, 1993. The children accompanied the driver and me to Nairobi to meet her. We slept in Nairobi. The following morning, we went to the airport to meet her. Her flight arrived as scheduled and after picking her luggage we set for Moi University campus. We had a pleasant journey with a lot of fun seeing wildlife animals grazing together particularly, Zebras, Giraffes, Antelopes etc. We got back to campus in the afternoon and our neighbors started coming to visit us. Amongst the first group of visitors were Dr. David Adamo and his family, George Njuguna and family, etc. When the news got the university community that my wife had come, we continued to have many more visitors. Mrs. Adamo and her children plus some female colleagues in the department particularly, Pamela and Mary became very close to my wife and children.

From July-November 1993 the Dean, Professor Okumu made me the Acting Dean while I was still the Head of the Department of Philosophy. As Acting Dean of the School of Social Cultural and Development Studies, I had ten departments under me. Coupled with my domestic responsibilities to my family, it became expediently imperative to assign to members in the department certain functions they could handle effectively with limited supervision. I had to adjust my busy schedules in such a way that I was fair in my discharge of duties, and I had good working relationship with students and colleagues; and at the same time maintained leadership discipline. I had very little time on my research and publications, but I was able to publish at least three journal articles. By October 1993, I began to think of leaving Moi University because of unnecessary politics that began to rear its ugly head. The academics at Moi University wanted to have a union like Academic Staff Union of Universities (ASUU) in Nigeria but President arap Moi government was not favorably disposed to it, even though Kenya constitution allowed freedom of association. The academic environment became tense with allegations of corruption amongst members of university management, palpable distrust and betrayal. I did not want any of such so I decided to apply for a job at National University of Lesotho Roma, Southern Africa. I was initially very optimistic that I was going to get a job in the Department of Philosophy given the impression from my interaction with the Dean of the Faculty of Humanities. Unfortunately, it did not work out as planned because, according to the Vice-Chancellor, the country was experiencing political instability. In view of what was happening in Lesotho, I made up my mind to go back to Nigeria by the end of 1993. The university management tried to resolve the internal allegation of corruption within the administrative organs of the university but it became politicized to the extent that it led to unsavory confrontation and I felt it was time to get out of the system. But meanwhile, my wife was about to put to bed and so I had to tread gingerly and be diplomatic as Acting Dean.

On November 6, 1993, she delivered a bouncing baby girl. We named her Temidayo Bimbola Ogungbemi, but our Kenyan friends named her Wanjiru, a Kikuyu name of a girl born on Saturday and Jebet, a Kalenjin name of a girl born on Saturday respectively. By early December 1993, I informed the university management that I was not going to continue my service and I thanked them for their hospitality and friendship. I then requested for the payment of my gratuity and planned to buy our return air tickets to Nigeria. But before my wife delivered our baby, I had informed the Dean, Professor Okumu, of my decision to end my service at Moi University on December 23, 1993, so that he could relieve me of the burden of an Acting Deanship position. I had a mixed feeling for the department because it needed an experienced, energetic and committed academic to carry on after my exit.

The processes and procedures I had to go through to get my gratuity and other entitlements were cumbersome. The tax deduction was high and getting the money paid on time was a painful experience. I thought I was going to get to Nigeria for Christmas but due to delays at different stages of disengaging my services made it impossible. Meanwhile, friends from West Africa and colleagues at Moi University organized a sendoff party for me. I was honored and humbled with all the beautiful words of encomiums plus the beautiful gift of souvenirs, which made me feel that my services were counted worthy of recognition and acknowledgements. Friends and colleagues at University of Nairobi organized a similar sendoff party at Hotel Milimani in Nairobi January 2, 1993, the eve of my departure for Nigeria. We left for the airport very early in the morning on January 3, 1994, to catch our Ethiopian Airline flight. I couldn't wait to get back to Nigeria with my family as we boarded the plane. We made it safely to Lagos and went by road to Ogun State GateWay Hotel, Ijebu-Ode. The following morning my friend, Dr. Muyiwa Ogunlade came to visit us and persuaded me to move to his house where I would have comfortable accommodation and my family would interact with his wife and children. After some deliberations we decided to move temporarily to his house in Ijebu-Ode.

LOOKING BACK AT MOI UNIVERSITY

The three years of my service at Moi University Eldoret Kenya was one of the most productive and memorable times in my academic career. I have always attributed it to the good weather conditions but beyond that, there was a significantly creative human factor, my students and colleagues. As I reflect on the events of the time and the progress of some of my students and staff, I am glad my services were not in vain. Two of my postgraduate female students in the Department of Philosophy and Religious Studies: Mrs. Eunice Karanja Kamaara and Mrs. Mary Aoya Nyanwegso Wangila caught my special attention for their academic and research achievements in their specialized fields. The former is a Distinguished Professor of Religious Studies at Moi University Eldoret, Kenya and the latter is a Professor and Peel Distinguished Chair of Religious Studies at East Carolina University Greenville, North Carolina, USA.

Chapter 14
LAGOS STATE UNIVERSITY OJO, LAGOS

"Since the 1980s, African universities have been devastated by the weakened African economies…universities have been victims of general economic decline and state mismanagement. Grossly underfunded, they lost their prestige, ability to sustain growth, and capacity to perform their minimum functions."

~Toyin Falola

Lagos State University (LASU) was established in 1983 as a multi-campus and non-residential institution during Governor Lateef Kayode Jakande administration. Its main campus is at Ojo along Badagry Expressway, Lagos State. It has two other campuses: Faculty of Engineering at Epe and College of Medicine at Ikeja respectively. The Department of Philosophy, Faculty of Arts is at the main campus, Ojo.

The above quotation from Toyin Falola explicitly explained what I found when I resumed at Lagos State University Ojo in January 1997 because it was established in 1983. The Jakande administration that established the institution was not unaware of the state of Nigerian economy and that was probably what informed its non-residential policy to address the large number of qualified candidates without university education. When Lagos State University was established, Governor Jakande was not anticipating a military takeover in 1983 and when Buhari Military government took over the reign of political affairs in the country on December 31, 1983, he too was not anticipating a coup but within two years, Ibrahim Badamasi Babangida took over from him in August 1985. So, political instability in the country contributed to the poor state of university education in the country.

MY EXPERIENCE AT LAGOS STATE UNIVERSITY

Professor Peter Akinsola Okebukola was the outgoing Acting Vice-Chancellor at Lagos State University Ojo in 1997 and the substantive incoming Vice-Chancellor was Professor Fatiu Ademola Akesode who resumed in February 1997, Professor Christopher Olubunmi Oshun was the Dean of Faculty of Arts and Dr. Maduabuchi Dukor was the Acting Head of Department of Philosophy when I resumed early January 1997. Dr. Dukor introduced me to some of the academic staff in the department, namely, Dr. Olajide Ojo,

Dr. Wale Olajide, Mr. Sunday Oke and Mr. Olalekan Rafiu Ayodele-Oja amongst others. He also introduced me to the Dean who welcomed me very warmly and prayed for me in his office.

Lagos State University lacked basic infrastructural facilities including office spaces for Lecturers. Dr. Dukor shared the departmental office space with me pending the time when an office would be allocated to me. It took a while before an office space was found for me. It was a cubicle, but it was better than sharing the departmental office with the Acting Head of the Department, Dr. Dukor. After a week of resumption, I began to write down some critical areas the department should address: computation of students' results, departmental program, Long Essay writing manual and regular departmental meetings. As I was deliberating how to make some useful contributions to the department there was a fundamental challenge on campus: Cultism. I had never witnessed students killing themselves anywhere until I got to Lagos State University in 1997. It was the first time in my life that I saw the kind of brutality and horror some students inflicted on one another. I saw three students killed with inflicted bodily injuries and their bodies thrown into the bush opposite Faculty of Arts building. I could not stand the shock of the ugly carnage. I went back home. Similarly, on the very day that the new Vice-Chancellor, Professor Fatiu Ademola Akesode resumed, his attention was drawn to suspected brutal and graphic cult rivalry that led to about five dead bodies near the university gate. It was unpleasant scenery but then, concrete evidence that the university administration of Professor Akesode had to face squarely the challenge of cultism on campus. Professor Akesode was happy to see me as an academic staff on campus because we had been together at Ogun State University Ago-Iwoye, Ogun State. Within a year of his administration, he had brought normalcy on campus as cult activities were on constant security surveillance.

Apart from the challenges of cultism, the Vice-Chancellor was concerned about the results of students that had not been brought to the Senate and the Department of Philosophy, was among them. The Dean of Faculty of Arts called a meeting to address the delayed results of students in some departments. For the past three years, no results of philosophy students had been taken to the Senate. I couldn't address the issue because I was new in their system. The department was mandated to present their result at the next Faculty Board of Examiners meeting. The department could not present its results to the Faculty Board of Examiners because of the HOD's inexperience and incompetence. The VC was under intense pressure from students and their parents on the issue of their results. After several letters to the HOD through the Dean and no positive result, the VC felt there should be a change of leadership in the department. So, he appointed me as HOD of Philosophy with a mandate to produce all the outstanding results in the department particularly, the results of final year students.

After I got my letter of appointment as HOD Philosophy, I went for a brief meeting with the Dean, Professor Christopher Olubunmi Oshun. He congratulated me for the appointment and promised to work with me on a quick solution to the delayed results of students of the philosophy department. I called a departmental meeting to let members know the urgent need for the department to produce results of students that had not been presented to the Senate for approval. I appealed to Lecturers to submit the scripts and marks to begin the process of computing the results. We then allocated administrative responsibilities to each member of the department; particularly those who will begin to compute the results at each level. I told them that results would be computed using registered courses on their registration forms and not what students brought from their Lecturers. I got all the materials for the computation of results from 100 Level to 400 Level. I set the example and worked late in the evenings and when the Dean saw what I was doing he assisted me with the electric lantern when the light went off. Some of the students who appreciated what I was doing came to advise me not to work late in the evening because there was a plot to eliminate me. I later got a letter of threat to my life on campus. I showed the letter to the Dean and the VC and requested for protected I took on. Some of the students advised me not to be on campus beyond 4 p.m. and to their advice. I began to wonder why anyone would want to eliminate me for performing my duty as expected of me? Who was behind the plot? I thought of contacting the police, but I was advised against since the VC had been adequately informed, and he had assured me protection. The department was able to present the results of 400 level students to Senate and they were approved. The students were the first philosophy graduates in 1998. The rest of the 100-300 Level students had reached an advanced stage. One of the best graduating students, Miss. Philomena Parfait and a Lagos State indigene, Michael Aina Akande, who also one of the best graduating students in the Department of Philosophy at Obafemi Awolowo University Ile-Ife, wanted to join the department and approached me for consideration for appointment as Graduate Assistants and I told them to apply. They applied and I recommended them for the post of Graduate Assistants to the VC through the new Dean, Professor Muhib Omolayo Opeloye. They were offered the job at the same time but, local politics reared its ugly head and Mr. Akande was dropped. Miss. Parfait resumed on August 3, 1998, and subsequently became the first female Lecturer in the department. Mr. Akande took his case to the VC for review and subsequently got the job; and resumed in January 1999. Mr. Alloysius Shaagee Ihuah from Benue

State who was a Ph.D. student at University of Lagos, Akoka was also appointed Lecturer 11 in the department in 2000.

I wanted the department under my leadership to standout as the best in the university and to do so, there were areas of challenges to be properly addressed, for instance, moral discipline among both staff and students, staff development, office space, marking schemes, course outlines, sales of handouts to students, computation of results, admission racketeering, etc. Recognizing the economic hardships in the country that made many people find different means to make ends meet, I felt academics who belonged to the middle class should not be found wanting in their attempts to meet their daily needs. The university itself was engrossed with indiscipline, but eliminating corruption at the time by anyone who wanted to clean up the mess would meet a strong brick wall. I was determined to make a difference no matter how little; I believed that the crusade from my department would have an impact on others in the system.

My appointment as Head of Department was for a year but renewable at the instance of the VC on the recommendation of the Dean although not necessarily in all cases. The VC had the prerogative to appoint anyone he felt could do the work satisfactorily, as in my own case. Given the short time of my headship and the threat to my life on campus,

I felt it was necessary to prioritize a few things I intended to accomplish: (i) Regular departmental meetings, (ii) B.A. Philosophy program, (iii) Office allocation, (iv) Course registration forms, (v) Computation of results, Course outlines, (vi) Marking schemes, (vii) Long Essay writing manual, (viii) Stoppage of sales of handouts to students, (ix) Admission allocation quota, (x) Staff development and (xi) Academic moral discipline. In a normal academic system, all those things listed above are accepted as given because there are rules, regulations and norms that form academic culture in the Ivory Tower but that of Lagos State University, Ojo, Lagos State was an exception. I chose to deal with the challenges above by having regular meetings where issues were deliberated upon and collective decisions arrived at for positive and proactive actions. We made tremendous achievements to the extents that our students were commending our efforts in the organization of things in the departments and results were produced. The Dean and VC were proud for the remarkable strides we had made. Be that as it may, there were three difficult areas where we made a little dent but not good enough to be considered remarkable achievements and they were: Stoppage of sales of handouts to students, Admission allocation quo and Academic moral discipline. These three issues were more of a general cankerworm in the university. The abuses were generally pervasive and any effort to deal with them in a decisive way at the departmental level would not be effective because other departments and faculties were equally engaged in academic misdemeanors. The department felt that they were Senate matters to be handled and enforced. But the question was, could the University Management and Senate deal with it decisively? A senior Senate member gave a vivid characterization of the behavior of young Senate members as 'Academic Baby Tigers' who would surreptitiously work against Senate decisions because they were difficult to cage in the system. They had formed a dynamic caucus within the university system like a 'mafia' that could penetrate any office on campus to decipher information they needed to advance their course of action. They had collaborators among non-academic administrative staff that helped them perpetrate their mischief. There was one of them who came to visit me when I was head of the Department of Philosophy and boasted that on this campus nobody could discipline him because he had 'his boys' who would deal with the person. I was told that 'his boys' were the cultists on campus. During the admission exercise he and his colleagues came to me because they heard that we were not going to admit more than 26 candidates for our department. He asked a rhetorical question from me: "Does a trader or market woman complain she has too many customers?" I then asked him: "Is admission in the university system a business?" He did not answer my question. I couldn't fathom why the university had become an extension of Alaba International market or Okearin market in Lagos Island?

It was later that I knew exactly what they thought about me and that was why they came visiting to know my views on some of their academic lifestyle. I was perceived as their 'business spoiler'. They opined that was the reason the VC, Professor Akesode brought me to spoil their business!

Academic moral discipline was at very low ebb in my department. There were instances that a senior lecturer awarded marks to a female student for elective courses she did not register for in other Departments and Faculties. Another lecturer was in the habit of awarding marks to students arbitrarily depending on how much the students were ready to pay. There were two other lecturers who were employed full time in the department but worked part-time. When these cases were reported to the Dean of the Faculty, some efforts were made to investigate the matters and when they found out that they were true the cases were buried underground. Similarly, students who violated university rules, for instance, cheating during examination, were given preferential treatments based on their parental personality on campus or in the State.

There were concerted efforts made to tarnish my leadership success by unseen human forces, the ritualists. It was a day I did not go to the office because I brought some files home to be treated. By afternoon on that day a colleague in the department called me that there was a ritual object put in front of Dr. Dukor's office and the Dean, Professor Opeloye, had written a memo to me and reported the case to the VC. Immediately he told me what the Dean had done, I knew it was a conspiracy theory to malign my fight against corruption in the system. I dressed up and went to my office. On getting there the ritual object had been removed from where it was initially kept. When I got back to my table the office secretary gave me the memo written by the Dean and a copy of a memo he wrote to the VC. I went to meet the Dean to know exactly what happened and to ask him why he did not allow the department to investigate the matter before reporting it to the VC? I went back to my office to reply to his memo and then called an emergency meeting. The department did not find any reason for the ritual object to be place in front of Dr. Dukor's office and that it was not true that only in the Department of Philosophy that such ritual objects had been found on campus as alleged by the Dean. I went to meet the VC on the matter, and he told me to ignore it. I believed he had been briefed about it and he simply considered it a conspiracy. Several weeks after the incident, it was rumored that Dr. Dukor was behind the blackmail.

The students and many others were happy that my leadership in the department and faculty was fighting injustice in the system. The VC stood by me but the 'Academic Baby Tigers' and their collaborators considered my action as a cog in the wheel of progress, a 'business spoiler'. I ended my service at Lagos State University, Ojo in December 2000 at the expiration of my appointment. On March 30, 2001, the VC, Professor Akesode suddenly died. When students heard of his death, they trooped out and started cursing those who killed their VC, a man of their heart. He was a liberal or moderate Muslim who mixed very freely with people of different faiths. He was buried according to Islamic rites. I witnessed his funeral and burial. He was a great medical academic whose moral principle of peace and kindness was taken as weakness. I believed someday justice would reign supreme at Lagos State University when another Pharaoh would come who did not know Joseph like the case of the Israelites in Egypt. About four years after the death of Professor Akesode, Professor Lateef Akanni Hussein was appointed Vice-Chancellor of Lagos State University, Ojo who like the Biblical Pharaoh did not know Joseph brought transformation to the institution. All the 'Academic Baby Tigers' were dislodged and some of their collaborators had to seek refuge in other institutions elsewhere.

MY REFLECTION ON MY ACADEMIC AND ADMINISTRATIVE SERVICES AT LAGOS STATE UNIVERSITY

My leadership role in the Department of Philosophy gave me an inward look; the imperative of having a morally principled and charismatic leader to champion the right direction to follow amongst colleagues whose perception of academia was in many ways different from mine. All the senior colleagues in the department had left the system except the two young graduates that I recommended for appointment as Graduate Assistants Miss. Philomena Parfait and Mr. Michael Aina Akande; both have got their Doctorates. Miss. Philomena Parfait is married, and now addressed as Dr. (Mrs.) Philomena Aku Ojomo; a Senior Lecturer while Mr. Akande is now addressed, Dr. Michael Aina Akande; a Lecturer 1. Mr. Alloysius Shaagee Ihuah that I mentored is a full Professor at Benue State University Makurdi, Benue State. He is a prolific writer and scholar. Mr. Olalekan Ayodele-Oja left LASU for further studies in Singapore where he got his Doctorate and has been an academic staff of National University of Singapore. All these scholars that I mentored at LASU have continued to add values to scholarships wherever they are and contributing to knowledge production; and serving humanity. I believe the staff strength in the Department of Philosophy at LASU has increased due to students' soaring population.

The civilian government under the administration of Governor Raji Babatunde Fashola and Governor Akinwunmi Ambode had paid necessary attention to the basic infrastructure on campus at Ojo and the two campuses at Ikeja and Epe respectively; and it has improved the aesthetic ambience of the institution. The progressive development witnessed in the institution could be attributed, in my opinion, to the priority the governors had given to quality education in the State.

Chapter 15
ADEKUNLE AJASIN UNIVERSITY

In human affairs, we can see that there are forces making for happiness and forces making for misery. We do not know which will prevail, but to act wisely we must be aware of both.

~Bertrand Russell

The historical background of Adekunle Ajasin University Akungba-Akoko is like a child of unusual circumstances. The institution was established by the first civilian administration of Governor Michael Adekunle Ajasin in March 1982 as Obafemi Awolowo University, Ado-Ekiti in the old Ondo State. Unfortunately, the civilian administration of Governor Ajasin was short lived because the Military coup and a new Military Governor, Navy Commodore Michael Bamidele Otiko took over the administration of Ondo

State Government and in 1985 he changed the name of the institution to Ondo State University Ado-Ekiti. As destiny would have it, the creation of Ekiti State from the old Ondo State led to the relocation of the institution to an obscured small community called Akungba-Akoko under the leadership of the new Governor of the State, Chief Adebayo Adefarati on December 1, 1999 as Ondo State University. In 2004, the administration of Governor Adefarati changed the name to Adekunle Ajasin University in honor of the late Governor Adekunle Ajasin.

APPOINTMENT AT ADEKUNLE AJASIN UNIVERSITY

Given the traumatic experience I went through at Lagos State University Ojo, Lagos it was not my interest to seek a permanent appointment in any Nigerian university. When I wrote a letter to Professor Funsho Akere who was the VC of Adekunle Ajasin University in 2004, I applied for a visiting position, which was for a year with the intention that if I encountered similar challenges like that of LASU, I was not going to renew it. Professor Akere replied to my letter and told me his first name and that I should send my Curriculum Vitae (CV) to him, and I did. I was not really expecting a prompt response from him after I sent the CV but surprisingly, a colleague of mine, Professor Campbell Shittu Momoh in the Department of Philosophy at University of Lagos Akoka, called me, as I was returning home after dropping my children at their school, to say that the VC of Adekunle Ajasin had been expecting me to report for work there. I told him that I had not received a letter of appointment, however, if I did not get his letter, I would go there after the Easter holiday. I went home for Easter holiday to spend the season with my dad, an Elder in the Baptist Church who was probably the oldest Sage in the community. When the festival was over, I told him of my plan to visit the VC of Adekunle Ajasin University but unfortunately, I did not know its location and how to get there. He told me how to get there and, surprisingly, I did not miss my way. He was over 100 years old then with such a retentive memory; it was incredibly amazing to me. The university campus was in need of basic infrastructural development, but one could appreciate what was on ground. I asked for the office of the VC and someone showed it to me. Surprisingly, on getting there, it was my sister-in-law, Mrs. Taiwo Akinbulumo, that came to receive me but unfortunately, the VC had not returned from Easter holiday, however, she told me he was on his way. Meanwhile, I went to the Department of Philosophy and Religious Studies to meet the HOD, Professor Gabriel O. Abe, who was my classmate at University of Ibadan. He told me that the VC had acted on my application and had forwarded it to the Coordinator of Philosophy program to act on it but there was no trace of where the application could be found. It had been kept in abeyance. I went back to the VC's office and Mrs. Akinbulumo advised me that I should come back the next day. Mr. Ola Akinbulumo came to welcome me, and we both went to their house where I spent the night with them. The following morning, I went to meet the VC and he was delighted to see me. He told me that after getting my CV, he was impressed with it and Professor Momoh spoke highly of me and that was why he wanted my service. He told me when to expect my letter of appointment. I thanked him and came out to meet my sister-in-law. I was impressed with the hospitality of my sister-in-law and her husband. I left the university campus at Akungba for Lagos and got back to the house in the evening. My wife was anxious to know the outcome of my trip to Akungba and I told her that we should keep our fingers crossed. On August 13, 2004, I got the letter of appointment from Adekunle Ajasin University. A week after I got the letter, Professor Momoh called me to find out when I would be going to report for duty there. It showed how concerned he was for me to be there. I went to resume on August 24, 2004, and I later called Professor Momoh that I was already at Adekunle Ajasin University Akungba-Akoko. When the VC realized that I had resumed duty, he sent for me, and I went to see him. He told me the reasons why he hired me for the job, and I promised to do my best to be part of his success story in building the university to a lofty height.

COORDINATOR OF PHILOSOPHY UNIT

There were four young academics on ground in the philosophy unit namely, Benson Monehin Akinnawonu, Stephen Olusegun Taiwo, Sylvester Lucky Dada Itanrin and Solomon Akinyemi Laleye. They were still in the process of getting their doctorates to enable them to meet the basic requirement and become full academics in the university system in Nigeria. So, the unit had to embark on staff development and recruitments of some senior colleagues. And as I resumed, we had to prepare for the National Universities Commission's (NUC) accreditation exercise. All the relevant documents had been sent to the unit before I resumed, and it became imperative to get prepared very well. Having been involved in the accreditation exercise in the previous institutions that I had been HOD, it was not something difficult for me to handle. So, with my background experience, we were able to prepare fully well for it. While getting things tidied up, I opened a drawer and surprisingly I got my CV that Professor Akere requested from the HOD Philosophy and Religious Studies for his comment. The HOD sent it to the Coordinator of Philosophy Unit for his comment before sending it to the Dean and finally to the VC. I drew the attention of Mr. Olusegun Taiwo to what I found in the drawer, and he told me that he was aware of those who decided to keep it in abeyance because they feared that my coming would probably make some of them lose their job. I did not know that the news of the reformation I did at LASU had spread to Akungba to the extent that I was considered a dangerous academic species among colleagues that I came to advance their good course. I believed with time; they would begin to know the true nature of my academic worth in their midst.

On the day of the accreditation exercise some Professors appointed by NUC and its Officials from Abuja came and met with the HOD before meeting all members in the department. We were well prepared for them and as they started, we were told to return to our offices and if they needed anything the HOD would let us know. When they finished with the Religious Studies Unit, they came to the Philosophy Unit. As they entered my office their leader said that the voice of one of us resembled that of Dr. Segun Ogungbemi at Ogun State University and I told him I was the one. He told his group that having known him for quality leadership there; their work had been made easier. When they finished, he expressed satisfaction with the Unit. My colleagues were happy to have me with them because they had not got enough experience to handle the rigor of the exercise. Having said that it was the collective effort that made the exercise successful to the admiration of the NUC accreditation leader.

STAFF DEVELOPMENT AND RECRUITMENT OF ACADEMICS

My plan to move the Unit forward was to create an enabling environment for unity and gain the confidence of my colleagues. The accreditation exercise provided the platform for me to have access to their files and know their academic qualifications and where they had enrolled for further studies including their individual progress reports from their supervisors and Heads of departments. Knowing the needs of the lecturers was key to being able to offer useful suggestions on their programs and provided them with relevant research resources at my disposal. Immanuel Kant whose metaphysics of morals is that 'nothing is good in itself as the goodwill'; informed my goodwill for the academics in the Philosophy Unit. My goodwill was to enhance the import of collective responsibility and the ability to work together for the common good of the Unit and the department. Once I knew their academic challenges, we were able to work together to achieve their academic goals. I made my library open to them and where necessary, I made contacts with some resourceful colleagues abroad that could offer different forms of assistance in terms of books and other research materials. I was looking for some more academics with intellectual zeal and creativity with firebrand cutting-edge values. There was a young lady, Ms. Irene Omolola Adadevoh who surfaced by a circumstance and approached me to ask if she could be considered for appointment in the department. I was interested in having female lecturers in the Unit, and I asked her to apply for the post because she knew she was qualified. When I got her application letter with the CV, I discussed her case in the Unit before taking it to the HOD and she was recommended for appointment. She got the job and joined us in 2005. Mr. Cyril Mary Olatunji also applied in 2005 for appointment as lecturer in the department and he got the job as well. The appointments of these two young Lecturers rekindled the need to have a philosophy journal in the department. In 2006 we had a maiden edition of JAPHIL: Journal of Applied Philosophy in the Department of Philosophy and Religious Studies. In 2007 we had Professor Nkeonye Otakpor on sabbatical from University of Benin, Dr. Yinusa Kehnde Salami was appointed as Visiting/Adjunct Lecturer and Dr. Alloysius Ihuah was also appointed Lecturer in the Department when I was the HOD. As part of my tradition, Mr. Sunday Layi Oladipupo, the best graduating student in philosophy who did his National Youth Service Corp in the department as a Teaching Assistant 2006-2007 was given an appointment of Graduate Fellow in 2008 to encourage students in the department; and to prepare him for future academic career in the university system. With this number of Lecturers in the philosophy Unit we were able to cope with the surging population of students admitted for the philosophy program. In 2009 we had Professor Samuel Ade Ali from Olabisi Onabanjo University Ago-Iwoye on Sabbatical.

The Headship of the Department of Philosophy and Religious Studies was rotational between Religious Studies Unit and Philosophy Unit. In 2007 it was the turn of the Philosophy Unit to produce the HOD. I was the most senior person in the Philosophy Unit and its Coordinator so I became the HOD. The first appointment I recommended was that of Mr. Olorunsegunota Bolarinwa who wanted to be reabsorbed into the department after the expiration of his political office as Speaker of Ondo State House of Assembly. Religious Studies Unit had a comparative advantage of more academic staff than Philosophy Unit except no female Lecturers, so my headship from 2007-2009 was gender sensitive; and I had Dr. Mrs. Theresa Adeseju Asojo appointed a Visiting Associate professor of Philosophy of Religion in the Religious Studies Unit.

With the number of Lecturers in the Philosophy Unit, we felt it was necessary to propose a new department of philosophy. I decided that another senior colleague would be necessary to make our case stronger. Professor Samuel Ade Ali whom I knew very well at Ogun State University now Olabisi Onabanjo University Ago-Iwoye, Ogun State was my choice. He was appointed in 2009 as a Visiting Professor for a year and when he resumed duty, we discussed the modality to have a Philosophy Unit as a Department of its own. Our colleagues in the Department of Philosophy and Religious Studies warmly received him. The Philosophy

Unit therefore set up a committee to explore the viability of becoming a Department of Philosophy. Professor Ade Ali was made the Chairman of the Committee. He had the power to co-opt any members in the unit that were not in his committee. They were to submit their report to me before presenting it to the unit and the department. Within three weeks their report was presented to me, and we had a meeting to deliberate on it and the unit unanimously approved it. To create a department in the university is one of the most difficult tasks because of the procedures and stages it must go through before getting to the university Senate for approval, which is another big hurdle to pass through. But members in the Unit were resolutely determined to face the task and accomplish their primary objective. With the support of members of the department and Faculty of Arts the request was presented to the university Senate for approval under the leadership of a dynamic, resourceful, charismatic and visionary Vice-Chancellor, Professor Oluwafemi Mimiko and it was approved on Wednesday, May 26, 2010. The VC thereafter appointed me as Head of the Department of Philosophy. I believe it was in recognition of my academic leadership and administrative dexterity to be appointed twice as founding Head of Department in two African public universities: Moi University Eldoret Kenya in 1992 and Adekunle Ajasin University Akungba, 2010. There were some driving forces that made me to accept these appointments: First and foremost, the VC of Moi University, Professor Keya was interested in the program and in the case of Adekunle Ajasin University, the VC, Professor Mimiko was committed to creating a department that could revolutionize the mindsets of students and staff of the institution in the pursuit of his vision and mission tagged 21st Century University Properly Called.

I was also committed to promoting African Philosophy because there was a school of thought that claimed there was nothing called African Philosophy because it did not exist. It was an affront on the intelligence, wisdom, rationality and sensibility of Africans; that those of us trained as philosophers should challenge such ignoble thoughts; with concrete evidence and logical argumentations because all humans were created with natural capacity to reason. It was a call to change social and intellectual orientation of values using necessary philosophical tools of knowledge for them to reject western stereotype, and more importantly to give them recipes for human values of capacity building and sustainable development, which was in tuned with the VC's mantra: AAUA 21st Century University Properly Called. All this required adequate funding for infrastructural facilities, staff development programs, robust and relevant academic programs, strategies to enhance hard work and commitments of staff and students in the environment conducive to achieve them. The VC was mindful of all these requirements as he shared his views in his first address on January 4, 2010, with a belief that the university community was ready for his vision and mission. In my view he was addressing a congregation of an aggrieved community whose salary arrears and allowances had not been paid for months. What they anticipated from him was the payment of their money with concrete assurance that subsequent monthly salary would no longer be paid in arrears, more so that his senior brother was the Governor of the State and Visitor of the university. Given the mental construct of the audience that I was conversant with, it was clear to me that they did not understand what a standard 21st Century University Properly Called was and the VC simply assumed that they understood his laudable intentions. If they understood it at all, it was an inconceivable apocalyptic paradise. A Utopia! After his address, I asked if he believed his audience understood him. He was optimistic that they understood because it was not difficult for them to comprehend him. I kept quiet because I knew it wouldn't be long before he realized what I meant. On my part I had to concentrate on building the new department in line with the vision and mission of the VC that I was not only aware of but also keenly interested to be part of its realization. One of the first things I did was to hold a brief departmental meeting to deliberate on the needs of individuals and the department. The immediate needs were office space and equipment, Lecture rooms and teaching aid, administrative staff and logistics. The university management of Professor Femi Mimiko took a proactive action on our immediate needs to make the young department function well.

As the department was brazing towards a 21st Century University Properly Called, the University administration felt it was compelling to enforce NUC minimum teaching qualification requirement, which was a Ph.D. degree. In addition, the University administration policy was to appoint HODs from the professorial cadre. Since the university had very few professors on ground it became compelling to hire some retired professors of national and international reputes on contract to boost the quality of the teaching and administrative staff and above all to carry out the reforms inherent in the philosophy and objectives of achieving the mantra: AAUA 21st Century University Properly Called. One of the cardinal reforms was admission of students. University admission was henceforth by merit only and furthermore, no admission of candidates on Governor's list or any list within and outside the State was acceptable. Heads of departments were to follow the guidelines of Information and Computer Technology (ICT) when producing students' results that put an end to manual computation of results. This policy received opposition from a few academic staff because they felt the system was not ripe for the effective implementation of the policy. The persistence of the VC and cooperation of most of the senior professors who were HODs including the

Acting Director of ICT, and his staff there was no turning back on the directive. It was indeed a herculean task. On the part of the department some decisive actions were to be implemented based on the realities of direction of the University Administration:

1. Staff Development / Promotion

Given the rural location of Adekunle University Akungba-Akoko, it does not attract senior academics and very few indigenes were interested in the academic discipline of philosophy. Most people are not aware of the discipline let alone its importance to human capacity building. A few people who have been acquainted with it have a negative attitude to it because of their wrong notion that it leads people astray from God. This misinformation about the nature of philosophy is prevalent in society. From the foregoing, it explains why staff development becomes imperative if the department is to grow and flourish. All the academic staff from Senior Lecturer cadre and below needed mentoring and those without a minimum university teaching requirement had to enroll in other universities for their doctorates. The appointment of new academics had to be generally skewed in favor of the indigenes of the State for strategic reasons, for instance, accommodation, transportation and several other environmental considerations for sustainability. Above all, staff development and promotions were meant to motivate, encourage and reward their dedication, commitment and service to deserving academics and they were clear indications that the department was following the requirements of the NUC for accreditation of the program.

2. Students' Results/External Examiner/Examination Board of Studies

Producing of students' academic results electronically as opposed to manual system became mandatory and as Head of the Department, I had the obligation to see that the directive was complied with. It was one of the agonizing moments for everyone in the university because some of the members were not computer literate enough to know how to process their results. With the training sessions made available it did not take long before everybody keyed into it. Once the results were processed normal procedures to produce them were followed as laid down by the University Senate. Only 400 level students' results required External Examiner assessment and report as demanded by the NUC. It was when the Senate had approved students' results that they were considered authentic and official.

3. Revision of the B.A. Degree Program

If the Department of Philosophy was to key into the vision and mission of the new university leadership whose mantra was: building a 21st Century University Properly Called, therefore we must initiate new courses rooted in African ideas, philosophy, moral, cultural and aesthetic values. The innovation was gradual because building a 21st Century University Properly Called was not to be achieved in a five-year leadership term of the initiator, Professor Femi Mimiko.

My original intention was to do away with a few courses in Western and Oriental philosophies in our B.A Philosophy program and introduce more courses in African philosophy. I, however, had two major obstacles: all my colleagues were schooled mostly in Western philosophy with very limited concentration on African philosophy; and only a few of them had some knowledge of Oriental philosophy that was not sufficient to be considered as experts in the field, and besides if I introduced more courses in African philosophy, who would teach them? I studied the emotional tempo of the time and decided to introduce more courses in African philosophy piecemeal without violating university procedures for introducing new courses. More importantly, I had to carry my colleagues along with a team spirit. We were aware that each Department could review its B.A degree program every two years, however, a department could add new courses with approval of the Faculty Board if they were considered necessary but subject to the University Senate ultimate approval.

4. Departmental Seminar, International Conferences and Workshops

In all the three public universities that I had served in Nigeria, it was in their tradition and policy that each department should hold departmental seminars, workshops and international conferences but due to paucity of funds the latter were rarely held. With the support of the Vice-Chancellor, Professor Femi Mimiko the Department of Philosophy like other willing departments in the university had a boost to have all these departmental responsibilities functional. As a matter of fact, it became part of the conditions for promotion of members of academic staff. The department had a roster of presenters of departmental seminars each semester and presentations were made voluntarily, and it worked most of the time. Most of the best papers that met local and international standards were published in different journals and those that were not able to meet the standards, the owners of the papers were encouraged to be reworked and resubmitted to peer reviewers for assessment and possible publication in our local journals. The department organized its first international conference in November 2014 to celebrate **Philosophy Day** established by United Nations Educational, Scientific and Cultural Organization (UNESCO) to commemorate the significance of the discipline to human civilization. It is the only academic discipline that has been given that honor among all the academic disciplines in the world by the organization. We hardly had departmental workshops because our faculty; Faculty of Arts usually had Workshops. Members of the department were encouraged to attend workshops organized by the Faculty of Arts and in other universities within and outside the country. Participation in International conferences outside the country was mandatory under the leadership of Professor Femi Mimiko for all senior academics for promotions in addition to a certain number of publications for different levels and categories. There were funds made available to assist academics for each year. It was the best period of my administration as HOD of the Department of Philosophy because several members attended conferences in Europe, America and other African countries, the outcome of which soared the numbers of them to six in all who became Professor, Associate Professor and Senior Lecturers and at the lower cadre, several of them moved to the level of Lecturer 1. For those who could not be promoted due to their inability to live up to the policy, it became compelling to pull their academic straps up and meet the daunting challenge for the next academic annual review exercise.

5. Departmental Journal

Having a departmental journal that is self-sustainable was my dream as HOD but there were apparently unimaginable obstacles that bordered on economic and moral pebbles that I never thought could inhibit the laudable dream. Normally, creativity is part of academic activity for its own sake and for humanity and publishing the inspired research work by the author gives a comfortable soothing and satisfaction when colleagues near and far read them as references. What I experienced at Akungba and elsewhere in Nigeria was that when promotion exercise was approaching, that was when a few Lecturers desire to write and publish in the departmental or faculty journal and thereby put unnecessary pressure on the editor(s) to have their papers published. They were ready to pay extra charges to the editor(s) for the reviewers of their papers if the result would be positive. That was, in my view, how they found the easiest way to fulfill righteousness to the mantra, **publish or perish** in the academic circle. If, however, some of their papers were not accepted for publication, the editor(s) of the journals would become what they called, 'enemies of progress'. There was another hurdle to cross before a paper was accepted for publication, the authors had to pay a fee and, if not, it would not be published. There were, however, several departmental or faculty journal editors that did not charge any fees for the assessments and publications of accepted papers in Nigerian universities and yet they were self-sustaining. I felt the two journals that we had when the department was a unit in the defunct Department of Philosophy and Religious Studies would be self-sustaining but unfortunately, they did not. When copies of the journals were sold the plan was to deposit the money into a department account in the bank but to my amazement, it was not done. What went behind the scenes was that when some members in the department were broke, they would go to the treasurer in charge of the sales of the journals for soft loans without interest. The treasurer used his prerogative to give loans without the authorization of the department. They probably felt that both the department and its privileged members in the department were one and the same thing. All the initial efforts to get the treasurer to give an update on the sales of the journals and the amount of money at hand were cleverly postponed till the next meeting. When the next meeting was held; instead of making the report on the sales of the journals it would be listed as the last on the agenda of the meeting or it would be brought forward for the next discussion. But when I insisted that the treasurer should give an update on the sales of the journal, he did. He gave his report and names of those who took loans and had not paid back. There were some individuals who sold copies of the journals and were yet to remit the money to the treasurer. The department resolved the case, but it became clear that it was impossible to make the journals sustainable. Another crucial issue that plagued the departmental journals was politics of self-interestedness rather than academic research seriousness. As the Editor of the journals, I knew it was worthless pursuing the dream of a sustainable departmental journal.

6. Departmental Responsibilities/Discipline and Leadership by Example

Members of the department took their responsibilities with enthusiasm and commitment regardless of the teething challenges faced by the emerging institution of the 21st Century Properly Called. For the department to function very well, regular departmental meetings were necessary because as HOD that was how to coordinate all the planned actions effectively. It was, in my view, how to demonstrate to members of the department leadership by example. I believed we ought to work with principles or moral virtues like integrity, hard work, courage, determination, decisiveness, consistency, perseverance, resilience, commitment, accountability, friendship, generosity, sympathy, empathy, discipline, equity, transparency, honesty, obedience, truthfulness, respect, team spirit, good-will, fairness and justice. These moral values or principles I have held dear to my life as leadership mechanisms in running the affairs of the department.

7. Regular Departmental Meeting

Everything was not smooth sailing at times during our meetings. Some members who did not take their work seriously enough were reprimanded. There was an academic member who was notorious for collecting money from students and altering students' marks as he deemed fit. One interesting thing about him was that whenever he was caught, he was quick to admit the allegation and begged for pardon.

8. Postgraduate Program (M.A. Degree)

As the department was growing very impressively the department decided to have a postgraduate program. We put all our resources together and wrote the M.A degree program. It was presented to the Faculty Postgraduate Committee for approval, and it was approved. We presented it to the Postgraduate School Board and got it approved. The Dean of Postgraduate School presented it to the Senate and it was approved.

We advertised the program and we got several candidates screened for admission. We picked the best candidates and within the stipulated period of completion, two of them graduated namely, Sunday Layi Oladipupo and Moses Biodun Jinadu. They were subsequently appointed as Assistant Lecturers in the department. Before my retirement in 2016, another brilliant student, Joseph Babalola Balogun enrolled in the program and competed and graduated and he has since been appointed a Lecturer in the Department of Philosophy at OAU, Ile-Ife in Osun State.

ADMINISTRATIVE SERVICES IN THE FACULTY OF ARTS

I was never interested in the contest for the Deanship of Faculty of Arts at all but when some Deans were elected in the Faculty of Arts and appointed by the Vice-Chancellor, I was ready to give a temporary service as Acting Dean when they needed my service. Amongst the Deans that found my services worthy were, Professor C. A. Daramola, Professor Francis Oyebade and Professor Oluwayemisi Adebowale. They did not hide their feelings and appreciation for my good services when they were away.

I also held several administrative positions in the Faculty of Arts such as: Member of Faculty Board of Examiners, Member of Faculty of Postgraduate Committee, Member of Faculty Promotion and Appraisal Committee etc.

ADMINISTRATIVE SERVICES IN THE SENATE AND UNIVERSITY MANAGEMENT

Senate in any African universities where I had served was and still the most powerful organ institution responsible for dealing essentially with academic matters. I was a member of the Senate at Adekunle Ajasin University.

When the Senate decided to have a Business Committee in 2008/2009 to process students' results under the administration of VC/Professor Philip Abiodun, I was one of the members representing the Faculty of Arts. When Professor Mimiko took over as VC in 2010, I felt relieved because I did not want to continue to serve on the committee because it was time consuming and tedious. When VC reconstituted it and later found that I was no longer a member because I had influenced the Faculty of Arts to appoint another colleague and it was done, he reappointed me to serve on the committee. There was a six month National ASUU strike in 2013 and its Branch at Adekunle Ajasin University wanted to halt all academic and administrative activities that involved academic staff on campus. Recognizing its negative impact on the students and the displeasure it would arouse in the State, particularly, stakeholders, the VC directed that all Professors on contract, some of whom were members of Business Committee of Senate, should process the results of final year/graduating students for NYSC and Faculty of Law students going to the Law School. He gave the directive on the strength that their contract appointment was predicated on agreement of non-unionism on campus. Some of the professors who were not members of the committee were co-opted to boost the morale of the members and expedite action on getting the results out promptly without compromising academic and efficient standards. As we were planning for the best strategy of action, we were mindful of what the management of ASUU on campus could do to frustrate the processing of the results on campus. I felt it was possible to avoid confrontation with the management of ASUU on campus by interacting with some of their members who were moderate and had respect for me. As I was driving out of the Faculty of Arts to go home, one of the moderated ASUU management waved me down and I stopped to hear what was on his mind. After a brief friendly chat, he said, 'Prof. Please tell your friends to find a neutral place outside campus to use for your assignment and security because we respect you all.' I thanked him and made a call to the Chairman of our committee, Professor Fasidi and told him what the young man said and that we should consider his advice and look for a neutral venue. The University Management took a wise decision and relocated our office to a temporary secured university property outside the campus. Before we moved to the private place to do our work the management of ASUU on campus wrote a stinker to every one of us on contract appointment. The VC was furious when he read the letter, but we prevailed on him not to take any punitive action on our behalf. Professor Mimiko (2017:249) writes in his book entitled, *Getting our Universities Back on Track*: "Some retired professors that were with the University on contract appointment, who by their terms of employment were not supposed to go on strike, were mobilized to process some results for us, upon which ASUU did a two-page query to them for having the audacity to work for the administration during a strike action!"

We considered their behavior as a manifestation of youthful exuberance to be ignored so as to concentrate on the assignment before us.

As we moved our materials to a serene private location outside university campus and from any interference, we made sure the materials were well secured. Members of the University Management paid us impromptu visits to know the progress we had made and to ensure our safety. With the support of ASUU management and the University Administration we felt insulated from any interruption or violent attacks from within and outside the campus. Alas we were not absolutely secured from reckless drivers whose behavior on the road near where we were working could have a boomerang impact on the gate of the university property that subsequently threatened our safety. Yes, one day it happened when we were in the depth of our work. We suddenly had a loud bang on the gate, and it caved in and a car was heading towards us and 'miraculously' it stopped at the entrance of the gate without causality. People around started to make unscientific insinuations by attributing the accident to a metaphysical power, which I found ridiculous to believe as a philosopher with a scientific bent. We called on the university security men and local police to handle the impact of the accident on the university property. On the second day we carried on our primary assignment because time was of essence. We completed processing results of the final year students to enable the successful amongst them to graduate. It is significant to mention the best Law student, Opeyemi Akeem Longe who made the university and Ondo State Government under the leadership of Governor Olusegun Mimiko very proud became a testimony of the university achievement. The CV/Professor Mimiko said, "Mr. Opeyemi Akeem Longe who had won nine awards out of 29 handed out at the Nigerian Law School and, in 2014 Bar Examinations, had the best overall result nationally in the examination." It was a unique opportunity and experience for me to work with all the committee members particularly, professors Ishola Fasidi (Chairman of the committee), Jacob Remi Ogundari and Nathaniel Oluwadusi Ajayi. In 2014 I was amongst members of the committee awarded, Adekunle Ajasin University Distinguished Merit Award for Excellent Services.

The VC/Professor Mimiko also appointed me Chairman of Ceremonies Committee to handle convocation activities and university Inaugural Lectures with a mandate to produce a template for convocation planning and when we finished, he commended our efforts and said, "It was one accomplishment I felt very proud of." It is equally important to note that there were several other achievements we made as Chairman and members of the Ceremonies committee that the VC was 'very proud of' namely, convocation lectures, quality of publication lectures, organization of the convocation arena, honorary doctorates awards: Professor Toyin Falola in 2013 and Dr. Akinwumi Adesina in 2014, etc. There were some members who stood by me most of the time to do extra assignments to enhance the quality of the convocation's products, namely, Tolulope Maiye (now Mrs. Tolulope Maiye Olajide residing in Chicago, Illinois), Sola Imoru, Victor Akinpelumi, Professors Ajayi (DVC), Oluwayemisi Adebowale and Olu Aboluwoye.

I was also appointed as a member of the University Library Committee. In 2014, Professor Mimiko nominated me for the post of Deputy Vice-Chancellor, and I stepped down on the floor of the Senate for the female candidate, Professor Oluwayemisi Adebowale who became the first female Deputy Vice-Chancellor (Academic).

Professor Femi Mimiko also set up Invigilation Examination Committees headed by Senior Professors to check incessant misconduct and absenteeism of Lecturers on duty during semester examinations. I was a member of the committee for Faculty of Arts and Chairman of the committee for Faculty of Science respectively.

Between 2015 and 2016 the new VC, Professor Amos Ajibefun appointed me Chairman of the Panel set up by the Senate on Students' unrest that led to the death of a student outside the university campus. The VC also appointed me as:

Member of University Quality Service Assurance Committee and Member of Committee for the proposed establishment of a Secondary School respectively.

All these services were in addition to my Headship appointment. I could not fathom where I got the time and energy to effectively perform those functions as I did and still got time for my research and family affairs.

NATIONAL UNIVERSITIES COMMISSION (VERIFICATION/ACCREDITATION EXERCISES)

One of the cardinal functions of the commission is to "Ensure quality assurance of all academic programs offered in Nigerian universities." Verification/Accreditation of academic programs of universities in Nigeria is an attempt to ensure the quality of the programs. In its effort to achieve it, the Commission appoints from time-to-time credible professors in their professional fields to help them perform this important function. I was involved in this exercise from 2011-2017. I was also invited by the Commission to attend their Conference at Abuja in 2016. I have found the experience very rewarding in the sense that it made me keep abreast with some of the myriad challenges bedeviling the citadel of learning in Nigeria.

REFLECTION ON MY 12 YEARS OF SERVICE

I considered my 12 years of meritorious services at Adekunle Ajasin University the most challenging and very rewarding. There were oppositions and counter-oppositions along the way, but I was resolute on my vision and mission. The appointment of Professor Femi Mimiko as Vice-Chancellor and his vision and mission of making Adekunle Ajasin University a 21st Century University Properly Called ignited the burning flame of unprecedented success the institution has ever had to date. The iconic Senate building, the first of its kind in any State and Federal owned institutions epitomized his vision and mission. I had a very good working relationship with most, if not all the colleagues, non-academic staff and students. I cracked jokes with people on campus and I was nicknamed by Professor Mimiko, Yemoja High Priest, others called me Baba Ogun while others called me Baba Irunmole and Professor Toyin Falola at University of Texas at Austin called me Irunmole of Africa and now 'the Irunmole of the world'!

Before my final exit at Adekunle Ajasin University in November 2016, Department of Philosophy witnessed a rapid development in terms of academic and non-academic staffing as provided for in the university establishment, students enrolments at both undergraduate and postgraduate programs, Benson Akinnawonu, late Irene O Adadevoh, Cyril-Mary Olatunji, Solomon A Laleye, Olorunsegunota

Bolarinwa, Sunday Layi Oladipupo, Sylvester Dada Itarin and Moses Abiodun Jinadu got their doctorates, which subsequently led to their promotions. For instance, Dr. Benson Akinnawonu became a full Professor; late Dr. Adadevoh was a Senior Lecturer, Dr. Olatunji, Dr. Laleye, Dr. Bolarinwa became Senior Lecturers and subsequently Dr. Laleye was appointed Acting Head of Department. Academic colleagues made more presentations of papers at local and international conferences, NUC accreditation of Departmental B.A Philosophy program among others made the Department of Philosophy one of the best not only in the Faculty of Arts but also in the University at large. In recognition of my good leadership in the Department some members decided to honor me on my birthday in 2016 with a book titled, *The Polemics of an African Philosopher: Essays in Honour of Professor Segun Ogungbemi*, (eds) Solomon A. Laleye and S. Layi Oladipupo but unfortunately, I had to go back to the US for health reasons. The amazing thing to me when I got a copy of the book, there were 25 contributors from 21 different universities in Nigeria. It is awesome!!! I was and I am still humbled by the editors and contributors of this FESTSCHRIFT because it delineates their perceptions of my moral life, quality of academic and administrative leadership plus recognitions of my profound contributions to scholarship, some of which are truly polemic.

While I appreciate all the university community at Akungba,

it is worth acknowledging some who made it possible to be there and had contributed to my success story. I am very grateful to Professor Funso Akere, who was the VC of the university when I applied for appointment in 2004. I read in the Nigerian Tribune newspaper that he was the VC, but his full name was not written. So, when I wrote to him and addressed the letter as Professor Akere VC Adekunle Ajasin University, Akungba he replied and gave me his first name. I was impressed by it, and I had a feeling that he wanted me in the university. Interestingly, he went to find out about me from a colleague, late Professor C.S Momoh at University of Lagos where he was a professor in the Faculty of Arts. Professor C.S. Momoh gave him a very good report about me, and he invited me to Akungba and I became one of his academic senior staff in August 2004. Professor Femi Mimiko became VC of Adekunle Ajasin University, Akungba in 2010. Before then he was Deputy VC under Professor Akere. As VC, Professor Mimiko surrounded himself with the best Professors he thought could help him achieve the lofty goals he had set for himself, and I was one of them. He created an enabling environment for me to operate that enabled me to reach the apex of my academic career. He made many of us willingly support him; and when we felt he was making some unpopular decisions, late Professor Olu Aboluwoye and I were there to tell him and with superior logical and persuasive arguments he would change his mind. Professor Aboluwoye was one of my best colleagues on campus because he was honest, bold, courageous, forthright, trustworthy, generous and kind. He never hid his feelings when confronted with issues of common interest about the university community. He had planned to launch the FESTSCHRIFT in the university in 2016 unfortunately, I had to leave the country for medical treatment in Houston, Texas and by the time I came back he and the new VC, Professor Amos Ajibefun were not good bedfellows. Professor Aboluwoye would not eat or drink in any office apart from mine. The news of his death in April 2020 shook me to my bone marrow. A few other Professors that made my stay at Akungba very interesting and fruitful were Olusola Ibukun, Isaac Rotimi Ajayi, C.A. Daramola, Oluwayemisi Adebowale, Francis Oyebade, Isola O. Fasidi, Kole Omotosho, Niyi Akinnaso, Nathaniel Oluwadusi Ajayi, Adewale Taiwo, Funmi Emma Ogunbodede, Ade Ali, Alloy Ihuah, etc. Dr. Sunday Layi Oladipupo and Dr. Solomon Laleye, Dr. Olusegun Taiwo, Olukayode R. Adesuyi, Aanuoluwapo Alafe, Abiodun Paul Afolabi amongst others in the Department of Philosophy were very precious to overlook their dedication, commitment and loyalty. Two non-academic staff, Mrs. Bosede Olaniran and late Mrs. Grace Orunkoyi served the department satisfactorily.

The first female Registrar, Mrs. Bolatito Adenike Oloketuyi, former Registrar, Mr. Bamidele Olotu, former Librarian, Mr. William Abiodun Akinfolarin, former Bursar, Mr.

O.T. Akinteriwa, former Bursar, Mrs. Olubunmi Veronica Ologun, Mr. Tobi Irina, Mrs. Bolanle Debo Ajaguna in the Bursary, Mr. Sola Imoru (PRO), Mrs. Tolulope Maiye-Olajide now in Chicago and Victor Akinpelumi etc. did contribute significantly to the good working relationship I had in the university and even after my exit in 2016.

It is significant to mention that some of our best students who wanted to be in academia to pursue their interest were absorbed namely, Cyril-Mary Olatunji, Sunday Layi Oladipupo, Moses Abiodun Jinadu, Aanuoluwapo F. Alafe (female) and Abiodun P. Afolabi. One of our best students that we could not absorb on time, Babalola Joseph Balogun got an appointment in the Department of Philosophy at Obafemi Awolowo University Ile-Ife, Osun State. A few of our students who graduated decided to set their own businesses while others are in different economic and political sectors of Nigeria proving their worth as true ambassadors of the Department of Philosophy, Adekunle Ajasin University Akungba-Akoko, Ondo State. Therefore, reflecting on my 12 years of meritorious service at Adekunle Ajasin University was a rewarding experience of successes, happiness with satisfaction.

CREATION OF DEPARTMENT OF PHILOSOPHY AT FEDERAL UNIVERSITY OYE (FUOYE)

After my final disengagement at Adekunle Ajasin University Akungba in November 2016 at the age of 70 years, I tried to explore a possibility of one-year temporary appointment at a newly established Federal University at Oye, Ekiti which was about a two hour drive from my house at Arigidi-Akoko, Ondo State. I was aware that there was no philosophy program there but my intention was to meet the Vice-Chancellor, Professor Kayode Soremekun and impress on him to have a department of philosophy. In March 2017, I had an appointment with him and we deliberated on my mission and its importance to Liberal Arts and Humanities, Law, Natural Science and Social Sciences etc. He was delighted in the program. I wrote the B.A degree philosophy program with my team, Dr. Laleye, Dr. Oladipupo, Prof. Ali and Prof. Balogun. There was a long delay on the part of the university to get serious with the program.

On July 9, 2020, Professor Akintayo got back to me and rekindled my optimism that the program was receiving positive attention. On December 9, 2020, the NUC Verification team was at the institution for the verification exercise; Professor A. Ihuah from Benue State University led the team. I was informed in March 2021 that approval of NUC for the university to establish the department of philosophy had been received and that an advert to admit students was made public on March 26, 2021. The Department has been established with admission of about 30 students. I was delighted to hear the development but it was too late for me to be part of its takeoff.

I also made an attempt to get a department of Philosophy established at Federal University of Lokoja under the former Vice-Chancellor/Professor Angela Freeman Miri, but it did not materialize before the expiration of her term. Happily, the new Vice-Chancellor/Professor Olayemi Akinwumi in 2021 created a new department that incorporated philosophy as a unit. Hopefully, soon the philosophy unit will become a department.

REFLECTION ON MY MARITAL LIFE

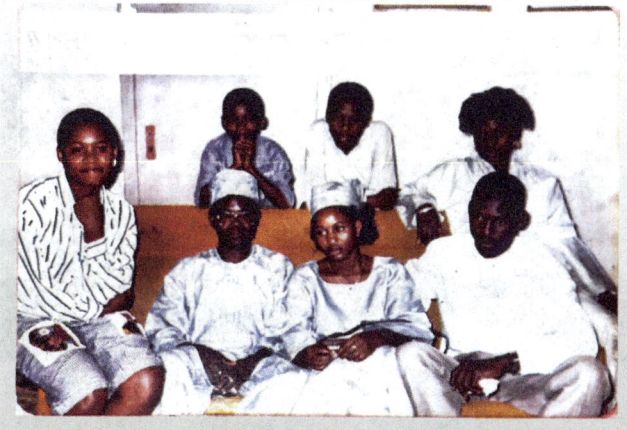

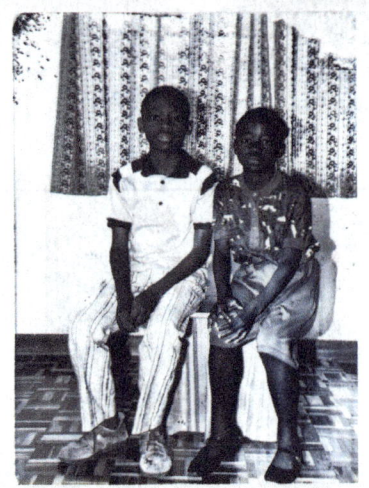

SEGUN OGUNGBEMI I, II, III

PART EIGHT

MY SERVICE TO COMMUNITIES

Chapter 16
IDOFIN-ISANLU COMMUNITY

"It's better because it is home."

When I visited my son Segun Bidemi Ogungbemi Jr. in Houston some years ago and I was going back to Nigeria, he felt it was time for me to stay back in the US and I told him 'Home is the best'. His question was, Dad, but the US is better, and I told him Nigeria is better because it is home. As I was leaving, he sent me a three-page goodbye message entitled, 'It's better because it is home'. The interpretation of this idea is significant because it is not Nigeria that I really have in mind but my communities, Idofin-Isanlu, Yagba East Local Government, Kogi State and Ere Yagba West Local Government. Because Idofin is home, it is therefore imperative to make my modest contributions to its development just as our parents did when we were growing up. My contributions to Idofin community began in 1956.

Member Of Sudan Interior Mission Church Choir

As we were growing up in the early 50s, the main reason for going to the Sunday school on Sundays was to get their beautiful cards after reciting the memory verses in the Bible. I did not understand the Yoruba of the missionaries. We did not know that the Christmas and Easter old cards were used to entice us to come to the Sunday school. So, in the early 50s, we had one Henry Daniel Osaniyi a native of Ejiba, a nearby community who took over from the missionaries. He was employed to teach in the Sunday school and Kindergarten 4-6 pm from 1952-53. I became more attentive to his teaching because I could understand him better because he was teaching us both in Yagba and Yoruba languages and more importantly; we were living in the same Odeko ward. I perceived his proximity to our house; and closeness to my father as a kind of control of my behavior in the kindergarten because my father would always ask him how I was performing in his class. When I was about 10 years old, I became a member of the Church choir.

Being a member of the choir from 1956 to early 1963 was a unique experience even though I did not know that I was using the gift of my voice to serve the congregation and the community. I could not quantify the tangible and intangible impacts my role in the choir had on the people but what I still remember was that missionaries and members of the congregation used to commend the choir members particularly, Elijah Abiodun Daramola (Choirmaster), Oni Omodara, Joseph Noah, Benjamin Abegunde, Isaac Abegunde and me after singing some beautiful songs in the church on Sundays during and after church services. We were singing inspiring church songs, which appealed to their existential and collective spirituality; and morality to enhance quality of life and harmonious peaceful coexistence. The religious impulses or reflections were the least on the mind of anyone of us as members of the choir and probably the congregation at large. We were more of heavenly bound than this worldly bound. In other words, our songs were in accordance with the tenets of the church as directed by the missionaries since this world, as they taught us, is not our home, heaven is our eternal abode where there will be no sorrow, pain, agony, sickness and death. Heaven is a blissful haven to aspire to be after the journey is over on this planet earth. My contribution as a member of the choir upon reflection was serving both Idofin community and their final destiny in the world beyond.

SECRETARY-GENERAL OF IDOFIN DESCENDANTS UNION (1966-1974)

My education as a pupil at S.I.M Central School Isanlu from 1958-1962 exposed me to the importance of unionism, having seen what the young elites at Makutu conceived of the Idofin community to be in their mindset as one of their wards. It was there that we formed a union to create awareness to correct their erroneous idea and created a distinction between a ward and a town; and we called 'Idofin a city', hence the popular name, Idofin City. Let me reiterate once again that; it was our performance in the school that gave its popularity because we were among the very best in our classes. Mr. J.L Osho the Headmaster of Isanlu Central School preferred to call us; 'Idofin City' rather than our individual names. It was at Makutu in the 50s that the idea of Idofin Descendant Union was born and nurtured. I did not become very active in the union until in the 60s.

When I was a student at Igbaja Bible College in 1966, I did not have a clue that someday I would become Secretary-General of Idofin Descendants Union. However, it happened at the annual general meeting of the union in December 1966. The people at that meeting unanimously elected me. I was speechless because I was not expecting to be elected because I knew it was very demanding and being a student, it would take away the time that I should devote to my studies. The functions of Secretary-General were spelt out in the constitution. I made sure that annual meetings were held yearly and with constant reminders of our branches in Lagos, Ibadan, Ilorin, Kaduna, Kano, Jos, Sokoto, etc. Each branch was to send at least a representative with their branch annual bill. I made sure there were annual activities each year. It was during my time as Secretary-General that we had the first and second Miss. Idofin in the persons of Miss. Grace 'Kosiji Ogunbiwaje and Miss. Florence Boja Balogun respectively. We had some humanitarian services to the sick, widows and poor parents in the community. Our pupils in primary school at home were motivated in their studies to pass the yearly common entrance examinations because education was key to self and community developments. It was essential to constantly rekindle the awareness of parents of inherent values of educating their children both boys and girls because the slogan that education was not profitable like learning a trade and becoming an entrepreneur, which could not bring much development to the community. We also focused on providing healthcare services to the community and decided to have a maternity and dispensary as a self-help project. One of the things to motivate our people and generate funds was to have annual almanac, which we produced for a couple of years. We made some progress in those days with a collective resolve and determination to continue to do more every year. When we became very popular in our vision and mission there were members amongst us who wanted to be in the driver seat and the baton of Secretary-General had to be passed to another person in December 1974. The new leadership did not live up to expectations hence, several years things started changing for the worse and there were no annual activities. As time went on, Idofin Descendant Union became moribund; and a new one was formed as Idofin Development Union under a new leadership. At that time, I was already pursuing my further studies in the United States of America. When I returned to Nigeria in 1985, Mr. Daniel Awofenka Awogbenja was the President of the new union. The major focus of the executive of the union was the electrification of the community because all the immediate communities from Egbe to Ejiba in Yagba West LGA and Mopa to Makutu-Isanlu in Yagba East LGA had been enjoying light except Idofin and Iddo-Ojesha located on the land of Idofin-Isanlu. I was aware of the problem but I couldn't participate in the fundraising because I had an appointment in Kenya. I left Nigeria for Kenya to teach at Moi University in 1990 and came back in January 1994 and our communities were still without electricity. I was not aware that Providence had planned that I was going to be the instrument to accomplish the yearnings of the people. How he was going to do it was not known to me but at the appropriate time he acted in the community history.

ELECTRIFICATION OF IDOFIN-ISANLU AND IDDO-OJESHA COMMUNITIES

When I returned from Kenya in 1994 with my family and we had to go to Idofin, I knew my children would be very uncomfortable living there without electricity. Luckily my friend Mr. Joseph N. Molemodile had a small generator in his house, and I decided we should stay there until I leave for Ijebu-Ode where were staying with my friend Dr. Olumuyiwa Ogunlade. While at home, I decided to go to Abuja and one of my friends Dr. John Laoye wanted me to meet his Boss, Dr. Samuel Ogbemudia at Nicon Nuga Hotel Abuja. We got there and he introduced me to him. As we were chatting, I told him I planned to go to National University Lesotho. He said why and I told him the reason. He then told me to meet him in his office in Lagos and he gave me his phone number to call him. When I went back to Idofin, I told my wife we must shorten our stay and returned to Lagos because I had an appointment with the Honorable Minister of Labour and Productivity, Dr. Samuel O. Ogbomudia. On returning to Lagos, I called the Honorable Minister and he gave me an appointment to meet him in his office at Federal Secretariat Ikoyi, Lagos. When I went to meet him, we exchanged pleasantries and he appointed me as one of his Senior Special Advisers in charge of research. I was delighted to get the appointment and when I told my wife and children, they were very happy. I was not aware from my wild imaginations that the appointment was going to be a stepping stone by which Providence was going to use me to make electrification of Idofin, Iddo-Ojesha and the environs a reality.

There were several efforts made by Mr. Joseph N. Molemodile and Idofin Development Union under the leadership of Prince Bamidele David to raise funds and use manual labor where necessary to start the project before asking the State Government for help. Meanwhile, Mr. Molemodile had used his contact with Governor Abubakar Audu to get a donation of a transformer for both Idofin and Iddo-Ojesha communities. The transformer was kept in the premises of the late His Royal Highness, Oba Moses Ibitoye of the town and protected from being stolen by anyone. The Idofin community was undoubtedly encouraged, hoping that soon the State Government would do more than a donation of a transformer. Political instability in Kogi State further caused the delay in getting more help from the administration of Governor Audu. Be that as it may, Idofin Development Union rose to the challenge by getting each branch of the union to have fundraising for the project. When I attended the meeting of Lagos branch and heard what they were doing, I felt otherwise. Was it not because we did not have any influential Idofin person in government at the Federal level to get the electrification done; and that was why the people resolved to use their very limited resources on a huge project like rural electrification? I did not want to discourage them, but I was not going to be a party to such a futile community project. I felt the government at an appropriate time would do the project. Chief Jide Omokore also made some frantic efforts to get the people he knew in the Ministry of Power and Steel, and he was assured that it would be included in their budget. With that assurance, he believed, that the project had been included in the budget but there wasn't any visible evidence that the Ministry of Power and Steel was serious on the project because there was no letter from the ministry as evidence that it was in its budget because no survey had been done and without the survey, it could not be included in the budget.

When I took the appointment as a Senior Special Adviser to the Honorable Minister of Labour and Productivity during the Military regime of General Abacha, Head of State of Federal Republic of Nigeria in 1995, it was my intention to use it as leverage to attempt the electrification of Idofin and Iddo-Ojesha communities. On August 17, 1995, I called my brother Chief Jide Omokore that I was going to the Ministry of Power and Steel to pursue the electrification of Idofin. He told me that it was already in the budget and that I could ask one of his friends in their office. When I got there and introduced myself and told them that Chief Omokore requested me to interact with them on the electrification of Idofin community since he was told that it was in their budget. One of them told me "Jide was told that it was in the budget, but the truth of the matter was that it could not be included in the budget because there was no survey carried out on the project." He then advised me that if I wanted the electrification of Idofin done, I should go to the Director-General (DG) of Power and Steel, Mr. Geoffrey S. Sekoki who was the former DG of the Ministry of Labour and Productivity. I went back to my office and looked for the handbook of the former senior staff particularly, the former DG and I found his name there. I then made a call to his office and his secretary put me through to him and I told him that I needed his help and I wanted to meet him. He was receptive to my request and asked me to come on August 17, 1995, in the afternoon.

I went to meet Mr. Sekoki in his office as scheduled and he welcomed me very warmly and asked me what I wanted him to do for me. I then narrated the ordeal of not having electricity in our two communities. He asked me to put in writing and address it to him. I thanked him and left. On August 18, 1995, I wrote the letter and took it to his office. Within three weeks I was called to come and get a letter. I was not sure what it was, but the lady online told me that my request had been granted and I should come for a copy of the letter. The letter was dated September 4, 1995. I was told to take my copy to Engr. Ogedengbe, NEPA Head Office,

Awolowo Road Ikoyi. It was one of the greatest and happiest moments in my life. I collected the letter and sent a small note of appreciation to the DG, Mr. Sekoki.

I made three photocopies of the letter and gave Prince Bamidele David, President of Idofin Development Union, Chief Jide Omokore and kept the third copy for Mr. Joseph Molemodile who was in Lokoja, Kogi State. I asked Prince David to accompany me to NEPA Head Office Awolowo Road, Ikoyi and we met Engr. Ogedengbe and his colleagues who arranged for the survey of Idofin and Iddo-Ojesha communities. It took almost two weeks before it was completed. When they were done, they told me to take it to their branch office at Omuaran, Kwara State and someone would follow me to do the survey. Prince David and I went in his Beetle car for the survey. Chief Omokore gave us (N2000) for fueling his car and Mr. Molemodile sent a vehicle to assist us when we got home. The survey was completed within two days and the report was sent to Lagos. It was after the survey report was sent to Lagos that the cost estimate was made and a copy of the survey and cost estimate: N26, 887,614.43 (Twenty-six million, eight hundred and eighty seven thousand, six hundred and fourteen naira three kobo) was sent to the Honorable Minister of Power and Steel on October 13, 1995 for approval. It was thereafter that it was put in the budget. When the project was about to be awarded to a contractor, I was with the Chairman of

Implementation Committee on Rural Electrification, Engr. Nggada, and I gave him my preferred company, Destiny Works Ltd that was famous for quality service without delay. He was familiar with the company and its owner, Mr. Olu Komolafe from Ogbe in Yagba West LGA. The work was completed and listed among the 'Completed Rural Electrification Projects between May 1999 and February 2002' as Number 260, in *Sunday Punch* August 18, 2002, at the cost of over N32 million (Thirty-two million naira only). All the letters I wrote to the DG, Ministry of Power and Steel on the project and responses from the ministry including its subsidiary, NEPA in this chapter serve as evidence of how Providence had used me to accomplish the task of electrification of the two communities including Ajuru and Surulere, which Makutu to Mopo Isanlu communities also became its beneficiaries. It must be noted that it was not the achievement of any political party or any other individual that began the project and competed it apart from what I have narrated in this book. That is why no political party or any other individual or group of individuals could use it for their political propaganda and to harass anyone who is not in their party to be denied access to electricity in the communities.

RIPPLE EFFECTS OF ELECTRIFICATION OF THE COMMUNITIES

There have been steady increase in development projects since the electrification of the Idofin, Iddo-Ojesha and Ajuru communities namely, modern architectural housing structures, Churches, Private and Government boreholes to alleviate the burden of using stream water for domestic purposes, Computer training in the Secondary School, Establishment of ECWA Theology Seminary at Ajuru, Bio Resource Development Center of National Biotechnology Development Agency (NABDA) that is sited at Idofin by the Federal Government of Nigeria under the leadership of the former Director-General/CEO of the Agency, Professor Bamidele Solomon, Small and Medium Enterprises (SMEs); hospitality industry, Pure water, Supermarkets, etc., have contributed job opportunities with modest economic and health prosperity to individuals and the communities at large. The communities have witnessed steady demographic increase of people namely, Yagba indigenes, Tiv from Benue State, Ebira largely from Okene, Kogi State, Igbo from Southeast Nigeria amongst others.

SERVICE TO ERE COMMUNITY

Chief E. Bolaji Iyekolo was admitted at a New York University for a summer course in publishing and when he completed his program, he paid me a brief visit in Dallas. I was rounding up my Doctorate at The University of Texas at Dallas, Richardson, Texas. During our conversations on what I could do for Ere community, he opined that I should get First ECWA an Organ and books for Okutadudu High School where Elder Silas Oshajare was their Principal. I told him that being a student at that time could be a challenge but as soon as I finished my program something positive would be hopefully achieved. As I was preparing to return home in 1985, I got help to donate the Church Organ to First ECWA Church Odo-Ere, formerly S.I.M where my grandfather Pa Joseph (Alaawo) Ogungbemi was an Elder in the Church. I bought some books and got Sunday Afolabi in Stillwater, Oklahoma to donate books as well. He brought a lot of books but, I could not afford to take all of them because of the weight and my space in the container was limited. I was, however, able to bring most of the books to Odo-Ere and delivered them in 1985 to the institution and the Church Organ to the Church through Chief Iyekolo the initiator of the projects. Chief Iyekolo told me that the Church invited me to their service, and I attended it but to my surprise it was in their plan to show appreciation for the Church Organ and the books donated to their school. I was honored and humbled by their encomiums.

Chief Honorable David Ekundayo Ogundipe, a community leader in Oke-Ere, invited me to give a public lecture on

December 26, 2015. I accepted the request and as I was going there, I stopped at Odo-Ere to ask my brother, Mr. Isaiah Kayode Ogungbemi to accompany me and he did. The occasion was well attended by eminent people including HRH, Titus Makanjuola, the Elere of Ere and his Olori. I addressed the community on the importance of education for rapid development. I addressed the people in both English and Yagba languages. I was overwhelmed by their appreciation for the lecture.

REFLECTION ON MY SERVICES TO MY COMMUNITIES

I wish I could do more for my communities than what I have modestly contributed to their development. The overwhelming acknowledgements of what I have done in the areas of education and infrastructural developments have been very encouraging. It is morally imperative to recognize most passionately the commitment of Prince Dele David. Throughout the time the electrification of the communities was completed, I was amazed that he never, for once, asked for monetary gain. Both of us were apolitical about the project because none of us was interested in using the project when completed for any political interest at national levels. From my perspective, he deserves an award and what I have written about his contributions to the project serves as a prestigious award! It is morally compelling to reiterate my profound gratitude to Mr. Geoffrey Sikoki, former Director-General of Ministry of Power and Steel whose role made the electrification of the communities possible.

It is noteworthy to mention the 1996 Ere Pacesetters award given to me in recognition of my contribution to Education growth in Yagba land. I want to recognize former Miss. Bukola Kowantan and other Executive members of the organization for the award. That the Youths of their generation could think me worthy of the award was remarkably significant and treasured. On April 14, 2017, in a surprised manner HRH Oba Tajudeen Olatunji Taiyese I, The Eleri of Odo-Eri Land, Yagba West LGA awarded me a traditional Chieftaincy title of Bobajiroro. There were other awards that I turned down because I was not interested in them due to unforeseen circumstances, I found myself at the time. The import of these awards and the general appreciation expressed to me, seem to suggest, that I have contributed to their meaningful existence.

As I conclude this chapter it is necessary to note the source of my idea of service to my communities and humanity. The irresistible and inspirational impulses of my existential responsibility to the community and people around me found its roots in my parental upbringing and institutions attended particularly, Igbaja Bible College, which instilled in me Christian discipline, service and leadership in my early 20s when I was energized by two youth organizations namely, Boys Brigade and Fellowship of Christian Students. As I advanced in academic pursuit and interaction with people of integrity, discipline, empathy, generosity, etc., the dynamic of my vision and mission towards humanity became more profoundly aroused and morally compelling.

PART NINE

THE PATH OF EDUCATION

Chapter 17
SELF-REFLECTION

"Give me education and I will find my way in the wilderness of existence."

SELF-REFLECTION

I believe the essence of education is, in part, for self-reflection using all the cognitive apparatus to do justice to one's experiential background and modest achievements in the pursuit of education; with intention of bequeathing a reasonable footpath as a legacy for others to learn from. With a preponderance of inner conviction my father was right when he told me, 'I have sent you to school to acquire knowledge of Western education, which my time denied me so that you could someday become an elite like them'.

The import of the reason why he sent me to school to acquire western education resonated with me for the rest of my life and the quotation above is a product of his primary objective. His idea of western knowledge was equated with 'western trick': that is western technology that made them not to be afraid to navigate the big waters like Atlantic Ocean, ability to produce airplanes for transportation that could fly in the sky like birds with higher velocity without being lost in the natural wide space was an incredible magic worthy of learning; the secret behind western knowledge of medical sciences, knowledge of arts and humanities of literary world could be added to what was already acquired locally and traditionally. But the question is: did I understand his ideas of western education and its importance and benefits to my life at that early development? Of course, I did not. I preferred western education to going to the farm because subsistence farming was to me a dirty job and its physical demand was energy sapping. But the irony of it all was that I liked harvesting the crops when they were ready because they provided us with foods and health benefits. Let me reiterate here the two types of education: traditional or cultural education that is indigenous that predicates itself on the principle of *Omoluabi*, meaning the acceptable human conduct or character. Properly conceived, *Omoluabi* is also a Yoruba philosophical concept of an ideal moral norm for the well-being of individuals in the corporate existence. It is a cultural and environmental value for prudent-existential orientations to promote understanding of harmonious relationships with fellow human beings and nature for mutual benefits without creating unnecessary conflicts that could be dangerously destructive to both parties.

TRADITIONAL SYSTEM OF EDUCATION

1. Family Relationships/Peaceful Co-existence

I derived my biological and sociological existence from my parents, the first contact to the wilderness of existence that made modicum provision of comfort of survival and environmental ambience for my early growth and development in life. But in our culture, one's nucleus parents were in my generation not necessarily the only parents I had; grandparents on both paternal and maternal sides were grandparents, close relations to these 'parents' were automatically mine as well; nephews, cousins, uncles, aunts, deceased ancestors, etc., became my 'nucleus family'. It is a complex family circle, but it is real and nobody undermines this ingrained understanding of family because it is our historical great chain-of-beings that enhances a peaceful co-existence. It is consummated with a unique cultural distinguishable identity of family as *Soko oligbo edun*, which is distinctively a praise chant trademark that individuates its members from others in the community. The family tree of *Soko oligbo edun* has many branches of distinctive and distinguishable identities, for instance, our ancestral branch is famously branded, *kasinuawo* and its short form is *Kasi* depicting the form of leather entrepreneurship or leather industry of our ancestors. Don't let me be self-praising here because mine is not the only one in Yagba/Yoruba cultural customs. It is fundamentally a general cultural and social intrinsic and extrinsic value that permeates noetic structure of Yoruba life.

2. Moral Values/Knowledge Acquisition

In each family structure, there is always a chain of command that is generally recognized and respected beginning from one's parents. Their authority and commands are in most cases sacrosanct. Human learning system began first and foremost from parents particularly, mothers, 'the institution of knowledge, wisdom and customs. In my generation, every elderly person in the compound or ward had the right to inject social values into the cognition and discipline of every child as an introduction to a peaceful co-existence. In the early life of every child moral behavior was given a priority training in terms of storytelling, proverbs and pithy sayings. As I grew in knowledge and understanding Yoruba customs and values, I always remember the Yoruba words of wisdom in Chief Folahan Odunjo's *Yoruba folklore of wisdom* becomes more instructive:

Yoruba Language	Transliteration into English Language
Ise loogun ise	Work is the cure for poverty
Mura si ise ore mi	Be hard working my friend
Ise la fi n di eni giga	Through working you become great
Bi a ko ri eni fi ehin ti	If you do not have a helper
Bi ole laa ri	You seem to be a lazy person
Bi a ko ba ri eni gbokan le	If you do not have a supporter
A tera mo ise ni	Be passionate about your work
Baba re lee lowo lowo	Your father may be rich
Iya a re si lee lesin leekan	Your mother may have a horse
Ti o ba gboju le won	If you depend on them
O te tan ni mo so fun o	You will soon be put to shame
Ohun ti a ko ba jiya fun	What you do not labour for
Se ki lee tojo	Will not last long
Ohun ti o ba fi ara sise fun	It Is what you work for
Loun pe lowo eni	That endures tides of life
Apa lara	Your arms are your

	relatives (supporters)
Igunpa ni iyekan	Your shoulders are your relations
Ti a ba n fe o loni	If people cherish you today
Ti o ba lowo lowo	f you have money (you are rich)
Won a maa fe o lola	They will still cherish tomorrow (more)
Tabi ki o wa ni ipo atata	Or you are in high position of honor
Aye a ye o si terin-terin	The people will cherish you with laughter (delight)
Je ki o di eni ti o n rago kiri	If you then suddenly become a poor person
Aye a maa yinmu si o	The people will wince at (despise) you
Eko si tun n soni doga	Learning makes you become great
Mura ki o ko daradara	Ensure you learn it thoroughly
Bi o ba si ri awon eniyan	If you see persons
Ti won n f'eko s'erin rin	Making jest of learning
Dakun, mase fara we won	Please, do not emulate them
Iya nbo f'omo ti ko ko gbon a	Suffering is imminent for child that is not wise
Ekun nbe f;omo ti o nsa kiri	Weeping is imminent for

a	child wandering about
Ma f'owuro sere, ore mi	Do not play with your youthful time, my friend
Mu ra si ise, ojo nlo!	Work hard, time is far spent!

The folklores of wisdom are embodiments of Yoruba ontological concept and moral principle of *Omoluwabi*. One of the goals in life of my parents was to make me imbibe Yoruba fundamental human values to greatness.

3. Spiritual Forces and Holistic Wellness

The Yoruba holistic indigenous medical therapy is both physical and spiritual. It was part of my growing up experience under the parental health care system in my family, which was common to other children in the community as well. It was difficult for me to fathom the causal connection between my headache or fever or malaria and an offering of a chicken to unseen spiritual forces for the speedy recovery of my illness. As far as I could recollect in those days, that was one of the most efficacious medical methodologies and remedies used by traditional 'medical intellectuals' available to assist my parents when I urgently needed health treatment in my early life. I was made to respect places of worship like shrines, sacred places where offerings were given to deities, ancestors and offerings at crossroads. I was told it was forbidden to blow whistles at certain places in the community in the daytime or in the evening. As a growing up child, I was fully aware of the culture of not asking inquisitive questions without getting unexpected knocks on the head as a warning and not as punishment. So, I was made to believe that those things were real and indubitable because they contribute to human wellness, harmonious relationships and prosperity.

4. Respects for Natural Environment

I was very close to my father from childhood being his first son and that was why I went with him to his farms, forests and rivers around us to expose me to the beauty of the natural environment as the abode of indwelling spirits and they must be approached and treated with caution. These spirit-beings as far as my father was concern had enormous spiritual capabilities to bless or punish individuals as they wanted, if their rights were obeyed or violated, beyond human comprehension. I watched my father with admiration as he attempted to clear any farm areas for cocoa in the forests, yams in the savannah and catching fishes in the rivers. He would first make appeals to the spirit-beings that dwelled in those places and asked for their permission and sometimes with propitiations and sacrifices of food items to get their favors. I never saw any spirit-beings coming out to eat the food items given to them. I knew that the rest of the food items would be for both of us; so, my patience was not disturbed. I believe my siblings probably had the same experience when I was not around with them. What my father did in those places became clearer to me later in life in terms of education and training of traditional ethical methods and principles of dealing with the natural environment for peaceful coexistence. It was what I have called traditional common-sense ethics or nature-relatedness. Did my father receive any appropriate or significant reward for his obeisance? I did not ask him, but I was aware he had good harvests each year, which to him, was some form of sufficient evidence that his efforts were rewarded to his satisfaction. The import of all this to me was to have respect for the natural environment and not to exploit it in such a way that it becomes inimical to my life and corporate existence.

WESTERN EDUCATION

1. Church Kindergartens

My early contact and experience of western education began in the Church. Initially I did not know it as western education but rather as an institution to enable me stay away from farming. It was erroneously conceived, in those days, in the community as an institution of escapism for 'lazy children' who abhorred farming. It was a church rudimentary school under the leadership of a pastor who doubled as minister and teacher. It first began in the Baptist Church in the early 50s with only two of us: Bamidele Shaba, now Prince Bamidele David and me. Interestingly, both of us started as friends until we later discovered that we were cousins. It was customary for our parents to escort us early in the morning to the minister/ teacher in his 'parish' and leave for their farms. We were only left to play until we became tired or hungry and we would be told to go home to eat. But from 1952-1953 I was enrolled at the Sudan Interior Mission (S.I.M) Church Sunday School/ Kindergarten where Henry Daniel Osaniyi was the teacher in the evening 4-6 p.m. We were taught Yoruba alphabet and stories in the Bible. We had to memorize everything and recite some passages in the Bible. That was the foundation of my early Christian knowledge and spirituality introduced by western European missionaries.

2. Native Authority School (1954-1957)

There was no established government institution in our community until 1954. My community was in the erstwhile Kabba Province, Northern Nigeria under the administration of Sir Ahmadu Bello, Premier of Northern Region that failed to embark on free primary education. The community had to build the first classroom in 1956 and parents had to provide tables and chairs for their children, pay school fees, buy school uniforms, books and stationery supplies. All the pupils were charged with cleaning the premises of the school every year without compensation. The mode of teaching was different from my experience in the Church institution. We were taught English Language, Reading, Writing and Spelling, Arithmetic, Yoruba Language, Music, Geography, Handwork/Artwork, etc. There was strict discipline and disobedience was met with severe punishment. The school had zero tolerance for indiscipline. The teachers were revered, as they were the 'intellectual demiurge' of their time. We were introduced to British imperialism by celebrating the birthday of the Queen and the Empire Day every year. Frankly, I did not know the meaning and implications of those celebrations until after Nigeria's Independence from British colonialism in 1960 and in 1963 when Nigeria became a Republic. It took many years later before I fully understood what was going on in those dark days! In this public school, school discipline sort of obliterated my previous background of religious spirituality.

We had only standards 1 and 2 from 1954 to 1957 so we had to repeat the same class several times until we were able to travel to a neighboring community, six miles to enroll in the next class, Primary 3.

3. S.I.M Isanlu Central School (1958-62)

Bearing in mind the warning message in *Yoruba folklore of wisdom* my father dissociated himself from those who spoke disparagingly or scornfully of western education in the community, hence, he was ready to take me to the next level of my education pursuit at a mission school; Makutu-Isanlu in 1958, over six miles. There were no adequate vehicular transportation systems in those days unlike today. Trekking short and long distances without shoes, on untarred and dangerous narrow roads, was most often the mode of getting to one's destinations. My father had no relations at Makutu who could accommodate me and cater for my feeding. So, he had to go there to plead with those who could give me a helping hand on condition that he had to provide raw foods and money to make feeding a joint responsibility. That was what my father did for five years; and on my part, I had to carry the raw foods on my head every week during the school sessions, just like other pupils from our community. Reflecting on this traumatic experience, reminds me the Yoruba idiom that what you don't work hard for, you don't have value for it. What you labor for is that which has lasting values.

My five years of study in the mission school at Isanlu combined liberal education with moral discipline and individual spirituality. In other words, both forms of education have secular and theological components that emphasize the importance of spirituality in human endeavors; and they have contributed to my knowledge; as path of education to explore and exploit for survival and to leave behind, as immortalized legacy. My parents' investment in my elementary education did not yield any financial turnover to alleviate their economic deficit and impoverishment but it did not dampen their spirit of courage and perseverance with fervent hope that the future would bring prosperity, happiness and satisfaction. After my graduation in 1962 at

S.I.M Isanlu Central School, my parents resolved to support me with prayers and best wishes because that was their limit of financial resources for my education. I could understand their dilemma. Having lost their cocoa farm to a fire disaster in 1956 without compensation from the government with attendant responsibility for care and education of my three siblings, I was left in the hands of Providence.

4. S.I.M Igbaja Bible College (1966-1970)

Yes, Providence intervened in my pursuit of education at Igbaja Bible College by using American Peace Corps: Ruth Bowden and Rosalie Peterson who paid for my tuition and fees for four years while Kenneth Koosman gave a helping hand in 1969. My advancement in theological studies had its background at Igbaja Bible College. It was here that gave me rigorous challenges in terms of moral discipline, hard work and exposure to theological variants of conservatism and skepticism. This institution was a unique stepping-stone for me to other institutions of higher learning in Nigeria and the United States of America.

5. University Education

i. University of Ibadan, fondly called UI, Premier University:

University of Ibadan was the first prestigious degree awarding institution in Nigeria. The Federal Government of Nigeria established it in 1948 as University College Ibadan affiliated to University of London; hence it is called Nigeria Premier University. It became an autonomous full-fledged university in 1962. It has been the most prestigious University in Nigeria and one of the most prestigious institutions in the continent of Africa. Getting admission to university of Ibadan in those days was like going to Harvard or Yale in the United States of America. It was highly competitive. It was the only university in Nigeria I had passion for because of its serenity and environmental ambience. Of course, beauty they say is in the eye of the beholder. In this case, it was beauty in the eyes of the academic beholders. The primary objective of going there was to acquire more knowledge that would change my status and improve my economic condition in the society. I found the institution as an entry-point to ideologies: Western Capitalism, former USSR Socialism and Communism, Marxism, Pan-Africanism, Black Nationalist Movement, African-Militarism, Students-Unionism etc.

In other words, acquiring university education, therefore, was a renaissance, with the goal to provide a 'meal ticket', meaning, a necessary baseline of comfortable income for self-sustainability, social status-driven with influence in the society; and to accumulate wealth with enviable respect.

In general terms, however, for my generation in those days, university education was a renaissance to provide leadership assets for national growth and development. As I was preparing to leave our hall of residence, Independence Hall in 1976, I told one of my roommates that I would like to proceed for further studies in the United States of America even though I had no slightest idea where the scholarship for the laudable dream would come from.

ii. American Universities (1978-1985):

Southern Methodist University Dallas (S.M.U) and The University of Texas at Dallas (UT-D) made the greatest impact in my pursuit of knowledge in the United States of America.

My studentship in the above institutions exposed me to more than ever before; to a magnificent powerhouse of generative ideas instituted in the university system. It is the empirical outcome of these generative ideas that brought about modernity with amazing infrastructural developments and its maintenance that consequently became part of my 'intellectual inheritance' for reference. I came to the actual realization of the import of American capitalism with the widespread of infrastructural developments in American institutions. It was capitalism with inbuilt social infrastructures of human values that propelled both political and economic influence of the country as the most powerful nation in the world. I came to realize why it was possible for American oil companies to exploit Nigerian crude oil to the benefit of their people and to some extent Nigerian elites who studied in the United States institutions and subsequently became leaders today. As students in those days, we had the benefit of studying American system of democratic governance, though not perfect, but it provided mechanism of dynamic and enduring institutions to guarantee stable governance of mutual benefits to its people and international students. It was consciously and unconsciously a form of 'intellectual colonization' that was meant for us to support and promote American democracy and its values after graduation, as we returned home to our country, because it was the best political and economic system of governance. The propaganda of the American communication and information systems constantly drumming the scientific and technological greatness of United States of America, for instance, after their astronauts landed on the moon on July 20, 1969. This form of self-glorification became an obsession in this country to the extent that the rest of the world saw Americans to be unnecessarily arrogant. But if Americans didn't blow their own trumpets of achievements, who was going to blow it for them? It was the cold-war period of a fierce show of strength between the erstwhile Soviet Union and the United States of America. Even after the cold war on December 3, 1989, was over American self-glorification continues like an endemic infectious disease. There was no better place to witness its infectious disease, in my time, than in their university system. The university system has continuously encouraged the human mind to think, reason and research with the primary objective to overcome any obstacles that stand to defeat the egos of his superiority to nature and any other living beings on this planet earth. And to do this, they have instituted the ability to conquer fear because it is an impediment to progress. Therefore, knowledge acquisition has no limit. It is my belief that that is the fundamental role of university education for trajectory transformation of human knowledge for social change, cohesion and development.

My studies in those days enabled me to see in a wider spectrum some of the contradictories and challenges of social and moral behaviors of white racism and its political, social, psychological, spiritual, economic impacts, mostly on African Americans that were seen as counter-intuitive and counter-productive in a Christian and democratic political system. It was what I called evils of socio-political and economic capitalism that emanated from human tragedy of slavery and ignorance. This human tragedy of ignorance and arrogance led to the forceful grabbing of lands of Native Americans by the European warlords with attendant gruesome killings of the owners of the lands without moral conscience, as it was justified by one of the foremost British philosophers, John Locke in his book, *Two Treatises of Government*. One wonders with curiosity, if in the remote and imaginative future, Native Americans have political power to take their lands back from the generations of intruders? Will Native Americans treat generations of intruders kindly or otherwise? Will they agree to a peaceful reconciliation and harmonious co-existence like that of South Africa? Nobody knows for sure if it will ever happen because its probability is very remote. But if it happens, I foresee a massive migration to Africa because of its land mass or to other planets as alternative options or solutions. After all, Africa is believed to be the origin of human existence. But there might be those who will prefer a new planet rather than Mother Africa. One is not sure if this is not one of the reasons for the 'supersonic search' for other habitable and heritable planets by American scientists. I am just being curious in my wild imagination!

From the foregoing, studying in American universities brought me closer to the knowledge of what made my father to marvel about western education and its modernity: it is the education system of western capitalism. It is education that tends to glorify human knowledge as power to conquer the world. It is indeed education with inherent power of moral courage and ethical compass to navigate the meandering roads of existence. It is a holistic form of education with religious and theological components that emphasize the importance of spirituality in human endeavors.

Yes, I have a penchant for quality of life that is worth living, which I want to bequeath to my children and humanity. It is predicated on ontological humanism of existence that treats human life with respect and dignity. It is like Sidney Poitier's perspective of life when he says, "I have this feeling that life is so magically created that if I respect it, that respect will come circling back to me in ways I don't even know." (*The Oprah Magazine* (October 2000).

PART TEN

BECOMING A U.S. PERMANENT RESIDENT

Chapter 18

BECOMING A U.S. PERMANENT RESIDENT

The idea of becoming a United States of America resident later in life was not at all on my priority list; and that was why it had no strong force in my plan, although in my mind, I had a weak contingency possibility of it because no condition is permanent. And that was why I decided to have another child in Plano, Texas, so that preadventure, there could be a good reason to wanting to come back here later in a remote future; he/she could file for me. So, on October 23, 1983, we were blessed with a baby girl, Yetunde Bosede Ogungbemi who was born at the Methodist Hospital Dallas, Texas. I made sure I got her an American Passport when she was a baby. Unfortunately, that plan of action was not to materialize due to unforeseen circumstances. The irony of it all was that my son, Segun Ogungbemi Jr. who was born in Nigeria when I was a student at S.M.U Dallas, and I got him and his mother to join me in 1979 was later in life became the instrument to fulfill that aspiration at the fullness of time. The intuitive and nostalgic feelings plus emotions with a compelling psychological passion for innate oneness in human relationships, particularly between children and their parents explain, as it were, the indwelling mechanisms in human nature. And until these yearnings for oneness are placated in terms of reunion, there will always be a psychological restiveness. That was exactly what happened between my son and me when he had to join his mother in Houston in October 1995. Having lived for seven years in Nigeria and three years in Kenya, he only, relatively speaking, enjoyed the short period we were at Moi University, Kenya. Apart from the three years that he was with me at Moi University Eldoret, Kenya where he enjoyed the serenity and beautiful cool weather in the Rift Valley and his good friends, the two children of Njuguna family, he probably never enjoyed living in Africa. Being a scholar, I enjoyed traveling abroad to attend international conferences and workshops. The country I preferred most was the United States of America so that I could spend a few days after the conference/workshop with my children in Houston, Texas. After attending a conference at The University of Texas at Austin in 2011, he thought it was better for him to file for my green card so that coming to the US for whatever reason would not warrant going to the American Embassy/Consulate office for visa every two years. I appreciated his concerns, but I was not enthused at that time because the university still needed my services and my two young daughters were still in school; and my wife had spent only two years on her job in the Federal Government service in Lagos and she was passionate to have more years of experience that would enhance her being appointed Head of her department; and to reach at least 10 years to qualify for retirement benefits. But the economic conditions and insecurity in Nigeria were getting to a disproportionate degree; and the warning signs of looming dangers ahead were vivid and scary. But the most significant and compelling traumatic experience I had at the Methodist hospital in Houston, Texas in 2014 where my son had a very close shave with death; with its subsequent reoccurrences in 2015, 2016 and January 2017; though were not deadly terrifying like the first in 2014 but they were serious enough signs for me to expedite action and relocate to Houston to get acquainted with the cause and nipped it in the bud. Therefore, relocating to the United State of America was one of the most difficult decisions I have ever made without any regrets, however.

So, in 2016 my son decided to file for me to become a permanent resident in the US. At that time Temidayo had been admitted for postgraduate studies in Public Health at Western Kentucky University, Bowling Green, Kentucky; while her younger sister Tinuke was in Senior Secondary (SS

2) in the 2016/2017 academic session at Greater Tomorrow International College Arigidi-Akoko. In all these, Providence, I believed had mapped out his plan for the success of this possibility.

In 2016, I came for the Annual Africa Conference at The University of Texas at Austin, Texas with my wife, Olori Olayemi Ogungbemi with the plan to spend a few days with my son in Houston before going to attend the conference at Austin. The conference was for three days and after the conference we returned to Houston. Before leaving for Nigeria, my son decided to file for my permanent immigrant status. He invited me to join him to meet his Attorney, Shola Sutton in his office in Houston to complete the application. I was delighted to meet his Attorney who warmly welcomed me to his office and told me details of what to do. We completed the necessary forms, and I was told of other documents that were required to complete the process. On getting back to Nigeria, I mailed all the required documents at my disposal to complete the process. Within several weeks, I was told that the application had been approved but I needed to send police reports from Kenya and Nigeria having lived in the two countries for more than three months. One of the things I tried to avoid in my life was to have anything to do with police anywhere particularly, the Nigeria Police Force because of their reputation for corruption and crude treatment of people perceived as criminals when arrested with impunity. Of course, there are very good and professional policemen among them.

POLICE REPORTS

1. Nigeria

I initially thought getting the police report from the Nigeria Police Force office would be a herculean task, given daily experiences of Nigerians with them. But I was proved wrong the day I went to their office in Ikoyi, Lagos to get the report. I was given my due recognition and respect as Professor in a Nigerian State University. The process and service were prompt without asking for a bribe! I got the certificate the same day I applied for it. I felt the most difficult hurdle was over.

2. Kenya

The Kenya High Commission Office in Queen's Road in Ikoyi Lagos had relocated to Abuja but its Consular Office remained in Lagos. So, in my view, it would not be necessary to go to Abuja for a police report. I went to the Consulate Office to inquire how to get the police report in Kenya. Surprisingly, their officials in the Consulate in Lagos could not handle the case hence; I had to write to the Police HeadQuarters in Nairobi. It took several months to get feedback and when I got it, I was told to pay 500 Kenyan Shillings. I did not have

Kenya Shillings and I was wondering whom to contact for help. I remembered that my friend, Chief Ezekiel Okeniyi and his wife could come to my rescue. I contacted Chief Okeniyi and he responded and gave me the money. I sent it to the police Headquarters in Kenya. After several months the money was returned with a letter that I had to pay 1000 Kenyan Shillings. I had to ask Chief Okeniyi for help again, which he did. I then wrote back to them in Kenya about the frustration I was getting over a police report. It was after that that I was directed to the Kenya High Commission Office in Abuja. The Police Headquarters in Nairobi forwarded the Kenya Sh1000 to Kenya High Commission in Abuja for further transaction. The Kenya High Commission in Abuja returned the fee of 1000 Kenyan Shillings to me. I was told to pay for the fee and services for the police report in Naira. When the police report was ready, I got a message to come to collect it or pay for them to send it by courier service. I opted for the courier service. I got the police report within four days. It was a big relief to me because what I thought would be an easy transaction became the most difficult one. It is significant to note that on one of the trips to Abuja, my wife decided to go with me in the heat of kidnappings on the road. We left Abuja around 4: p.m. for Arigidi where we lived in Ondo State. It was about a 4-hours journey on rough and dangerous roads Kabba–Lokoja through Obajana road. We, however, had journey mercies of Providence!

Because it took several months to get the police report from Kenya, I had to get a new one from the Nigeria police office again because the two previous ones had expired after three months. I got another one and mailed the two police reports to my Attorney's office in Houston. It wasn't long when I received a letter for my interview at the Consulate Office in Lagos with an instruction to go for a medical test at a designated hospital in Victoria Island, Lagos. When all these requirements were met, I was told that the American Consulate Office in Lagos would contact me for the scheduled date of my interview, which came within several weeks. My wife accompanied me to the American consulate office, Victoria Island, Lagos for the 7:30 a.m. appointment on March 21, 2018. I was confident but not overconfident that my interview would be successful. And yes, it was successful! It was one of the happiest moments in my life. My visa was dated March 21, 2018, and it expired on August 5, 2018, which meant that I had to travel to the US before its expiry date. I had a short time to prepare for my journey although I had prepared my mind to leave in May 2018, but I wasn't sure of the actual date. I had a short time to make a strategic and careful planning so that my family did not lack some basic needs particularly, our daughter, Tinuke (TK) who was preparing for her West African Senior Secondary School Certificate Examination (WASSCE) at Greater Tomorrow International College, Arigidi-Akoko, Ondo State after leaving the country. And when I finally decided on the probable date of departure, my wife and I went to the airlines vendor's office at Ikeja, Lagos State, to book for the air ticket. I was booked for May 5, 2018, and to arrive in Houston on May 6, 2018.

DEPARTURE FOR HOUSTON

On May 5, 2018, I left Lagos for Houston with the hope to begin a new of life as a resident citizen of the United States of America. As expected, my wife, Olori Olayemi Ogungbemi, our daughter, TK, my sister-in-law, Mrs. Wunmi Adesokan and her daughter Dumininu graciously escorted me to Murtala Muhammed International Airport, Lagos. As I checked in my luggage and hugged each one of them and got ready to leave for the boarding terminal, I had an existential feeling of anguish with attendant shedding of tears. I took courage as a weapon to face every existential condition and then, moved on. I, however, took solace that my wife and daughter would soon be coming to join me in the U.S. for the graduation ceremony of our daughter, Temidayo Ogungbemi at Western Kentucky University, Bowling Green in May 2018.

The boarding protocols and procedures were usually cumbersome because of the huge number of people traveling to the U.S. from Lagos and European countries. Bearing in mind the long queue, I decided to stop at the African restaurant to eat solid food to get enough stamina to withstand the odds before getting to the boarding terminal. The restaurant had varieties of African foods and I hardly knew what to choose. Given the nature of impatience of Nigerians on the queue, I hurriedly chose eba and okra soup with assorted soft meat and a bottle of Eva water. I didn't bother about the cost because I was exhausted and hungry; coupled with the fact that it was the only place, I could get that kind of African food to eat. After eating my food, I went to join the queue to go through the protocols of checking passports, hand luggage and other personal effects before getting to the final boarding gate where another routine of checking before boarding. When everything was done, and I boarded the aircraft it was then I had some respite to relax and rest before the take off at the terminal. We left Lagos at midnight with a two hours stopover in London Heathrow Airport. After a stopover in London, we continue our journey to Houston, Texas. I arrived in Houston on May 6, 2018, and had to go through their security protocols. It wasn't long before I got my passport stamped and a photo taken to produce my Green Card. I couldn't wait to be with my son to thank him for making the right decision and action to file for my U.S. resident citizenship. When I called him that I was already waiting in the airport, he sent Uber to pick me up. It took about an hour and half to get to his house in Richmond, Texas. He has his sister Yetunde, I fondly call Yeti and several of friends living in his house with him namely, Bisi Onitiri and Morano Mohammed Moses. I was delighted to see my daughter Yeti. It was a happy moment of reunion as a family under the same roof belonging to my son, since she relocated to the U.S. in 1995. I couldn't wait to see my grandson, Segun 111 and her mother Jackie. As I was busy relating with my children and grandson and others, my mind was not unmindful of my wife and TK in Nigeria and Temidayo at Western Kentucky University, Bowling Green. Later in the day I called my wife and told her that I was already in Richmond, Texas. She was happy that I had journey mercies to the U.S. The question of when to get the Green Card and Social Security card was lurking in my mind as I went to bed. Expectedly in June 2018, I got my Green Card and the Social Security card in July 2018, respectively. Having got the resident citizenship status, the question is: do I want to begin to live permanently without going back to Nigeria? To continue staying in the U.S. without going back to Nigeria would be a deliberate moral violation of the reason why my son filed for me. How can I be trusted again, if after making promises, I reneged to fulfill them? Will my integrity not hang in the balance; insofar there are no justifiable and compelling reasons to renege on my promise to my son? As parents of moral conscience, we do everything possible to lead by good examples.

Meanwhile, I needed to concentrate on how to relax after leaving Nigeria, a country of social tensions, upheavals and insecurity. One of the ways to relax was to spend some time with my grandson and get acquainted with his ideas and behavioral temperament, his progress in mathematics, reading and comprehension, etc. I got him to walk around the lakes and had him play with other children at the mini park. It was fun to see him running and jumping, playing pranks to deceive me as I attempted to catch up with him before getting to traffic stop signs in our street, Parkway Lakes Lane, Richmond, Texas. I was delighted to watch him while practicing on his piano with his dad and creatively amusing everyone. In response with admiration, his dad would clap for him and take pictures to encourage him improve his skill, while the mother was taking note and nodding her head, whenever he played according to instructions in his piano handbook.

Segun has several friends who lived with him because of his understanding, tolerance, accommodation, generosity and friendship. They occasionally cooked in turns but generally; Bisi Onitiri was a volunteer chef of the house. He has dexterity for cooking delicious Nigerian varieties of dishes without asking anyone for help in its preparations and when everything was done, he would invite everyone to the kitchen. In most cases, however, the aroma of the soup and stew usually made everyone join him in the kitchen.

Since we were in the summer, everyone enjoyed going for exercise to burn out some of the calories in his body. I could not join their rigorous exercises because of age and medical advice of my medical doctor but I envied their determination to do it almost every day to keep fit. They are all intelligent, brilliant and smart guys but some of their lifestyles of youthful exuberance, which I had experienced at their age, made me tolerate them even though they were unacceptable, but it did not stop me from giving them fatherly advice. My presence in their midst was tolerated with mixed feelings and more importantly, they were aware that I would soon be going back to Nigeria, where my disciplinarian tutoring is mostly warranted and respected. But I know that truth will always overtake falsehood on the racecourse of life.

I had an intuition to check the date of my flight back to Nigeria. I, therefore, checked my Nigerian passport to know if I had spent at least six months in the U.S. since I got the Green card, I realized my return ticket to Nigeria was December 4, 2018. I told my son the date of my departure to Lagos. He told his friends and each one asked me about the news about my departure. I knew they were happy to hear that I was going back to Nigeria. They nevertheless expressed their nostalgic feelings: oh we will miss you! I also told my daughter, Yetunde, that I was getting ready for my journey back to Nigeria. I taunted her if she would accompany me to Lagos. She busted to her usual infectious laughter and replied no Dad. Of course, I was aware what her reply would be, having lived in Nigeria where basic infrastructures were scarce and far in between.

In my preparation for the journey back home, Segun asked me to go out with him for shopping, which had been his practice so that I could get things for our people at home, friends and myself. I got as much stuff that I had allowance for by KLM airlines. On December 4, 2018, at 1: p.m. I left for George Bush Intercontinental Airport, Houston, Texas to catch my KLM flight. I missed the KLM flight, but I got checked into Air France airlines. The flight was turbulent faraway Bermuda Triangle. It was the most turbulent experience I have ever had. We got to Lagos on December 5, 2018, in the morning. My wife and her friend came to pick me up at the airport.

I was glad to be back home in Nigeria, particularly to see our daughter TK who was planning to further her education in any of the American colleges/universities. My wife had done everything within her ability and financial capability to make it possible for her to realize the objective. I was glad to see she had been admitted at Lee University, Cleveland, Tennessee. Her mind was not prepared for the interview at the U.S. Consulate Office, Lagos and that psychological trauma had to be resolved before the date of the interview. I was glad I came at the right time for us to assist her. I suggested an option for her to seek admission into another university for Fall semester 2019. With that in mind she was ready to wait and plan for the U.S. interview for a student visa in Lagos. I also advised her to go for the second choice of university. Luckily, she got admitted to Fisk University Nashville, Tennessee with a full scholarship. I immediately decided to pay the acceptance fee for her admission. She was excited about it and within a couple of days I noticed she informed her friends of the good news. She was full of excitement and to my amazement we started having several of her friends come to our house for discussions on what to do in preparing for their student visa interviews at the American Consulate Office, Lagos. While that mood was a sign of good omen, we had to caution her not to over blow her luck.

As December 2018 was coming to an end and everyone was expecting what the resolution on the application would be, I got a call from one of my neighbors at Arigidi asking me whether I had returned to Nigeria and when would I be coming to the city. I told him I would soon be at Arigidi-Akoko, Ondo State, Nigeria. I had an invitation for a wedding of one of my family friends on December 29, 2018 but it became clear that I would not attend it. The night of that wedding some burglars chose to break into my house opposite of where the event was taking place and on Sunday, December 30, 2018, when people were in the Church, the burglars drove into the compound that was fortified with a fence round the house and carted away my property worth millions of Naira. As a result, all the doors leading to each room were rendered disabled, and the window of my library was pulled down, and the cabinet vandalized. One of the neighbors called me to break the sad news about the incident and reminded me that; that was the second time the burglars had broken the house. The first time was on August 24, 2016 when I was in the U.S. for my eye surgeries and a burial ceremony was taking place in the same house opposite of mine at Arigidi-Akoko, Ondo State and the daredevils burgled my house and went away with my laptop, an expensive electric rotor of a sewing machine and other valuables. The damages to the house were baffling and costly to fix. Perhaps the burglars chose the time of the ceremonies to perpetrate their evil acts. It could be the case that some of the neighbors were involved in a coordinated fashion. The two cases were reported to the police and their verdicts were that the insiders in the neighborhood were involved. Some sympathizers felt that traditional means should be utilized to apprehend or curse the burglars. Given my experience in the community, all the burglars and thieves apprehended, their parents, relations and influential personalities were used to plead for their pardon. And my case would not be treated differently and using a traditional device that could be deadly was not going to serve any useful purpose to me. I told those suggesting that I should use metaphysical powers of Yoruba deities to punish the criminals that I would prefer they asked Olodumare, the Supreme Being to change their minds rather than wishing them dead. As painful as those two terrible experiences at Arigidi were, I was of the view that; that is one of the dangers of living in the existential wilderness of existence. Besides, one is not to expect successes and prosperities without some hiccups and what happened to my properties at Arigidi were some of the hiccups and I had to move on. And to move on required that I concentrated on my family and plan for my return to the U.S. as soon as possible, which would probably reduce the momentary psychological trauma of the worst robbery of my property at Arigidi-Akoko on December 29/30, 2018. But I couldn't leave for the U.S. without fixing the damages done to the house and having an inventory of what was stolen. So, I went to Arigidi to do all that in early January 2019 before going back to Lagos.

When I got back to Lagos, I decided to return to the U.S. because President Trump's rhetoric of 'America will be Great again' was deceptive in connotation and body language. He had no good intentions for Africans and colored people living legally in the U.S. His policies towards nonwhites were perceived crude, cruel and inhuman. I called Prince Shola Sutton, one of the best immigration lawyers that I knew in Houston, to know if I could stay longer than six months before I returned to the U.S. and he advised that given the situation in the country, it was advisable to return as soon as possible but not after six months. I called my son to tell him that it was compelling for me to return to Houston as advised by my attorney. But I didn't want to leave until adequate arrangements were made for TK's student visa. When we had made adequate preparations that instilled confidence in her, I went to book my flight ticket for May 15, 2019.

LEAVING NIGERIA IN MAY 2019 FOR THE US

I had a premonition that electing President Muhammadu Buhari for a second term in 2019 would spell doom for the country. Meanwhile, his first term had nosedived towards economic disasters with high interest rate, high rate of unemployment, unstoppable corruption, etc. I doubted his second term mantra of Next Level, which was shrouded in deception, could not take Nigeria to its Eldorado. I went to several banks where I had some little money to close all the accounts because the devaluation of Nigeria currency was getting worse: the exchange rate in the banks on May 8, 2019, was 358 Naira to the USD. Considering the social economic indices and the ability of Buhari administration to radically reduce insecurity, I felt it would be necessary not only for me to relocate temporarily to the U.S. but also my immediate nuclear family.

On May 14, 2019, I began to arrange my personal effects to take with me to Richmond, Texas. There were heavy boxes that TK and I had to bring down from the top of the closet and when we couldn't bring them down because they were very heavy, we asked Oseni Hasan, the security guard of the house, to give us a helping hand. TK and I were packing and repacking my luggage because of the limited kilograms the airlines allowed every passenger to carry unless one wanted to pay for the excess luggage, which I couldn't afford. What TK and I did was preliminary packing and when we got tired, we left the rest till the second day, May 15, 2019. There was one concern still lurking in my mind: will TK succeed in her interview at the American Consulate Office? If she did not get a student visa, what could I do from the U.S.? But something instilled confidence in me that she would get her visa. I was careful not to share my internal pessimistic discourse so that she could have a pleasant night rest. After breakfast on Sunday, May 5, 2019, I brought my boxes to the living room and my wife and daughter, TK, came to assist me with logistics of packing the most essential things I would need in the two boxes allowed by the airline. I first set aside my traveling documents, Nigerian passport, US Green Card, air ticket and purse, before packing other important materials I would need because I wasn't going to come back to Nigeria soon. The documents of my houses at Arigidi and Idofin were kept among things that would not be needed in the U.S. I told my cousin, Sam Iyelolu to keep my Prado Land Cruiser in his house. So, I left its key with my wife to be handed over to him. I had only two boxes and a hand luggage. When it was about 5: p.m. Sam's driver came to take us to the airport. We got there on time to get the luggage checked in and we had some time to gist, but I wanted them to go back home before it was getting dark. I expressed my best wishes to TK on her interview at the U.S. Consulate office in Lagos and I would be expecting her at Fisk University Nashville later in August 2019. I promised to file for my wife as soon as possible in 2019 and hopefully she would join me in 2021. I was shedding tears after we exchanged best wishes and watched them leaving the airport lobby. Bearing in mind that British Airways was known for keeping to its schedules, I intuitively adjusted my nostalgic mood to face the reality of not missing my flight. By the time I got to the boarding gate, checking passengers for boarding had begun. I made sure my passport and air ticket for boarding were firmly held in my hand as we were checking in one after the other. We were checked in on time and the plane took off on schedule.

We had a stopover at Heathrow airport in London for a couple of hours and before boarding we had to go through security checks. After going through security checks we went to board and we were ready for takeoff to Houston, Texas. We made it to Houston in the morning of May 16, 2019 and I called my son to get me a transport to take me to his house, which he did. It was about an hour to get to his house and when we got there he came out to welcome me back to his house. It was a good reunion. After exchanging some pleasantries with him and his friends, he led me to my room for me to have some rest. I thanked him and he left to meet his friends. I called my wife and daughter to let them know that I made it to Houston safely. I was tired and needed some sleep. I had a week of jetlag but I was happy to be here because without being here it would have been impossible to have necessary and cogent firsthand information with pragmatic experience to navigate the storming water of deep-seated family feuds of yesteryears, and the wisdom to disrobe a pervading appeal of an 'idolized masquerade' with its deceptive aesthetic amusement and pleasure, with negative consequences in the U.S.

CHALLENGES OF YESTERYEARS

Given the fact that Segun and Yetunde went to be with their mother in the U.S., the promised land that many people continue struggling to be, but I was not unmindful of American policy of respecting freedom of children, which African parents would consider as extreme obsessions, but violating it could put them in jail. Bearing that in mind, I did not want my children to take liberty for license to misbehave to their mother. Therefore, there was always room for communication. In other words, there was no disconnect between us from time to time through postal services, and subsequently phone calls.

As a university teacher, the welfare and education of the

children were of topmost priorities in my mind, which their mother assured me of being capable of providing, when she requested to take custody of them. As Yoruba say: *ta lo mo' wo biko se iya olomo?* Meaning, who knows how wherewithal like the mother's child? That is why children in Yoruba culture, and in practical terms, usually go to their mothers for their needs/wants before going to their fathers, if and only if, directed by their mothers. I was happy that they were in safe hands with their mother and in a country where education is free from Elementary School to High School, and more importantly there is no power failure (Up NEPA!!), and medical services are probably the best in the world. Our daughter Yetunde had a very sensitive disposition toward the way she was treated among other siblings and if there was no compensation for her perceived unfair treatment, it could lead to a negative psychological mood. This became a teething problem between her and the mother, which lingered on for a while to the extent that she decided not to take it anymore; hence things started falling apart for her. Segun, her senior brother, had to take charge of the pieces after things had been 'falling apart and the center could no longer hold' for Yetunde. Coming back to the U.S. to stay would help me to understand the issues and challenges; and find a lasting solution for inner peace and happiness that Yetunde desperately needed to enhance her personhood.

I grew up in a culture that believes that however old or

mature or influential your child is in the society, he is not above reproach whenever he transgresses societal norms or injunctions of the parents and family elders. He is still a 'child', a matured child! But in the U.S. when a child attains the age of 21 years, he/she is considered an adult and parents can hardly tell them what to do because they are adults. You won't be surprised when you want to correct your child of 21 years or above, he or she will tell you in a conversation, Dad, leave me alone, I am an adult. Some African guys living in the U.S. assume that there are virtually not any moral values or experience to learn from their parents because they are adults. They are lured into American masquerades of deceptive pleasures. Coming from an African parenting background but conversant with American artificial masquerades of freedom and pleasure, I did not give my son and his closest friends a breathing space by diplomatically persuading them to beware of its red zone with health and untimely death consequences. It was really like 'sickness unto death'. As my father used to tell me when I was young, son... 'to obey is better than sacrifice, and to hearken than the fat of rams' (1 Samuel 15: 22). From reflection or hindsight, I strongly believe the ancient Biblical moral code has its universal imperative applications. That was what happened to my son recently as he reflected on his existential life:

"We've come to the sunset of another year. It is a time when most are reflective and think about the lessons learned from the year. For me it's simple. We are not invincible. As the years pass, we are grateful to be alive but also mourn the deaths of those we have lost. I lost a few people recently and it is a sobering realization that the most important asset we have is time. You know the saying; how you treat your car is how your car will treat you? This is especially true with our bodies. Unlike cars that we can trade in for a new one, we have only one body and how we treat it will determine the quality of life we live, if we are lucky enough to get old. This year taught me to be mindful of what I am doing in the moment and how it can affect me in the long term. Replacing bad habits like staying out late, over-drinking, not sleeping, eating unhealthy, smoking hookah, and other habits that nourish the brain and the body will help us not only in the short term, but in the long term as well."

If a child does not touch the red ball of fire; he will not know how hot it is and its consequences, but immediately he tries it, he doesn't need to be told because he has intuitively experienced its unfriendly nature.

Given the fact that Temidayo was and still in the U.S. and TK's successful interview at the US Consulate Office in Lagos, she would soon become a student at Fisk University at Nashville, Tennessee, I felt it would be morally inappropriate and logically indefensible not to have their mother to join us in the U.S. I discussed the proposed plan with our son, my landlord! He did not have any objection and I went ahead to file for my wife in 2019 because keeping the family together has its intrinsic and extrinsic values. But I was not unaware that considering human nature there would be occasional manifestation of pebbles of inconveniences but overall, it is worth keeping the family together. From my family background, the unity of the family is the bedrock of strength, joy, happiness, satisfaction, and pride in my paradoxical existential life.

PART ELEVEN

REFLECTION ON MY MARITAL LIFE

Chapter 19
REFLECTION ON MY MARITAL LIFE

Generally, in African culture, parents look forward to the time their children will get married and have children to give them assurance of continuity of descendants, so that when they die, they will be given a befitting funeral and burial rites, in order to become ancestors. My parents were no exception to this metaphysical assumption! They were looking forward to when I was going to have a wife and children but only when they felt I was mature enough with adequate resources to raise a family of my own. Let me reiterate this narrative here since it is very germane to this discourse of reflection on my marital life. When I graduated from University of Ibadan in 1976 and was employed by Kwara State Government and deployed to the Ministry of Education in Ilorin, and then posted to teach at AAAMCO Okene, formerly in Kwara State and now in Kogi State, my mother felt it was time for me to have a wife and children like my friends in the community. That had been her expectation and perhaps, existential yardstick of fulfillment of being a successful mother. My father agreed with my mother on her perception of my status in the society and the desire for me to have children but, he was not convinced I had sufficient knowledge and understanding the complex nature of women particularly, their emotions; and how I could live with a wife without the virtue of extreme patience, tolerance, accommodation and forgiveness at my age. At that time, I was 31 years old when my parents disagreed on the proposed idea that I should have a wife and children. On my part, I was not ready for marriage; my reasons were not based on my parents' own but on the fact that I had passion for higher education in Nigeria and preferably, in the United States of America. Getting married at that time would be counterproductive; that I was not ready to allow, in my wheel of progress. Besides, I had an inner feeling that any lady interested in me, as her husband, was not from commitment to genuine intentions, but rather from the benefits she would derive from my status and potential. My mother was in such a hurry to get things done to fulfill her desire for me, as if she had a premonition of her imminent death. So, I gave in to her pressure to satisfy her ambition and goal to make her happy. My mother and I then talked my father out of his uncompromising position but surprisingly; he gave in to my mother's proposal. By December 1977, I became a married man, even though I had been processing my applications to some American universities with the hope of getting admission and scholarship. Fortunately for me, I got admission with full scholarship at Southern Methodist University (S.M.U) Dallas, Texas in April 1978. By April 1978 my wife took in and my mother was full of jubilation thinking she was going to have a grandchild of her first son. Unfortunately, the gravity of death fell on her about a month before the birth of her grandson, Segun Bidemi Ogungbemi Jr. My mother was a lucky woman with double barrel blessings: her son gained admission and scholarship to SMU Dallas in the U.S. and a bouncing-baby grandson was born barely a month after her death. The boy is now an adult and has become a multifarious channel of blessings to us in the family, extended family, friends, colleagues and humanity. In 1983 we had another child, Yetunde Bosede Ogungbemi. These children remain critical to my joy and happiness.

The ideal of a traditional marriage has had impacts on me as I was growing up and witnessed different marriages. The traditional marriage between a man and a woman follows customary and cultural values in which marriage is for two families agreeing to remain as one entity to act as a bridge of mutual benefit to the couple and to mend fences where there are conflicts threatening the unity of their relationship. It is like a 'customary and cultural institution' to prevent divorce and to encourage healthy relationships for peace and happiness. That is why father and mother in-laws play a vital role in the marital conflicts in the home of their children but when such mutual understanding is lacking, then such marriage is built on sinking sand or a quicksand. That is why the Yoruba say, it is better to have a troublesome wife than having vexatious in-laws because they will do everything possible to inflame the fragile relationship between the couple. Rarely is divorce allowed in Yoruba culture because of its impacts on the children and the image of the family in the society. Sometimes, a peaceful mind would rather have a divorce than to allow unwilling and incompatible marital relationships to keep on dragging a tired horse until it dies and, more importantly, when any of the principal in-laws wants a divorce for their son or daughter. Once that happens, you must hands up and say, after all, everyone has his or her own life to live! This scenario has been part of my marital experience.

Having a life partner, one has to bear in mind some facts about what type of person one wants to live with? I believe in my own African experience: intelligence, respect, commitment, obedience, hard work, honesty, integrity, patience, faithfulness, kindness, empathy, resilience, generosity, spontaneity, forbearance, love and common interest. To begin a relationship some women, have semblances of these virtues but after getting married the desire to keep the momentum going starts weaning out and the true phenomenon of the woman begins to unfold itself. The relationship begins to drift towards a dangerous storm. Having children could impact the velocity of the drift because they bring happiness and joy to the family. So also, family in-laws who are respected by the wife could be a source of solution to the crisis and their intermittent interventions could be a healing balm to the aching body and distress. This is also my second marital experience. Our son and the two daughters, Temidayo Bimbola Ogungbemi and Tinuke Bisola Ogungbemi are fantastic children. They are my joy and happiness. And of course, my late father and mother in-laws, Chief Babalola Adeusi and Chief Jokotola Olaoba played a significant role in cementing the existing enduring relationship in my family. My wife's siblings, Olayinka Taiwo Akinbulumo, late Lanre Olaoba, Kehinde Olaoba, Ayotunde Olaoba, Olaitan Olaoba, Bola Babalola, Wunmi Adesokan and Bode Olaoba relate with us as one family. On my part, my late father and late sister Maroni Omokore and particularly her son, Asiwaju Jide Omokore, have been pivotal to our success as one family amongst others.

MARITAL LIFE WITHOUT DULL MOMENTS

I love sports and athletics because it kept me actively strong. I used to create jokes to make people laugh and perhaps forget their sorrows, and from tiredness, and a moody state of mind. But as soon as my wife and son joined me in 1979,

I did not have much time for those activities. I had to find other means to socialize to keep my family from boredom. We used to go shopping on weekends at Kmart, Sears, Sanger-Harris, etc. in Dallas and Plano, Texas. We attended several church services on Sundays in Dallas particularly, Tabernacle Baptist Church, 3403 McBroom St, Dallas Texas 75212. This Church was significant because of its uniqueness at the material time: it was an African American Pentecostal Church and the Minister was Rev. (Dr.) Moses Sr. a friend of late Rev. (Dr.) D.S. Moody back home in Nigeria. He gave David Adamo now (late Professor David Tuesday Adamo) the name and address of the church to him in 1978 when he was coming to S.M.U Dallas. We attended the church services together twice and he decided to attend a different church. When my wife came, we started to go to that church. They treated us so well that we became part of them. The wife of the Minister took my wife as her daughter and my son as her great grandson. Their children, Martha and Moses Jr. were special to us. They helped us to remove loneliness and dull moments on every Sunday that we attended their service. There were several First United Methodist Churches that immensely contributed to our happiness in Dallas and Plano, Texas. Edwin and Campton Sylvest invited us to their Church in Dallas and when we moved to Plano, Texas, Rev. (Dr.) Ben Feemster welcomed us to First Methodist Church Plano, Texas, where our son was attending the kindergarten Sunday school. When I visited the Church in 2019 some members still had faint memory of him, and they asked of his whereabouts. It is chronologically significant in this anal of my story to mention several individuals whose contributions to our comforts and happiness in an individualistic and capitalistic economy of loneliness in the U.S.: Ezekiel Okeniyi and his wife, Elizabeth, who on several occasions invited us to diners in their house in Dallas; Sam Olumoko who helped us to move to Plano; Mrs. Gay Dahlstrom who was like our mother in a foreign land; Ray & Jane Dubberly in Irvin, Texas treated us like their children; John Thornburg, Keith Morgan in Saint Louis, Missouri, and his parents, Ralph and Marita Morgan in Tulsa, Oklahoma; and Professor Louis P. Pojman and his wife Trudy in Dallas, amongst others.

In July 1985, I felt it was time to go back to Nigeria without any inkling of coming back to the U.S. because 'home is the best'. This historical narrative was the first face of marital experience as a student in the United States of America. The second face is slightly different because of several factors; namely, I became a substantive Lecturer/Professor in Nigeria and Kenya that gave me a better perspective with intensity to acquire more experience and understanding of women, as we had some of them as Lecturers and Professors. I was also more mature to reflectively comprehend why my father felt it was too early for me to get married in 1977. After seven years since I returned to Africa, it became more compelling to reconsider getting married again because my two children had grown up.

I got married in December 1992 and my wife joined us in early 1993 at Moi University Eldoret Kenya. A new family relationship took center stage with a series of activities that expanded for 30 years thus far. We went on safari to Nairobi several times to get out of occasional boredoms. At Moi University, the joy of expecting a new baby filled our hearts. The baby was born on Saturday, November 6, 1993, and our Kenya friends who were Kikuyu named her Wanjiru and the Kalenjin ethnic group named her Jebet; each name means a girl born on Saturday. As Yoruba parents, we named her Temidayo, Bimbola Ogungbemi. The fact that she was born in Kenya did not make her a citizen because her parents were not Naturalized citizens of Kenya. Unknown to us that Providence had designed the U.S., the most powerful nation in the world, to be our next destination as future citizens. In 2016, Temidayo resumed her postgraduate program at Western Kentucky University, Bowling Green after we returned from a conference at The University of Texas at Austin. In 2018 we went for her graduation together with Tinuke who was still nursing her ambition to study in any of the universities in the U.S. Tinuke was lucky to get admission and scholarship at Fisk University, Nashville, Tennessee in 2019. Our joy was full to the brim when our daughters got to the U.S. and commenced their studies. In early 2021 the traditional wedding of Temidayo and Ademola took place in Lagos and it was well attended despite the outbreak of COVID 19 global pandemic. We did a zoom video here in Houston to capture the event in Lagos. It was a huge success. We cannot forget the support of Asiwaju Jide Omokore and his Olori, Angela, Chief Tope Mark, Sam and his Olori, Toyin Iyelolu, my brothers, sisters, cousins, nieces, Iya-Alaje Anike Solomon, Kunle David, a.k.a Mr. White amongst others. On August 8, 2021, Temidayo and Dr. Ademola Oridate had their Church wedding in Houston, Texas with attendance of many family relations and friends in the U.S. and Nigeria. We cannot have everyone mentioned but a few members deserved to be remembered: Professor Toyin Falola and his Olori, (Dr.) Bisi Falola, Professor Joseph Abiodun Balogun and his Olori (Dr.) Adetutu, Chief Ezekiel Onaolapo Okeniyi and his Olori Elizabeth, Chief Segun Awo and his Olori Obiaderi, Rev. (Dr.) Olusola Adetiba and his family, Sam Iyelolu and his daughter, Tolu, Sonde Omokore and his family, Segun Ogungbemi Jr. and his son, Segun 111, Tinuke Bisola Ogungbemi and her friends, Ayotune Olaoba (Big Mummy) and her friends, Sade and her husband from Dallas, Mrs. Dupe Oridate, mother-in-law, Dr. Adedamola Oridate and family from Canada, Olori Makinde from Canada etc., were there to grace the great occasion with us.

And finally, my wife remained with us in Houston after

the wedding to get her immigration status changed to a permanent resident status to maximize the fullness of God with us. While here in Houston some individuals in the neighborhood added values to our lives: Chief and Olori Taiwo in Austin, Texas, Professor Toyin Falola and his Olori, Bisi Falola, Professor Joseph Abiodun Balogun and his Olori Adetutu, Chief Segun Awo and his family, Jackie Herrera, Navy Commander (CDR) Dayo Victor Lofinmakin and his Olori Dolapo, Modeleola Kayode, Olori Omolara Kowe and my unique landlord, Segun Ogungbemi Jr. and my grandson, Segun Cristian Ogungbemi 111.

PART TWELVE

MY BENEFACTORS

Chapter 20
MY BENEFACTORS

By nature of human existence, everyone however rich or poor his background is, has benefactors; apart from the Creator of everything that is. So, as I conclude this book at the age of 76 years, I looked back to my beginning where everything about me began and felt compelled to mention a few of them particularly, in my struggle to obtain the best in Western education. My first benefactors were my parents particularly, my father, Pa Afolami Ogungbemi who had been to the Yoruba towns and cities; and saw what Western education had accomplished in terms of development in those places like Lagos, Abeokuta, Ibadan, etc., in the defunct Western Region, now Southwestern Nigeria. The Baptist Church at Idofin became the beginning of my journey in 1952 where the Minister of the Church combined his ministry with teaching at his local parish. It was not a school but what one will probably call kindergarten even though it was recognized as its equivalence. The community decided in 1954 to make the Baptist Church a classroom during the week for a very few of us to pursue western education. Thus, both the Baptist Church and Idofin community are hereby qualified as my stepping stones, benefactors!!

There were three American Peace Corps that played a prominent role in my progression, and they are: Ruth Bowden, Summerfield North Carolina, the primary mover for my sponsor at Igbaja Bible College and the secondary mover was Rosalie Peterson from Lindsborg, Kansas, and third supporter was Kenneth Karl Koosman from Washington State. Mr. Koosman passed on in February 2022. He will always be remembered.

The mother of Rosalie Peterson raised funds for my studies at University of Ibadan in 1974-1976. I visited the family in Lindsborg, Kansas in December 1978. I was delighted to know them before they went to be with their Creator. Their monumental support will continue to be remembered and treasured. Pa Leslie Bello Obielodan and Rev. Dr. Nathaniel Olutimayin were the pathfinders of my journey to the U.S. in 1978.

Southern Methodist University (SMU), Perkins School of Theology Dallas remained my benefactor in 1978-1980. I was given a full scholarship that effortlessly opened the strong gate to the U.S. and thereafter to The University of Texas at Dallas (UT-Dallas) for my Doctorate in 1980-1984. There were individual benefactors I cannot forget in the institution: Campton and her husband, Professor Ed Slyest for their friendship and financial supports, Professor Joseph Allen, my Advisor at S.M.U, who after several years that I went back to Africa was still sending books to me for my research, Keith Morgan and John Thornburg were my schoolmates and best friends at S.M.U Dallas. Keith invited me to his parents' home in December 1978 and since then, we remain friends till today. His parents have treated me as one of their children; hence, I call them Mom & Dad till the moment. I have visited them several times in Tulsa, Oklahoma. I was introduced to their Church and the last time that I visited them in 2019, I interacted with Dad men's class. Mom also took me to meet a lady who took us for a tour of the main Church building. I was taken to a section of the Church preserved for sobering moment and a particular section of it where an individual had paid to preserve their remains after cremation. I was shown the one for Mom & Dad. I chuckled! Wondering whether I will be able to cope with the emotions that will overwhelm me when they pass away, and their remains will be in each box with their names conspicuously written on it. Mom took interest in reading some of my works because we share certain beliefs about our love for humanity regardless our different methodological approaches. We had gone to different places in Tulsa apart from their Church: Gathering Place, the biggest park in Tulsa, Oral Robert University, The University of Oklahoma, Farmers weekend market, Restaurants, Ice skating, Wellness Center, etc.

To be closer to UT-Dallas, I had to move to Plano to save cost on transportation and besides housing was easier and cheaper than living in Dallas and Richardson. I decided to relocate to Plano, Texas in 1981. After relocating to Plano, I decided to join the United Methodist Church that was not far from where I was living, and Rev. (Dr.) Ben Harold Feemster was the Minister of Church. He was very pleasant and kind to us. The congregation welcomed us very warmly. Our son became a member of the children Sunday school that he enjoyed because he had several friends. The church supported us morally and financially. In 1982 when I had to go to School of Oriental and African Studies (SOAS), University of London for 8 weeks, Dr. Feemster got the church to sponsor it and arranged accommodation for me at John Wesley's house in London. Dr. Feemster and his congregation contributed to the successful completion of my Ph.D. program at UT-Dallas. On October 2, 2022, as I was searching for his current address, I was stunned to know that he had passed away since August 5, 2005, at the age of 75. He and the Church in Plano will always be remembered as my benefactors.

Mrs. Gay Dahlstrom and her husband, a construction engineer were members of a Methodist Church in Dallas. Mom, as I fondly called her, was extremely helpful to me. She paid my monthly apartment rent in Plano and contributed to the production of my dissertation in 1984. When I told her that I was returning to Nigeria in 1985, she advised me to stay behind because she did not want me to go back where my family and I would suffer. The family is remembered as one of my important benefactors. In addition to the Methodist church family of benefactors were Mr. & Mrs. Ray and Jane Dubberly in Irvin, Texas. They supported me morally and financially in school and even when I was in Africa. They impressed on me that out of sight is not out of mind.

Outside the Methodist folks was Professor Louis P. Pojman, my teacher, mentor, friend and an academic icon who nurtured me with intellectual ingredients that made me to grow, and to attain academic stardom in life. He was not only my benefactor in all ramifications but also my existential hero. When I was arranging for his visit to Adekunle Ajasin University, Akungba-Akoko in 2005/2006, his death on October 15, 2005, struck me like a thunderbolt. Although Pojman is no more in this physical world, his contributions to humanity remain indelible in the anal of history of what constitutes the meaning and purpose of life.

APPENDIX

PERCEPTIONS OF SEGUN OGUNGBEMI

THE GREAT CHAINS OF FAMILY MEMBERS

Segun B. Ogungbemi Jr.

What can I say about a man who has reached the pinnacle of his success? From a young age I had front row seats to watch and learn from my dad and I am grateful to have been a part of his journey.

From the time I came to the United States at a very young age we were together while he was pursuing his Masters. You would think being a preschooler I wouldn't remember much of those times but that would be where you are wrong. Some of my fondest memories were staying up late with my dad as he prepared and defended his dissertation for his PhD. I loved staying late with him drawing Spider-Man with my assortment of crayons while he went to work.

I loved going to the university with him and sitting with him at the library, learning the value of hard work. That is one thing my dad never shied away from, the work it took to be great. He took his academic skills and his hunger to better Nigeria with him as we embarked on a new journey to the motherland. The level of sacrifice cannot be overstated.

He has always dreamed of taking what he learned from the white man to educate his own people so that we could thrive as a nation. There are many lessons I learned from him and this is one of the greatest, the lesson of personal sacrifice.

This was a lofty task, a one-man mission to go back home to educate his people. It didn't come without its own struggles as one can imagine. Nigeria is a country that lacks core values, structure, with deep-rooted poverty nearly made this an impossible goal.

But knowing the true nature of my dad, he didn't let that discourage him, in fact he took it as a personal challenge and built long standing relationships with people who saw his vision for the country and they were able to help him in several of his goals.

I am proud to say that my dad led a team of patriots to bring electricity to Idofin. Today the area is lit at night and people are able to work and socialize together past sundown. We are all very grateful to him for his efforts in bringing a much-needed resource to our small city.

Metaphorically speaking, he was also able to bring light to darkness by educating the thousands of students he taught over a 40 year period. From Ogun State University to Ondo State University, and across the pond all the way in Eldoret Kenya, he has touched many lives through the value of education and most of them hold him in high regard for his noble efforts.

Many of his students have not only graduated from his classes but they went on to become useful citizens of the country in different fields, many even took after him and became professors at the schools he taught.

As a father, he has influenced me greatly. He was always there with a stern hand to ensure we focused on our education. He would stay up in the middle of the night teaching us and helping us with our homework.

Most importantly, he taught us how to be good people. I am proud to say my dad has lived a life dedicated to being a good man. His core values are displayed not by his words, but by his actions. He is a man of integrity, kindness, dedication, and love. He is forever a student of academia. I am blessed to be called your son.

Yetunde B. Ogungbemi

My dad is the most loving, hardworking and smartest man that I know.

He raised four wonderful children and I am proud to be one of them.

I love you dad.

Temidayo B. Ogungbemi

Despite having different names, fathers play fundamental roles in the lives of their children. I can testify of the great roles my father has played in my life.

My father unhesitatingly sacrifices everything for me. He has an incomprehensible and unconditional love for me and for those around him. His love is not subject to only his biological children but to family and friends. I have never met a man that goes a great length to make people comfortable and happy. I am proud to have been born into the Professor Segun Ogungbemi family. Through him, I have known how to love, give, be humble, work hard, and be resilient. During my bad days, my dad will tell me everything will be alright and eventually everything gets alright. The words that come out of his mouth are full of wisdom, and never misleading. He is a man of integrity and truly the best example any man can be. A lot of people call him 'My Prof', and he is truly one; an exceptional teacher, an amazing father, a humble husband, a devoted dad, a fearless man and many more.

I love you so much dad, and I am grateful for your achievements and all you do for us. You are a rare gem and your light shines everywhere because you always make a lifelong impact in the places you go. Thank you for your sacrifices and support; I will forever cherish every moment we spend together.

Tinuke B. Ogungbemi

My Father is an amazing man. He is very passionate about his children, having a good education and he worked hard to give me a great education experience. He is a disciplinarian and always has a word of wisdom no matter your situation. My father is a hard worker and always passionate about what he puts his mind to what he is doing. He is a giver and he is unapologetic about it. He is ever loving and protective. Need I say that he is knowledgeable? I will say he is a genius. My father is a man that has worked so hard to achieve everything he has. He loves his children and always provides for our needs. Daddy, I'm so proud of you and I love you forever.

Ajayi Igununtoba

When I tell people about my incredible brother, I always say I have the best brother.

It gives my darling wife immense pleasure and me whenever you communicate with us. You are a whirlwind of pure love, passion, enthusiasm, warmth and humor that is contagious. I see you in the laughter and kindness of my precious family.

For me, this is a chance to say proudly that I feel so fortunate and proud to have you not only as a brother but also as a role model. You are resourceful, loving, devoted to the family, and no wonder at your youthful age you took us to Okene in order for us to go to school when you were teaching at

Abdul Aziz Atta Memorial College. There is no member of the family you have not helped in one way or the other.

Your wisdom, experience, foresight, and authenticity are inspiring. You have been an amazing role model, supporter, educationist, adviser and confidant.

Your love for education and foresight of the future made you to pay the school fees of many children in our small city, Idofin.

You are more than a brother to me. I can not forget the car you gave me which I'm still using. You are a loving brother and a disciplinarian.

Prof., indeed I am proud of you and l wish you more divine grace.

Iyabo Ogungbemi

"Any man can become a father but it takes someone special to be a DADDY". You are my daddy because you're special in all ramifications. Because of your sacrificial lifestyle, everyone in the family fondly calls you, Daddy. The love you have for family keeps me wondering the kind of man you are. Over the years you have taught me the importance of man and how well to treat family members.

From my personal experience, you have given me everything I needed as a tool to overcome a lot of huddles of life. You taught me morals and gave me a solid foundation to build on academically. One of the moral lessons I will never forget was the day I lied about losing the money I was given to plait my hair instead of telling the truth that I used it to buy biscuits. I had the beating of my life that day; it however, transformed my behavior of telling the truth no matter the circumstances.

As a father, you have provided a template for me to know how to live with people and the interpretation of "spare the rod and spoil the child…": the rod that you didn't spare me in my formative years.

Your encouragement keeps me strong to face daily challenges. Your ever-listening ears make home safe to come knowing that I have your backing always.

I'm blessed to have you as my big daddy and supporter over the years. You are a blessing to the family, community and humanity. Your legacy is written in my heart as a testimony of love and care of our big Daddy.

Moyin Afolami Ogungbemi

My sweet father is my hero and my guide in life. He is the one I look up to whenever I find myself in trouble. He has been the guiding force for all my major decisions in life and I have never regretted adhering to his advice because it has always worked for me.

I feel grateful that I have the opportunity to be his daughter and to be a part of a wonderful family that has a great father like him.

He is a dad of profound understanding and often politely corrected my mistakes without rancor in order to make me a better person in life.

My Dad is a person who does not like to sit idle. He is always up and doing academically and also carrying out his fatherly role. It is very clear that his professorship is well deserved due to his hard work.

He does not spend his money on expensive things. He lives an easy and peaceful life. Also, he doesn't shout on anyone of us.

He is my role model for many reasons: Firstly, I admire his passion for hard work and education, that's is why he is so respected by his colleagues.

Secondly, he has affection for his children and for their education.

Thirdly, he can go to any length to make sure people around him have quality education.

Fourthly, he can never sit and watch his family go hungry. Wherever foodstuffs are, he will provide it. I love and cherish our Dad for all these qualities. He is the best Daddy ever!!

Oluwakemi Omotayo

Uncle, I choose to call you my father because the word 'father' is the noblest title a man can be given. It is more than a biological role. It signifies a patriarch, a leader, a teacher, an exemplar, a confidant, a hero and a friend. The quality of a father can be seen in the goals, dreams and aspirations he sets not only for himself, but also for his family.

Father, you have a place in my heart no one can fill. You are a man like no other, if love, humility and compassion had a form in humans, then it's you, you are an icon worthy of emulation, a strong support system, a hardworking, honest, intelligent and strong individual who is always there for his family. Family means so much to you, you always want to know what is up our sleeves so as to put us through where the need arises, highly principled, lover of education, a philanthropist, always there for peace keeping and upholding family ties, you always stand firm for what you believe is in the general interest of everyone. There are no enough words to describe just how amazing you are, all the lives you have touched, what a powerful influence you are.

The morals and values you taught and are still teaching us will continue to be a guiding light in our lives. I personally cherish the relationship I have with you and will try my best to live by righteous virtues you've raised me with and most importantly a valuable life lesson that 'family is key to always stay together through thick and thin, and to support, love and respect each other.

Thank you sir for this privilege and I also want to appreciate you for all the support, kindness, loves, words of advice and encouragement. Thanks for believing in me and I promise to always make you proud. Thanks for always being there for my beloved mother Ms. Ibidun Ogungbemi, your sister. May Almighty God continue to strengthen you and answer your secret prayers. We love and cherish you so much.

Dada Koja Michael

Professor Segun Ogungbemi, fondly called Daddy Prof. was born on August 26, 1946. He is the eldest brother of my mother, late Mrs. Funmilayo Michael. I am one of his nieces.

From what I know about his family background, he is a man of several home backgrounds. He hails from Ere Yagba West Local Govt, Kogi State but by virtue of his parental relocation, he grew up at Idofin-Isanlu, his great grandma's home in Yagba East Local Government, Kogi State.

He is a philosopher and has lectured at several universities in Africa. His last place where he had lectured that I am most conversant of, because of my age then was Adekunle Ajasin University Akungba-Akoko, Ondo State, Nigeria.

Prof. being the most educated among his siblings has been more of a blessing to us his nieces and nephews. Daddy is not just an educationist but also a believer in family bonds. Perhaps his parental family background with his exposure, wisdom and intelligence influenced his promotion of love and unity among his siblings and their children. He took it upon himself to ensure we all spend quality time with each other, which has now become the family norm.

Big daddy as we call him. He became my mentor for the very beginning of my education and he played a wonderful role in the career path I have chosen. I must say I am doing very well in it. He has shown me how to live, love and discipline myself in life.

Less I forget my uncle is a sweet and caring father, he has a military trait in him. He is brave and courageous. He is a no nonsense man and he would dish out your due punishment as appropriate if you misbehave. Bearing that disposition of him in mind it made us composed ourselves around him. Daddy is also a moralist and a respecter of customs, traditions and culture of our people.

Growing up, I saw him as a difficult person but as time passed by he became my most favorite uncle. Thanks for the mentorship and discipline daddy made me to pass through, which has made me flourish thus far. One of my aspirations is to become an education legend like him that he can be proud of. May you live long daddy. I love you.

Mrs. Oluyemisi Ayodele

My dearest uncle, Professor Segun Ogungbemi who I fondly call "uncle mi'.

I thank you so much for your love and care. I know that I can always count on you for all the encouragement, enlightenment and understanding of realities in life.

My dearest uncle, for me you are already our second parent. Thank you so much for the effort that you've exerted in rearing us. I really appreciate all your love and kindness towards me and the family.

My dearest uncle, thank you for giving me guidance whenever I needed your advice.

Your words were so inspirational to me and I will keep your words of hope all through my life.

I have always counted and relied on your mentorships. Today I am better for it.

You really set a good example for us to follow, thank you uncle.

You have always been part of every important occasion and

event of my life. I cannot imagine life without your love and support.

You've always been there to lend a helping hand. You have never got tired of helping especially in times when I really need some support.

God bless you uncle for all your good deeds.

I deeply appreciate all the gifts that you gave me, especially my teaching appointment in Lagos State teaching service commission. I am now a Deputy Director of Education. A million thanks to a wonderful and unparalleled uncle, Professor Segun Ogungbemi.

Shade Omokore

I clearly recalled the first time I met Daddy (because that is what I call him) at the Adekunle Ajasin University many years ago. I had gone to write post UME exams to be admitted to the school. He is very intelligent and versatile. We talked about a lot of interesting things and even told me more about our culture because as at then, I had no idea (LOL). Another attribute of Daddy is that he is a disciplinarian but in a good way. He teaches discipline so that you can become a better person for yourself. Attitude and enthusiasm play a big role in his life. Everybody around daddy is his family. He cares a lot about people (related or non-related). He is very supportive and encourages young adults especially his nieces and nephews.

Iyelolu Samuel & Toyin

It is a great privilege to be able to comment on the autobiography of our dear uncle and mentor. We praise the name of God for the great opportunity to be able to document your life journey so far. E o pe fun wa!!

You have been a great pillar of support to us individually and collectively as a family. Through your relentless support and even in the face of being a lone voice you stood by us, and we are forever grateful to you. We have known you all our lives and we have watched admirably the way you support members of your immediate family, extended family and our community Idofin as a whole. Being one of the foremost scholars in the community you believe that the pursuit of academic excellence is the way out of poverty and with your support and encouragement many who bought into your vision are now professionals in various fields of human endeavor today.

We say big congratulations to you sir, and we wish you greater achievements in the future.

Obiaderi & Victor Awo

Professor Ogungbemi is someone that my family truly admires and respects with all our heart. We became close to

him after he visited us and spent two weeks in our house. I could feel his pure heart for humanity. He has such a simple, caring and humble personality. He is my native culture and language teacher. My first language lesson was "Ekuri gidi" meaning; you are doing a good job! We appreciate you sir, a loving uncle.

Chief Temitope Mark

I count it a great honor and privilege to have been given an opportunity to contribute to the autobiography of a great

Father, Uncle, Role model and the pillar of our dynasty in person of Professor Segun Ogungbemi (fondly known as Prof. by close friends and family).

Obviously for the reason of age difference, I did not have the opportunity to get to know him closely until 1988. I traveled to Ogun State to meet him in his residence where my older brother was already living under his mentorship. The memory of the thrill, warmth and hospitality accorded me still remains fresh. Prior to this time, my Late Father who was Prof's Uncle had always spoken proudly about him; a lot of us young kids back in our small city, Odo-Eri in the current Yagba West Local Government, Kogi State looked forward to meeting him when he would return from "abroad" (USA) where he was studying. Despite having never met him in person, mentions of his name and accomplishments alone offered great motivation to us and gave us great expectations for what life could offer.

Prof. is an extremely modest person with great strength of character. He is a very honest man who stands by the truth always and says things as they are. He readily identifies and stands with his people anywhere and anytime. He knows practically all his acquaintances by name, identity and peculiarities. We all run to him whenever we are at crossroads, confronted with difficult decisions. He also has a strong sense of humor and humility. I remember a particular incident where he laid flat on the ground despite his status to appease an Elder even when he was obviously not at fault. He is a man of peace.

Prof. is a strong believer in possibilities. He doesn't believe lack of an affluent familial background is sufficient reason to keep anyone on the ground. He would always say- "Everyone is born equal and there is no position one cannot aspire to in life with the right attitude and determination".

I recall in 1988 when trying to get admission into the accounting program at University of Lagos (UNILAG)- despite my seemingly brilliant performance at GCE "A" Level and desperate preference of UNILAG as a choice of university- was a challenge. His backing, encouragement and contacts fired me up even at low moments when I nearly gave up. While he saw the possibility, another elite reproached me for choosing a university considered too competitive and reserved (in his own opinion) for only the children of privileged few in the society. Prof. ensured I was considered for admission and I give glory to God for using him to allow me meet my aspiration and ambition at that point. Perhaps I would be far from whom God has made me today but for his intervention.

Before I conclude, I must mention that Prof. has a very strong sense of empathy. His empathy is a big reason why the cycle of poverty in the family has been broken. He aspires for everyone to live comfortably well.

He is a strong lover of education who wants everyone to become a professor like him. The day I told him I abandoned my PhD pursuit due to pressures of business ventures, I noticed a change in his countenance; He responded – "Why did you not inform me?". After that encounter, I was faced with no other choice but to go back to school to further my education despite my advanced in age. He is a very resilient person who does not give up on possibilities.

He is also a loving Father and Husband. His love for his children and family, which we all try to emulate, is unparalleled.

It is my prayer that Almighty God who gave our Fathers, Grand Fathers and Great Grand Fathers longevity of life and kept them in good health will extend the same grace to Prof. to continue his good works and lead us to a point where we would be strong enough to take over from him.

We are very proud of you sir and I will forever be grateful for all you have done and continue to do for us. I wish you continued to bask in the glory and goodness of Almighty God. I love you sir.

Olusegun Thomas Komolafe

Uncle Segun Ogungbemi, an elder brother, a Father by right, a Distinguished family Adviser, was raised in Odeko compound in Idofin-Isanlu. His father, Pa Afolami Ogungbemi of blessed memory, was a friend, probably the only friend I knew my Dad, late Pa Thomas Komolafe had. The two were

regarded as foremost disciplinarians who probably must have influenced the life-style of Uncle Segun Ogungbemi who seemed to have taken the right part of his late father, Pa Afolami, who was regarded as a no nonsense man. In those days we went to work on the farm to support our parents, mostly on weekends. I remembered Egbon as we fondly called him in those days at Sudan Interior Mission (S.I.M) primary school at Makutu-Isanlu about 6 miles away from our community, and returned every Fridays by foot. My age then was a barrier to know the reason while Egbon was not participating actively with his younger siblings, Luke and Joshua on the farm. I believe the author in his historical narratives would have directly or indirectly told us in the autobiography. It is also fresh in my memory how we were a liability to uncle Segun while working in S.I.M Bookshops in Ilorin. I vividly remembered how several of us went to his Emir's Road residence to enjoy free foods in the early 70s while I was an apprentice salesman under late Chief David

Akande in the same S.I.M Bookshops. Interestingly, and to the admiration of this gentleman he never said 'I am tired' and he never shied away from supporting people that came on his way. He has been contributing morally and financially to both his family and the extended one, which I belonged to. Sometimes I wondered from the way he had abridged knowledge of day-to-day activities at home more than those of us at home. I do ask, 'if this man is a spirit' because of his strong belief and conviction in African tradition. I am aware that he ctively supports and encourages devotion to Origba in our native community. Egbon is a man of many parts but I shall be failing not to acknowledge his simple lifestyle, commitment to humanity, and his compassionate disposition to issues and benevolence to all around him. I wish to congratulate him for embarking on his autobiography project. I also wish him longevity in good spirit and health.

Otunba Kehinde Olaoba

Professor Segun Ogungbemi is an in-law to me, having been married to my younger sister, Olayemi, nee Olaoba.

Beyond that, he's my teacher, senior friend, mentor,

benefactor, and my boss. If I chose to pen down on the What, When and How of all these several interactions and intersections, destinies and destinations, it would be tantamount to writing another biographical work. So, I will only write about the latter- as a boss.

On a bright Tuesday morning in 1994, Segun took me into the presence of the then Honourable Minister of Labour and Productivity, Retd. Brig-Gen/Dr. Samuel Ogbemudia. The venue was the ministry's Conference Room at the Federal Secretariat, Ikoyi, Lagos. He briskly, and in his jovial self introduced my shy and humble person as the Research Assistant! Thus for the brief period late Dr. S. O. Ogbemudia was a Minister, I was a Research Assistant to Prof. S. Ogungbemi who was then a Senior Special Adviser (Research) to the Honorable Minister.

In this trajectory, Segun Ogungbemi, whom in my admiration I call "Prof of the Universe", was, and still is, Brilliant, Dogged, Committed and Organized. He's a great teacher of trainable minds. He is also very confident, very brave, very conscientious and very blunt, a personality! He carefully assessed and ascertained situations thereby refusing to be a permanent critic of anything good. Like him or otherwise, to Segun Ogungbemi, a spade is simply a spade. These attributes endeared him tso the heart of the Honourable Minister, late Dr. Samuel Ogbemudia, thereby making several gang ups against him by some civil servants who chose to stay in darkness under lights!

More importantly, in this prism of building a wooden bridge across a ravine: "A bridge made of wood is worthless, but the wood that can support a wooden bridge in the ravine is very valuable!" Segun Ogungbemi will always remain to me that valuable wood that supports the wooden bridge across the ravine!

COLLEAGUES IN THE UNIVERSITY SYSTEM

Prof. Dele Balogun

Professor Segun Ogungbemi is a Professor of Philosophy, an erudite Scholar and a lecturer par excellence who loves knowledge. His benevolence as well as his passion for helping others is quite admirable and a trait worth emulating. He is a professor who is readily accessible to his students and those he mentors. He has been a great mentor to me over the years, and coming in contact with him has greatly influenced the kind of scholar I am today. He has had a positive impact on my career and life generally, and I can unequivocally say that an encounter with him will positively change the trajectory of one's academic pursuits and stir an individual in the right direction.

He is a man who has imparted the lives of all who come in contact with him with his vast knowledge and wealth of wisdom. He is truly a trailblazer whose life is a road map for those who come behind to follow.

Dr. (Mrs.) Philomena Aku Ojomo

Prof. Segun Ogungbemi was my teacher at the Lagos State University (LASU), Nigeria, during my undergraduate days. As Head of the Department of Philosophy, he recommended me for appointment as a Graduate Assistant. This opportunity marked the beginning of my academic journey in LASU. To ensure that I succeeded in this chosen career, Ogungbemi continued to follow me even after he left Lagos State University for another University. The encouragement I got from him contributed to the attainment of my PhD in 2016. Prof. Ogungbemi is a gift to humanity. He is a man of conscience – a man whose life is characterized by values such as fairness, honesty, kindness, humility and integrity. Segun Ogungbemi is a teacher and a leader per excellence.

I am one of his mentees. He gave me academic direction. I can't write my academic history without mentioning his name. I count myself fortunate to be associated with Prof Segun Ogungbemi.

Prof. Alloy Shaagee Ihuah

I first came in contact with Professor Segun Ogungbemi in 1999 when he recruited me into the Department of Philosophy, Lagos State University (LASU), Ojo as a lecturer in 2000. I later joined him at Adekunle Ajasin University Akungba, again at his invitation in 2008. In short, professor Ogungbemi is a Friend, a father and a mentor of quintessential standing. He is a man of healthy credit balance of mental magnitude, epistemic prowess, spiritual depth and high moral integrity.

For this man of letters, truth stands out as the alloy that binds social progress and economic power. I have come to associate him with a guiding philosophy of life that has oiled his entire long walk to good life which is that, "honor belongs to those who never forsake the truth even when things seem dark and grim, who try over and over again, (and) who are never discouraged by insults, humiliation and even defeat".

He is the very expression of humanistic will and a symbol of culture and dialogue backed by an unparalleled generosity of spirit. This existential quality promotes in him honesty, transparency and fairness throughout his entire academic career.

His persuasive critique of present day theory and practice of African philosophy and praxis which is the hall mark of his research has found a voice in his most recent book, *Deconstructing African Thoughts and Practi*ces in which he offered a ripened fruit of sustained reflection on the synergy between philosophy and culture. It is no exaggeration to say that professor Ogungbemi has upgraded the quality of scholarship that is found wanting in many contributions to contemporary philosophical studies in Africa.

In his intellectual journey that spans over three decades, he has articulated many of today's key moral, ethical, political and social issues with methodic and insightful analysis on topical issues in African Philosophy and culture. He is, to say the least, an intellectual colossus; the One- a great and good man; the benchmark, a father figure personality, humble, compassionate and a man for all colors. It's no exaggeration to say that Professor Segun Ogungbemi is one among the many great and good men; the benchmark against whom scholarship should be measured in Africa.

Prof. Benson Akinnawonu

Prof. Segun Ogungbemi is a cerebral and prolific writer, an advocate of justice and fairness whose passion for academic excellence has resulted into the production of many scholarly publications in African Philosophy, Theology and Ethics. He is indeed a forthright man with firm posture, uncommon bravery and unrelenting commitment to the development of reading materials in Philosophy and Religion for both students and the general public. I am one of the beneficiaries of his mentorship and academic material resources. His meritorious services as Professor and Head of Department of Philosophy at Adekunle Ajasin University, Ondo state, Nigeria are noteworthy.

Prof. Laleye, A. Solomon

An erudite scholar of African Philosophy, Ethics, Philosophy of Religion, Segun Ogungbemi is a Professor of Philosophy who has taught in several institutions that include; Ogun State University (now Olabisi Onabanjo University), Ago

Iwoye, Nigeria, Moi University, Eldoret, Kenya, Lagos State University, Ojo and Adekunle Ajasin University, Akungba Akoko, Ondo State, Nigeria. From available records, one of the common denominators deducible from almost all the institutions where Professor Ogungbemi had contact with as a teacher or consultant is his unrelenting quest to establish or consolidate the existence of a department of philosophy as an academic discipline. He believes that people, including the educated, risk self-destruction if they lack the knowledge espoused by philosophy. The pursuit of this tireless zeal to promote philosophy at Adekunle Ajasin University for instance culminated in the de-merger of the Philosophy unit from Religious Studies Units of the former Department of Philosophy and Religious Studies of the University. The historic approval granted to philosophy and religious studies departments as two separate and independent departments is widely believed to negate the initial positions of the University Council and, the then Visitor to Adekunle Ajasin University, Akungba-Akoko that insisted on a compact University. It is to the credit of Professor Segun Ogungbemi that the units were separated and made departments. Today, both departments are waxing stronger in terms of students' subscription, deepened curriculum and internationally exposed academic staff.

Another striking denominator common to the services of Professor Ogungbemi in these aforementioned Universities is the responsibility to head the various departments of philosophy and provide the needed leadership at one time or the other. Suffice it to say, Professor Ogungbemi offered selfless, visionary, transformative and purposeful leadership. He is a prolific writer of the critical school of thought. Many of his published works challenged the assumptions and presuppositions of African traditional belief systems and western religion. As a liberal-minded scholar, he encourages public debate and constructive critique of any view and thought thereby inculcating the philosophic spirit of critical thinking on students and colleagues.

It is worthy of note that Professor Ogungbemi detests laziness and indolence, indiscipline and corrupt tendencies. A positive moral virtue determines his level of association with students and colleagues. To him, integrity is earned only after having been tested and, it is an unpardonable contradiction for students and staff that take pride in a discipline that extols good ethical behavior to be found wanton in moral uprightness.

In all, Professor Segun Ogungbemi is a kind-hearted, articulate, highly resourceful, sagacious and inspiring scholar and administrator of great repute.

S. Layi Oladipupo, Ph.D.

My first encounter with Professor Segun Ogungbemi was in 2004. He came in as one of my undergraduate lecturers at the Adekunle Ajasin University, Akungba Akoko, Ondo State, Nigeria. Specifically when I was in 300 level as an undergraduate student. He taught me quite a number of courses in Philosophy at Undergraduate and Postgraduate Levels. At first, he appears to be a man not to relate with because of his hardcore principles that suggest a man that searches for perfection in a fallible world from a fallible being. Alas, this perspective was changed with time. I remember approaching him after securing a 'C' grade in PHL 318 - Research Method, the very first course he taught me as an undergraduate student to ask why the 'C' grade as I expected a better grade. His countenance changed, but for the courage I surmount to appeal to him with a view to knowing why the grade. I later got a fatherly response to my quest. Another earlier encounter with him was during a class at 400 level during PHL 406 - Philosophy of Mind Class. It was a class on Descartes' philosophy of mind. The lecture dovetailed to discussing the idea of God. After an exhaustive and interesting but intrigue lecture, I beg to differ with his take on the idea of God. We had different views and at the end his take through his word "that is why it is called philosophy of mind. Your view is fundamental, but I am not talking about your 'Church-God' but 'Philosophical-God'. Sit down," gives me confidence.

I was later redeployed to Ondo State for my one year National Youth Service Corp Scheme with my place of primary assignment being the Department of Philosophy, Adekunle Ajasin University, Akungba Akoko, Ondo State, Nigeria. It was during my NYSC days that I got to have a better understanding of who and what Professor Segun Ogungbemi is and stands for. He later supervised my Master Degree Dissertation and was very instrumental to my retention into the academic staff of the Department of Philosophy, Adekunle Ajasin University, Akungba Akoko where I am till today as a budding scholar building a career in the academic against all odds. His rich library has always been made available for my academic research and consultation. In fact, he had released his library collections to me for use while he enjoys his retirement in Houston, USA from full academic engagement. He is no doubt my indefatigable academic father.

In all, I can confidently say that Professor Segun Ogungbemi is a father, mentor, encourager, philanthropist, moralist, an existential agnostic, a man of an impeccable character. He is a unique and vibrant man of many parts, full of knowledge, wisdom and high spirit of guidance. He says things as they are; not minding whose ox is gored. His submissions on issues are always quintessential.

He is a man that believes so much in self-sufficiency, an advocate of equity, equality, peace and justice. He is also a man who abhors all forms of immoral attitudes. He is a man that sets standard for colleagues both junior and senior colleagues. Though, he is not a perfect being, but his humanistic life exemplifies a near perfect life worthy of emulation. He lives and believes that man should be the author of his/her destinies and that he/she should be allowed to exercise his/her freedom and be ready to take responsibility for his/her actions and inactions.

For me, Professor Segun Ogungbemi is one of the astute elders known to me on the planet earth. Baba Agbalagba, I fondly call him. It is my earnest expectation that his life will continue to motivate us to continue to be tolerant and accommodating the views of one another.

Prof. Bojor Enamhe

I knew Professor Segun Ogungbemi at the Annual Conference convened by Prof. Toyin Falola at Austin, Texas. I shall not forget his sense of humor and gentle demeanor at the Austin 2013 Africa Conference that got us talking about the home front. His passion for education and Nigeria on substantive issues endeared me to him. In the years that followed, it was an honor for me to communicate and be guided by him on academic scholarship matters.

There are some truly brave people in the world that you meet and you are forever changed for the experience. Professor Segun Ogungbemi is one of such. He is a teacher, a writer, a scholar, a strong academic, genial, who propels younger academics, literally whips them to success. He is a teacher of teachers, who relates in theoretical and practical ideas, an unrelenting researcher devoid of intellectual arrogance, without discrimination, a mentor to many.

Professor Segun Ogungbemi is not only an academic colossus, but has also reached the academic colossi. He has published widely and still publishing even in his well-deserved retirement. A professional critique of African cultural beliefs, endowed with cultural ambience and heritage; A reflection of African philosophy, ethics, African aesthetics, metaphysics, religion and politics.

As a hero, Professor Segun Ogungbemi is not only worthy of being immortalized in concrete mementos, his achievements should also be weaved into possible sculptures, paintings, folktales, songs or poems.

Professor Ogungbemi lives a simple and unassuming life; very noticeable are his cultural and traditional affiliations and testimonies in his publications. His books: *A Critique of African Cultural Beliefs, Philosophy and Development, God, Reason and Death* (Edited) and *Deconstructing African Thoughts and Practices.* His research and writing activities after retirement testify to his rich desire of intellectual colossus and humanistic ideals. He is energetic mentally and physically; a contributor to human essence, this authology therefore is fitting tribute to this man of letters, a scholar of the humanities – Prof. Segun Ogungbemi.

Prof. Samuel Oloruntoba

It is a great privilege for me to write this brief piece in honor of Professor Segun Ogungbemi. My first contact was at the Africa Conference organized by Professor Toyin Falola, Department of History, University of Texas in Spring 2015. Since that time, we have come to develop very deep connections through calls and email exchanges. His humility and simplicity are two qualities that stand him apart from many.

I was particularly drawn to him by his usual resort to Irunmole and Yemoja as the source of blessing and protection. As a former apprentice at the shrine of Irunmole in my Ajowa city country home, who is now a born-again Christian, I found this very intriguing. Thus, each time Prof. Ogungbemi calls me 'omo Irunmole'; I will retort that I am now omo Jesu. While I respect African Indigenous knowledge and belief system, my faith is rooted in Jesus Christ as the redeemer of humanity from the bondage of sin and oppression of the devil.

Professor Segun Ogungbemi is a repertoire of knowledge. As a well-travelled and experienced man, I have gained from his wealth of knowledge and wisdom. He is very caring and full of empathy and compassion.

As an academic, who is retired but not tired, Professor Ogungbemi is very prolific in African Philosophy. As a co-member of the USA-Africa Dialogue, I have benefited from his very rich and incisive contributions to topic issues of governance, identity and knowledge production.

I have no doubt that this autobiography will provide insights into his rich and illustrious academic career.

YOUNG AFRICAN ENTREPRENEURS AND PROFESSIONALS IN HOUSTON

Lieutenant Commander Victor Lofinmakin

Professor Segun Ogungbemi is a gentleman and a scholar. I have known him for 24 years now. He is the father of my best friend, Segun Ogungbemi Jr. Ever since I have known him; he has been an incredible mentor to me. I thoroughly enjoy our discussions on philosophy, life, policy, deity, etc. I have become a better person by being associated with him. One of the biggest lessons I have taken from him is to always live life according to my philosophy and not be overly swayed by others.

Adebisi Onitiri

Dr. Segun Ogungbemi is a tenured philosophy professor whose academic achievements are not just distinguished, but inspirational. His love for his family and country is undeniable just as his empathy for humanity. I've come to know him as my second father whose love and compassion I cherish very much. From fun stories of his childhood memories to ideological debates on politics, his unique views on life is evident in his literal application to how he carries himself. I always look forward to our weekly banter over the portrayal of African religions vs European deity transposed as true religion. He truly has reshaped my views on everything in life from personal responsibility, selflessness, and legacy. He is unequivocally the most observant, attentive and knowledgeable man I have met. Compassionate and humble, he represents the man I wish to be. To know him is to know happiness. He will literally give the shirt off his back just so you stay warm and clothed. There are too many fond memories I will forever cherish and I'm sure this book would shed light on quite a few of them, my prayer is that whoever is reading this book would be blessed with the wisdom, sadness and joy captured within the context. I'll leave you with this: picture the most charismatic individual in your life, someone with such an infectious smile and loud but warm laughter, it radiates the whole room, someone who wouldn't hesitate to correct any grammatical error even while you're giving a heated speech. You but have a glimpse of the most revered individual I've been most blessed with to have in my life.

Raymond Mbah

Professor Segun Ogungbemi, "Papa Segun", has been one of the inspirations in my life towards my pursuit for higher education. Many times he recounted his journey during our numerous enlightening correspondences. Fascinating, remains my sole impression of him. From the trials and tribulations faced studying in the United States in the 70's, to returning to his home continent and contributing across multiple higher education facilities. It is important when speaking on Pan-Africanism to highlight the vital role-played by educators like Mr. Ogungbemi. When you get right down to it, we all are astutely versed with the saying: KNOWLEDGE IS POWER.

SPECIAL FRIENDS

Rev. Rowland S. Babatunde Ph.D.

I am delighted to write what I know about Professor Segun Ogungbemi. He was one of the young and brilliant men who enrolled in Bible College of Sudan Interior Mission (SIM), but became known as the Society of International Missionaries, which subsequently was indigenized as Evangelical Church of West Africa, now the Evangelical Church Winning All (ECWA). Name adaptation has become ingenious and in keeping with the realities of the times and Ministries.

Segun's class enrolled at Igbaja in 1966. Segun, David

Medulu and I were roommates but I was their senior roommate. I found Segun to be respectful, dutiful, brilliant, jovial and loving. He could be hot tempered and react if pushed, but very amenable to caution and held no grudges. We lived together in harmony and understanding without any negative events throughout the years. Of his own volition, he called me "Oga mi" meaning, "My master " and keeps that designation of me till date, even in his exalted position as a Professor.

All along, it seemed, my brother was not really convinced that he was where he should be. Because of that, I guess, he was very critical about some School doctrines and some other things in the Institution. On a fateful day, he came to the room from Class, very furious and started packing his belongings to quit the School. I do not recall the specific issue, but I inquired and prayerfully reasoned with him to stay. He obliged and continued his studies performing as brilliantly as usual. At the end of the year our room changed and I graduated in 1967 while he continued his studies.

By the time he graduated (I am not sure which year), I was in the field and only heard that he went on to study at the University of Ibadan. Because of doctrinal differences, Department of Religious Studies, University of Ibadan at that time was not considered an Institution suitable for SIM members more so, a Bible College graduate. In those days,

SIM missionaries guarded their students and graduates very gealously against the possibility of doctrinal pollution. Our doctrine was and it still is that there is only one God and that the only way paved to Him is by the Lord Jesus, who made Himself a ransom for all. But the efficacy of the ransom is limited to those who will confess their sin, put their trust in Jesus Christ, and accept Him by faith. Bible reading and believing people do not accept Universalism as doctrine; we see it as a delusion. Each time we converse, I remind professor Segun of the gospel truth we learned and knew. Now that he retired, as a professor of philosophy I pray he would take time to properly reflect on the Bible and the claims of Christ to reactivate his faith in Him.

In all those years since we parted at school in 1967, we never called or communicated with each other. Therefore, I did not know how he got information that I had returned to Igbaja theological seminary for advanced studies. It seemed my own turn had come, and I had no intercessor! So I had to leave after Three years of the four years for which I enrolled to earn a B.Th degree. As a result of Dr. Teachout, my professor's counsel and a few good spirited elders, I was posted to teach in the Titcombe College, Egbe. When all roads seemed blocked to further education and future bleak, I received Segun's letter saying : "Oga mi, what are you doing in Titcombe College? Do you not want to come to America?" At that time I did not remember that there is a place called

America even after all these years of working with and serving American Missionaries!. So, I laughed and wonder whether Segun knew what he was talking about. I had put myself through to that level and could not contemplate going to the place for financial reasons. Therefore I laughed. But Segun Ogungbemi did not relent in his efforts. He collected application forms from several Colleges and sent them to me. Well, out of respect and obedience to him, not because I believe that it was possible, I filled the forms and released them. As responses came, I followed the lead of the one that seemed practicable to me and I got an admission to Trinity College, Deerfield Illinois, USA in 1980. To my amazement God enabled my wife and I to raise enough money from sales of family property to meet the financial requirements. It was like a dream came through; I flew out of Nigeria to America on January 12, 1980! This was made possible because God ordained it and because my brother Segun felt concerned, and acted to achieve results.

When I intervened in the hours of Segun's travails, I did not know that I did it for myself. If we had lived at variance and loggerhead in those days, fantastic things like these may never have happened. When I went to Fort-worth, Texas for a Master's degree, my wife and I visited professor Segun Ogungbemi in his residence at Dallas. As I made to thank him profusely for what he did for us, he interrupted me and stated: "No, Oga mi, what you did for me is more than what

I did for you " If that is the case, who did what for who? God did it all. If therefore, God put you in a position where it depends on you to turn things positively around, do not decline so you may not be found blocking your own way. Thank you for being our friend, Prof. Segun Ogungbemi.

Marita Morgan (Mom & Dad) and their son Keith Morgan

Segun is my only African friend. We met through my son who brought him to our home for holidays when they were in college together. I find Segun extremely capable in many respects. He is a brilliant philosopher, a compassionate humanist, a skilled communicator, and an open-minded individual. He seeks knowledge wherever he can find it. He and I have shared much information concerning our histories, families, faith, frustrations and hopes. In addition to all of these things, his laugh is contagious. I love Segun and he loves me.

Engr. Olukayode Owadokun

When I think of the word 'humanism' I think of Professor Segun Ogungbemi.

Prof, as we fondly call him by all and sundry in the family, lived in the same neighborhood with my parents when he was a professor of philosophy at Adekunle Ajasin University, Akungba, Ondo State, Nigeria. My late father and Mum would always talk glowingly and lovingly of their new neighbor, Professor Ogungbemi whenever I called them on the phone. Not too long ago, I had a great pleasure of meeting this wonderful man on one Christmas holiday, and ever since, he has become my mentor and ultimately, my father figure after my father passed on. Professor Ogungbemi Is an epitome of humility and decency that reflects the very best of the human spirit. He is a man not known to run with the hare and hunt with the hounds. An extraordinary being who embodies so much that is best for humanity. May I say here that he was and still always solidly there for my family, unbiased during our turbulent and trying moments. As a hero-soul, he resolutely stands for peace, truth, justice and fairness. He personifies trust, loyalty, integrity, kindness and devotion. Every chance I had to meet him on social-cultural and intellectual discussions, he exhibited an unequally great sense of humor that created a never-a-dull-moment clout of laughter. I have known him to be a dedicated husband and loving family man par excellence. His profound, rational approach and thoughts vis-a-vis humanism, existentialism, Olódumareism and other social-cultural issues are a reflection of his education and teaching in the realms of philosophy and theology. This, without ambiguity, has created a huge impact on my understanding of life and humanity. On behalf of my family: my late Dad, your friend, mum, sisters and brothers, I say thank you for creating the atmosphere of love which has made it possible for us to be part of your existence.

Prof. Oluwayemisi Adebowale

My personal office was beside that of Prof. Segun Ogungbemi in the new Faculty of Arts when he was at the Adekunle Ajasin University, Akungba-Akoko, Ondo State, Nigeria and we related well. Having him as the Head of the Department of Philosophy when I was Dean of Arts and working with him when I was the DVC (Academics) was great. He was ever ready to contribute towards the success of those at the helm of affairs in our

University. I know him to be a wonderful encourager who stands with anyone he believes in through thick and thin. Prof. Ogungbemi is a lover of the truth and no matter what happens, you'll always find him standing up for the truth at all times. Those who don't know him well think that he's a difficult man because he's too meticulous. Prof. Ogungbemi is not only thorough, he is very plain, sincere, humane and generous; he also enjoys lending a helping hand to anyone facing challenges. I can't but remember the case of a student in the Department of Linguistics & Languages who had serious issues with her father and who was not doing well in her studies. Although our amiable Professor was then a lecturer in the Department of Philosophy, he was moved when he heard about the challenges of this female student. As an African Philosopher who is also well grounded in Moral Philosophy, the father in him who knew the implications of a father's curse on a child came to the fore. Prof. Ogun Ogungbemi made serious conscious efforts by personally relating with the girl's father who was hundreds of kilometers away to appease him. His intervention yielded positive results, as the girl no longer manifested the traits of the spirit of epilepsy placed on her. There's no dull moment with Prof. Ogungbemi. This African philosopher calls women 'Om Yem ja' when greeting them but he generally greets people with 'Ogun a gbe o'. When he notices that someone is not warm towards such, he goes further to pray that 'o o ni rija Ogun o' ('May you not incur the wrath of Ogun the god of iron). His passion for tradition earned him a cognomen. Baba Ogun as he's fondly called is a great enthusiast, a selfless teacher and theorist, a man of honor, a compassionate counselor, a great nurturer and motivator of men. Prof. Ogungbemi is a man of integrity who is interested in the intellectual development of the younger ones. His amazing counsel for my second son is still fresh in my memory. This Professor of African and Moral Philosophy is retired but he continues to refire through his recent publications, as he is not tired of being exemplary. May he continue to positively impact humanity and may Olodumare grant our own Prof. Sọgun Ogungbemi, a man with a large heart, good health, peace and continued active conscience to sow more seeds of dedicated work to generations yet unborn.

Prof. Femi Mimiko, mni

I am excited that Professor Segun Ogungbemi found time to do this autobiography! The Professor of Philosophy is such a deeply knowledgeable man, with diverse experiences spanning several spatial realms and functionality, such that it would have been a disservice to humanity were he not able to make out time to write on himself. What forces shaped the life he lived, the choices he made, the profundity of his ideas (many of which are, of course, unorthodox), and elements that imbue him with his positive vibes and permanent amiable disposition, even under pressure, are all worthy to be read about, given how much impact such must definitely have on upcoming generations. As Vice-Chancellor at Adekunle Ajasin University, Akungba-Akoko, Nigeria, 2010 - 2015, I was privileged to work with Professor Ogungbemi. He is one person whose support for the broad outline of your vision doesn't preclude from inflicting the most caustic criticism on its finer elements, and the vehicles through which you seek to canalize them. I found such orientation invaluable, and a factor in the little we were able to achieve on that beat. This oracle of the Yoruba deity of 'Iyemoja,' (Yemoja) and the other 'Irumole' has thus remained an invaluable friend of mine since our paths crossed many years ago. His thoughts, carefully presented in "Living in Existential Paradoxes of Life: My Autobiography," in a manner that saves the general reader from the tedium of understanding the language, and internalizing the logic of philosophers, makes the book so compelling and an interesting read. I warmly recommend it to everyone desirous of a drink from one imponderable jar of wisdom that Baba Ogungbemi epitomizes.

Prof. Toyin Falola (TF)
Segun Ogungbemi: The Irunmole of the World

The Republic, a body of work by one of the greatest philosophers and proponents of theories and concepts to have ever lived, Plato, is a wholesome representation of the issues of the day, many of which are incidentally still issues of the day, lending credence to the fact that as evolved as the world has become — especially with technological advancements — we still have a long way to go in the advancement of our human societies and how they are ruled.

Away from the full contents of *The Republic*, one thing that has always struck me as ingenious is the proposition of the concept of the Philosopher-King. Plato's philosopher-king is that administrator or ruler whose prime and effective administrative and leadership skills are grounded in sound philosophical foundations. Plato posits that governance under a leader with such unique traits is the best form of governance anyone can have — one that would benefit all.

The concept of the philosopher-king, when brought into the world of academia, will depict an academic who has learned to combine a life committed to lifelong learning and scholarship with astute leadership and administrative skills, thereby being a delight within the classroom and to students at several levels of study, to colleagues and fellow researchers, to the university or universities where such a philosopher-king is privileged to work, and even to those who serve with and under such a person in several administrative roles. All do not necessarily love the personality of a philosopher-king, but their achievements, work ethics, scholarship, brilliance, and the outcomes they can consistently deliver are things that everyone appreciates and loves about them.

In looking at the life, work, and experiences of Prof. Segun Ogungbemi, I found it befitting to call him an Irunmole, the same meaning as an academic philosopher-king, because the bulk of his scholarship has been philosophy-related, but not only because of that, but also because he is a fine blend of academic soundness, administrative prowess, and sound leadership capabilities.

Prof. Segun Ogungbemi's academic sojourn started from his days at the University of Ibadan, where he studied for a diploma in religious studies. This multi-religious program served as the launch pad for what is to become a sound and vast academic scholarship. Going by the quality of scholarship and profoundness of the University of Ibadan's Religious Studies program, the years the professor spent studying for the diploma opened his eyes to fresher perspectives and newer horizons in studying humans, humanity, and human-related fields of academic endeavors. The eye opening must have marked a significant change in the trajectory of the professor's continued studies, as he went on to the State University of New York (SUNY) in Albany for a Bachelor's degree in Liberal Studies.

Liberal Studies is a multi-disciplinary academic program that encompasses courses in the humanities like literature, philosophy, history and languages, social sciences like psychology, and courses in the sciences and other fields of study. A four-year degree program in liberal studies helped Prof. Segun Ogungbemi build on the foundation that the Diploma in Religious Studies at the University of Ibadan gave him.

To bag a degree in Liberal Studies is to have been grounded in several aspects of academia. It is to have been baptized in epistemology, ethos and logic while taking lessons on world history and African history. It is to have critically analyzed the bodies of work by writers of different centuries and times. Galileo Galilei, Leonardo Da Vinci, Albert Einstein, Nikola Tesla, Socrates, and Plato — these people, among others, made contributions across verticals and in different fields. Each of them is known for more than one thing, from being scientists to being philosophers to being artists, inventors, and writers of classic novels and poems and drama. If we were to have a replication of any of these ancients who could and very well did contribute to several seemingly non-related fields, they would come as people who did a multi-disciplinary degree program at the university.

Profoundness comes with studying a course like that — it widens one's horizons, deepens one's perspectives on issues, and opens one to multiple narratives, all of which can help shape the quality of thought, expression, and academic contribution. An academic philosopher-king in this age and time has to be someone whose perspectives on issues are deep, profound, and vast, helped by the richness of their academic scholarship, and it does not come as surprising that Prof. Segun Ogungbemi fits the bill, seeing as his first degree prepared him for the sounder profoundness that was to come his way.

Prof. Ogungbemi returned to the religious roots for his first postgraduate degree, bagging a Master of Theology degree in Philosophical Theology and Christian Ethics at the Southern Methodist University in Dallas, Texas. He attained the pinnacle of academic study with a Ph.D. focused on the History of Ideas, Philosophy and Humanities from the University of Texas at Dallas. And so went successive years of academic pursuit and strategic grounding that laid the groundwork for what is to become successful and widely acclaimed and acknowledged academic life.

His sojourn in the world of academia — now as an academic and not as a student (although he remains a student of life like every one of us and has committed himself to lifelong learning — started at Bishop College Dallas, Texas, Ogun State University Ago-Iwoye, now Olabisi Onabanjo University Ago-Iwoye, Ogun State, bearing him to other institutions in Nigeria such as Lagos State University, Ojo, Lagos and the Adekunle Ajasin University in Akungba-Akoko, Ondo State. Prof. Ogungbemi's earliest years as university lecturer were spent at these four institutions, where he contributed to philosophy, religious studies, and history. As a philosopher-king, his contributions to the aforementioned institutions of learning went beyond academia, as he held several administrative roles in each of these universities.

Prof. Ogungbemi rapidly rose through the ranks, earning deserved promotions even as he continued his pursuit of knowledge, which saw him leave for Moi University in Kenya, and, finally his work as a professor of philosophy at the Adekunle Ajasin University, focusing on philosophy, theology, ethics, and religious studies. With a profound foundation laid in diverse disciplines of the humanities and social sciences, Prof. Segun Ogungbemi has dedicated his years of scholarship and academic acumen to the research of concepts and phenomena such as the African philosophy of history and its overarching significance on the larger African society, the African philosophy of religion and its significance for a heavily religiously Westernized Africa in the 21st century, among other Africa-centric scholarship and research.

This academic philosopher-king has proven that he is African by birth and ancestry and a true African breed through his work and contributions. The foundation and structuring of Ile-Ife, the ancestral home of the Yoruba people, culture, and civilization, resulted from the communal contributions of both old and young — wherein no contribution was too little, and all hands that were on deck went to work.

In the same vein, Prof. Segun Ogungbemi has contributed to the repair, reconstruction, designing, modeling, and building of African civilizations through his Africa-centric scholarship and research.

Can one truly be termed an academic philosopher-king if their contributions do not transcend academia, especially spiraling into administrative roles? Prof. Segun Ogungbemi has not only worked in academia but also has vast experience in administrative roles across several institutions and verticals. He has served on university senate committees, as a head of the department at several institutions, as a faculty dean, and as an external examiner for undergraduate and postgraduate studies at universities within and outside Nigeria.

Prof. Segun Ogungbemi has also held appointments on government-constituted committees, as a serial member of the National Universities Commission (NUC) Accreditation Committee to several schools, and as Special Adviser to the Nigerian Minister of Labor and Productivity, among several other administrative roles and appointments.

I find Prof. Ogungbemi's work on humanism, African philosophy, and African religions the most stimulating and profound, and there is no denying that it takes a deep level of scholarship, research, and ingenuity to consistently turn out work in these fields as Professor Ogungbemi has done. In a world where the struggle to find relevance and relatability for one's body of work and research is on the rise, academics like Prof. Segun Ogungbemi, whose lives have a fair share of both the academia and the professional and administrative world, have the leverage of relatability and relevance — having had contact with the town.

The title of academic philosopher-king is not one that I've chosen to call Prof. Ogungbemi out of a lack of names or titles. It is rather one that I chose to attribute to the name, the man, and the work he has done because it is befitting. Hearty cheers to more profound work and contributions, my dear friend!

GRADUATION CEREMONIES OF
TEMIDAYO OGUNGBEMI, TINUKE OGUNGBEMI, ADEMOLA ORIDATE, TOLUWALASE IYELOLU, AND OMOTOLUWAFE BALOGUN

WEDDING CEREMONIES OF
TEMIDAYO OGUNGBEMI, OLUWAKEMI OMOTAYO, AND IYABO OGUNGBEMI

MY 77TH BIRTHDAY

FAMILIES AND FRIENDS

FAMILY EVENTS

RECENT MEMORIES OF KENYA

BOOK IN MY MEMORY, AWARDS AND APPRECIATION/ ASUU

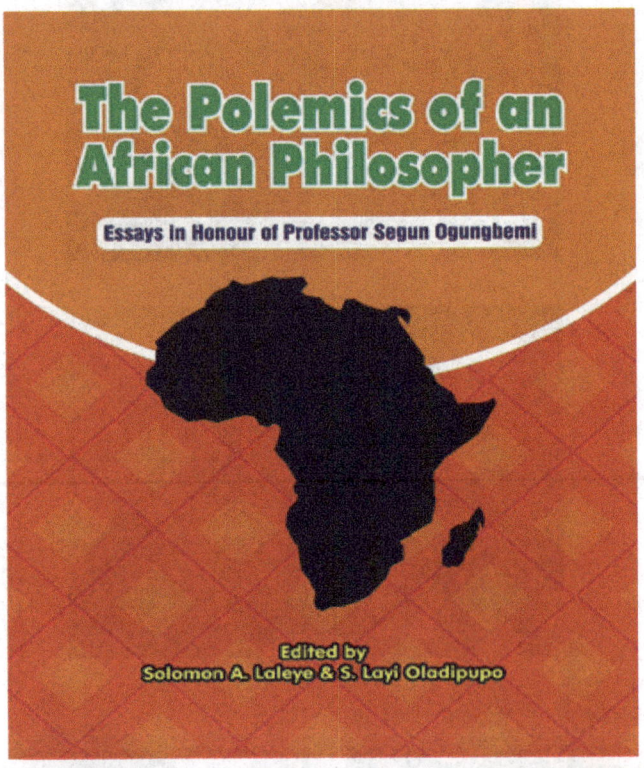

ACADEMIC STAFF UNION OF UNIVERSITIES

NATIONAL SECRETARIAT

Website: www.asuu-ng.org
Email: president@asuu-ng.org
admin@asuu-ng.org
info@asuu-ng.org
Direct Line: +234-9-2901318

UNIVERSITY OF ABUJA MAIN CAMPUS
AIRPORT ROAD, GIRI
P.M.B. 10, GWAGWALADA
FCT, ABUJA
NIGERIA

Our Ref: _____ Your Ref: _____ Date: _____

12th January, 2014

Prof. Segun Ogungbemi,
Adekunle Ajasin University
Akungba-Akoko (AAUA),
Ondo State

Dear Prof. Ogungbemi,

APPRECIATION FOR ROLE IN THE RESOLUTION OF AAUA CRISIS

On behalf of ASUU National Executive Committee (NEC), I write to thank you and other members of the Ad-Hoc Intervention Committee for the positive role played in resolving the lingering crisis between the University Administration and our branch at the Adekunle Ajasin University, Akungba-Akoko (ASUU-AAUA).

It is our hope that ASUU can continue to count on your support in promoting a vibrant and progressive unionism at AAUA for the benefit of all.

Once again, thank you and best wishes.

Yours in the struggle,

Nasir F. Isa, Ph.D
President

THE UNIVERSITY OF TEXAS AT AUSTIN

DISTINGUISHED AWARD FOR THE ADVANCEMENT OF PAN-AFRICAN DIALOGUE

Segun Ogungbemi, PhD

Please join me in welcoming Professor Segun Ogungbemi. He received his Ph.D. in Philosophy and Humanities at the University of Texas at Dallas in Richardson, Texas in 1984. Throughout his career, he has taught at several Universities. These include Bishop College in Dallas, Texas, Ogun State University now Olabisi Onabanjo University, Ago-Iwoye, Moi University in Eldoret, Kenya, Lagos State University in Lagos Nigeria, and he is currently at Adekunle Ajasin University, in Akungba, Ondo State, Nigeria.

Professor Ogungbemi has taught various courses in philosophy namely, Ethics, Metaphysics, Epistemology, Philosophy of Religion, Existentialism, African Philosophy, Social and Political Philosophy, Philosophy and Development, and Environmental Ethics. He has attended several local and international conferences in Nigeria, Kenya, Lesotho, and in the United States, and given public lectures at a plethora of venues.

He has several notable publications including the books, *The Yoruba Conceptions of Human Nature: A Philosophical Approach* and *Studies in African Thought and Western Philosophy*. In addition to these, his academic record features many journal articles and chapter publications across a broad range of domestic and international mediums. Apart from his academic credentials, Professor Segun Ogungbemi has served as the Head of Department of Philosophy in all the Universities he has taught in Africa. He was the founding Head of Department of Philosophy at Moi University in Kenya and the Acting Dean. He also served on various committees of Senate in all the Universities he has taught. Currently, he is working on a book titled, *Philosophy in the New Age*, and is set to release a contribution in an encyclopedic work on the Yoruba.

Beyond the academy, Professor Ogungbemi has held positions of influence in the Nigerian civil service. He was a special advisor to a ministry of labor in Nigeria and maintains several community leadership positions to this day. We are proud to recognize the multifaceted nature of his contributions.

Please join me in honoring Professor Segun Ogungbemi.

About the Author

Professor Segun Ogungbemi is a Distinguished professor of philosophy. He got his Ph.D from The University of Texas at Dallas, Richardson, Texas and has taught at Bishop College Dallas, Texas; Ogun State University Ago-Iwoye, now Olabisi Onabanjo University Ago-Iwoye, Ogun State, Nigeria; Moi University Eldoret Kenya; Lagos State University Ojo, Lagos State; and Adekunle Ajasin University Akungba-Akoko, formerly Ondo State University. He is the recipient of 2014 The University of Texas at Austin Distinguished Award for the Advancement of Pan-African Dialogue; and 2014 Adekunle Ajasin University Akungba, Ondo State, Distinguished Merit Award for Excellent Services. His most recent publications are: *Living in the Existential Paradoxes of Life: My Autobiography,* 2024, *A Critique of African Cultural Beliefs 2nd edition* 2022; and *Deconstructing African Thoughts and Practices,* 2022; all published by Cornerstone Publishing, Houston, Texas, USA. Some other books are:(edited) *God, Reason and Death: Issues in Philosophy of Religion,* (Ibadan: Hope Publications, 2008), Philosophy and Development, (Ibadan: Hope Publications, 2007), (First edition) A Critique of African Cultural Beliefs, (Lagos: Pumark Educational Publishers, 1997).

Several of his chapters in books include, "Traditional Religious Belief System" in *Culture and Customs of the Yoruba*, (edited) Toyin Falola and Akintunde Akinyemi,(Austin: Pan-African University Press, 2017). "Modern Science and Technology in Conflict with African Environmental Ethics" in *Readings in Philosophy: Problems and Issues*, (edited.) S. Ade Ali and Emmanuel O. Akintona, (Lagos: Triumph Publishers, 2015). "The Spirit of Pan-Africanism and Nationalist Consciousness: The Way Forward in the 21st Century" in *Pan-Africanism and the Politics of African Citizenship and Identity*, (edited) Toyin Falola and Kwame Esien, (New York: Routledge/Taylor and Francis Group, 2014). "African Women at the Receiving End" in *Beyond Tradition: African Women in Cultural and Political Spaces*, (edited) Toyin Falola and S.U.Fwatshak, (Trenton: Africa World Press, 2011); and "The Conflict in the Niger Delta and National Interest" in Oil Violence in Nigeria: *Checkmating its Resurgence in the Niger Delta* (edited.) Victor Ojakorotu and Lysias Dodd Gilbert, (Saarbrucken, Germany: Lambert Academic publishing, 2010) among others. He also has numerous articles published in reputable local and international journals.

He has served at the national level as Accreditation/Verification Member/Chairman of National Universities Commission (NUC) Abuja, (2013-2016); and former Senior Special Adviser to the Honourable Minister of Labour and

Productivity, Dr. Samuel Ogbemudia, Federal Secretariat Ikoyi Lagos,(September 1994-February, 1995).

He currently resides in Texas, United States of America with his family after his retirement in the university service in Nigeria.

Made in the USA
Coppell, TX
18 November 2024

40180649R10262